One out of every four girls and one out of every six boys are molested, with the average age being nine years old.

These numbers hold up worldwide, and they haven't changed over the years. But *we* have. We are not as numbed by the abuse of our children, we are not as tolerant of the misuse of their innocence, and we know the importance of protecting them. We now know we must stand up and allow the truth to be spoken. We know there is a road to healing and that healing *must* occur in order to restore a quality of life that everyone touched by abuse deserves.

If you were sexually abused as a child, please know it is never too late to begin your recovery process. *Healing Steps: A Gentle Path to Recovery for Survivors of Childhood Sexual Abuse* is a powerful and effective path to healing from the trauma of childhood sexual abuse and to regaining what you may have lost.

Thoughts from those who have already taken the Healing Steps path...

"The Universe gives us what we need to help us heal and become whole. [The author] experienced sexual abuse, as I did, and has done the work needed to recover. She knows the insidious effects of sexually dysfunctional families, and she offers tools for getting out of the victim role." — N.A.

"I highly recommend Healing Steps. It's one of the best things I've ever done for myself." — K.S.

"Thank you for holding our hands and helping to guide us down the long, narrow hallway. Thank you for giving us the safety of your light in order to allow us to explore the darkness." — N.W.

"I'm tired of accommodating to what molest has done to my life."
— L.W.

"This [series of exercises] made me aware of aspects of my abuse that I had considered secondary in the past." — L.H.

"I was given a structure that enabled me to stay on a healing path ... and it showed me how much resistance I had in certain areas of my healing." — K.D.

"I was very touched by [the author's] use of her own experience as a survivor – it is a tremendous gift she has given to us."
— C., therapist and survivor

"I'm very frustrated at not being able to articulate exactly what's happened to me [after Healing Steps], but my life has gotten easier, I'm able to see movement toward integrating aspects of my life that have not come together before. Some of the blocks to my creativity have weakened or dissolved." — an artist

"Before Healing Steps, I didn't realize I'd passed over fundamental aspects of my development that I needed to be a whole person. Now I can go back and take what is rightfully mine and not feel anything but good about it. The shame and the guilt are becoming memories." — E., a survivor

"Healing Steps changed my life. It offered a direction that was both educational and illuminating." — D., a therapist and survivor

"It was an invaluable experience that I could have never achieved through private therapy." — S.T.

"The Steps helped me understand myself and my acting out in a way I had never done before." — M.B.

"When you find out you're not alone, you begin to have a sense of peace. And I've had so many people tell me I seem to be so much more at peace with myself since starting Healing Steps. It was helpful to get in touch with the parts of myself that I'd lost during my childhood—and that had remained lost during my adulthood. I felt myself growing up!" — E.B.

"I am ready to accept that I was molested, and I need to work on reclaiming myself and my personal power. I am no longer willing to remain numb or spaced out. I am really angry that I have to do this work—and that so much of my life has been missed because I was not present to connect to other people. I am tired—physically, emotionally, and spiritually." — T.D.

"I want to do everything I can to help myself heal from this betrayal." — T.P.

"Getting support from others who have been through abuse can help you in more ways than you can ever imagine." — Rocky

"I now realize that the molester had sole responsibility for the molestation. I know that I have a right to experience a wide range of emotions, and that all my feelings are valid. I know that I can get beyond the experience and that it does not need to determine the rest of my life." — R.C.

"My therapist and my husband bullied me into it. I don't want to be who I apparently am. I am frightened, angry, and tired." — May, who stayed in a Healing Steps support group for years, by her own choosing.

Sharyn Higdon Jones, MA, LMFT

Healing Steps

A GENTLE PATH TO RECOVERY
FOR SURVIVORS OF
CHILDHOOD SEXUAL ABUSE

Inner Journey Publishing

SAN JOSE, CALIFORNIA

Printed in the United States of America.

ISBN: 978-0-692-15088-7

"A Common Prayer," by Michael Leunig.
Reprinted by permission of the author.

"You Turned Your Head," by J. Mirikitani.
Reprinted by permission of the author.

"Where Bodies Are Buried," by J. Mirikitani.
Reprinted by permission of the author.

"The Unbroken," by Rashani Réa.
Reprinted by permission of the author.

Cover and interior design by DianaRussellDesign.com
Author photo by Rod Searcey
Publishing strategist: Holly Brady

For more information:
www.InnerJourneyPublishing.net

Address permission requests to:
info@InnerJourneyPublishing.net

To purchase multiple copies of this book at reduced prices,
please inquire at info@InnerJourneyPublishing.net

Contents

Step Three
Confronting the Perpetrator: the One Outside and the One Inside ... 71

Step Four
Then and Now:
How the Ghosts of Your Past
Seem to Haunt Your Present ... 105

Step Five
Sex and Your Body ... 147

Step Six
Relationships: How Not to Bring the Past into the Present ... 189

Dedication

*To the two most important men in my life, my son Kevin and
my husband Ron, for encouraging me to give birth to this book
after a very long pregnancy.*

*To my daughter, Robyn, who is truly the wise one.
To my niece, Pam, who has always been my cheerleader.*

*And most of all, to the men and women embarking
on their own Healing Steps.*

*I am thankful to the many women who have participated in the
Healing Steps Workshops over the years as well as grateful to all the men
and women who have invited me to be part of their healing process.
I appreciate your trust and confidence as you have shared your wounds
with me. Together we have walked through stormy times on the
way to growth and acceptance.*

Preface

It's difficult to seek help and support when confronting issues around sexual abuse. I know because I'm a survivor myself. I'm also a licensed psychotherapist who has been working with sexual abuse victims for over thirty-five years. I feel privileged to have been a part of sexual abuse recovery work for so many years— and this book, and the approaches and procedures in it, are the culmination of my work throughout those years.

Healing Steps began as a series of workshops designed to help victims and survivors move through the many steps of abuse work. The workshops, seven in number, each lasting from 9am to 4pm, were spaced approximately a month apart so that participants had the necessary time to process and integrate the material. I required each participant to commit to all seven workshops, and I insisted that each participant engage in individual therapy over the seven-month period. At the end, several groups chose to continue meeting for themed work-shops, while others re-formed as ongoing support groups. Not surprisingly, the bonds that developed between these women while doing intimate and intense healing work were quite strong.

I remember well the day during my graduate seminars when a group of presenters from Parents United and the Sexual Abuse Treatment Program came to talk with us about an innovative, new program for families shattered by sexual abuse. The treatment was designed to intervene on behalf of families from the first incident report, through police interviews, experiences with the criminal justice system, and (sometimes) incarceration of the perpetrator; and ending with either reunification or dissolution of the family. Beginning at the moment the family was shattered by crisis, trained mental health professionals provided counseling and support to each individual. Peer counselors (active members of the treatment program) were also assigned both to the alleged perpetrator and to each adult member of the family, offering support and hope. Treatment, including both individual and group therapy, continued for all members of the family for a minimum of two years.

On that day, one of the presenting panel—a beautiful, soft-spoken adolescent girl—talked about how wonderful it was to be heard, to be believed, and to be supported in what was one of the worst moments of her life. And in a film shown later in the day, a group of molested women asked, "What would it have been like if there had been a billboard saying 'If you have been sexually abused, we are here to help. Call us.' " I was so moved by these powerful words that I found myself walking to the front of the seminar room. I approached the panel and asked how I could be part of this innovative program—and part of that "billboard." This was 1979, and sexual abuse and incest were not discussed in open forums. Most victims remained totally silent, hoping the memories would fade with time. I had been one of those women.

My offer was taken seriously. I was invited to a meeting of Parents United that week, and I was told that if after attending I was still interested in training, I could schedule an appointment for an interview. What I didn't know was how difficult it would be to sit in a meeting where approximately 250 adults were present—each of whom was either a perpetrator or the partner of a perpetrator. At that meeting, I realized the journey I was about to undertake was much more than training to become a specialist in this area: I had to confront my own unresolved issues, my own biases, my own fears, pain, longings, memories, anger—and all the demons in my life. After the meeting, I took a deep breath—and made an appointment for an interview.

All I can tell you is this was an interview like none other in my life. Not only did I interview with a group of dedicated professionals, including Hank and Anna Giaretto who started the program in 1976, but I also interviewed with the volunteer staff of parents, perpetrators, and victims who had gone through the program. The toughest part of the day was when I had to interview a perpetrator who had just entered the program. He was in the early stages of treatment, which meant he was minimizing what had occurred, he was blaming everyone and everything except his own compulsive behavior, and he was rather grandiose in his assessment of his own progress. I now know his behavior was typical—but at the time, I was appalled. After the perpetrator left the room, I told the staff that I didn't think I was meant to do this work. I couldn't feel the compassion I thought was expected of a therapist. I was angry at how he viewed himself and at what he had done to his daughter. I was frustrated with his excuses. I didn't believe him, and I felt our conversation had been meaningless. I was immediately offered an internship!

Thus began one of the most meaningful periods of my life. I met and worked with people who changed my life and my point of view. It was an exciting time: innovative work, intense training, and enough crisis management to last a lifetime. I worked not only with children and adolescents, but also with perpetrators (both incarcerated and living in the community) and family members, and with AMACs–Adults Molested as Children. I was trained by some of the best in the field. We tried different models, and different combinations of clientele, all with the hope of finding the most effective and supportive ways to heal the deep wounds left by abuse. I led groups of AMAC women and mixed groups of AMAC men and women, some of whom were both the molested and the molesters. Several attendees had to be released from mental health facilities in order to participate in the group. In the end, the program trained people from around the country and from around the world, all of us trying to offer what had not been offered before.

The next step for me was a difficult one. While doing work at what became known as the Giaretto Institute, I was also in my own therapy, which I had started in the early 1970s. During that time, I found myself wanting to limit my professional work in sexual abuse because I was beginning to see abuse and incest everywhere I looked. I'd see a father and daughter sharing a meal and wonder, I'd see a man teaching a boy to ride a bike and wonder, I'd watch soccer coaches working with kids and wonder—you get the picture. After much agonizing, I decided to begin a private practice while I continued my work at the Institute in order to create a more balanced professional life for myself. It was the right decision. After some time, I decided to leave the Institute and develop a full-time private practice. That practice thrived, as I thrived in doing my own healing work. That is, until December of 1987, when my life fell apart.

At the time, my children were beginning lives on their own, I was with a man I deeply loved, my practice was full, and I had wonderful friends. But suddenly I felt as though someone had pulled the plug and drained the energy right out of me. My spirit dampened, and I became afraid. I found it very difficult to get out of bed in the morning. I couldn't wait for the day to end so I could crawl back into bed. A touch of a persistent flu, I thought. Maybe too much work, too much prep for the holidays, too many clients, too many late nights, too many demands and too few resources to be able to respond. Christmas dinner was at a hotel because I was too tired to go to the grocery store, too befuddled to make out a menu, and too overwhelmed to set the table. There were days of appointments cancelled, social plans axed, reservations unattended. I didn't know what was happening to me. Finally, on February 6, 1988, I barely had the energy to lift my head off the pillow. I realized I needed help and called my doctor. I was diagnosed with chronic fatigue syndrome and began a nine-month odyssey of self-examination while stuck in bed with no distractions except for my constant companions—fear and despair. Hope was clearly on an extended sabbatical.

The saga of my dance with chronic fatigue syndrome is for another time, but I will say it was a real time-out in a life that had always been lived to the fullest. I had always jumped into endeavors with both feet and loved the anticipation of whatever was just around the corner in my life. Energy was always there, a clear head and the ability to concentrate for as long as I liked were givens in my life. So this was indeed shocking. I grieved the loss of energy, the loss of friends, the loss of possibilities; but most of all, I grieved the loss of the work that was so important to me. I didn't know if I would be able to work again; and if I could work, I didn't know if I could work in a constant, predictable way. And if my work was hit or miss, how would that affect my clients—that is, assuming I would have any clients after I returned. And if I did return, would the clients again trust I would be there? On and on marched the circle of questions with no answers and no assurances. I drove myself crazy as I confronted the primal issue that permeates all religions and all faiths: detachment. I feared detaching from my life as I knew it, detaching from my work and my identity with my work, detaching from the grace I felt in my work with survivors of sexual abuse, detaching from my tomorrows.

One day when my spirits were at their lowest and my bed-hair was at its most bizarre, I turned on Oprah. (Isn't that what we all do when we're having a sick day—or in my case, a sick year?) She had just gone public with her own sexual abuse, and she was doing a show on the effects of sexual abuse in adult women. Here were these courageous women sharing their stories, their struggles and their successes. I was deeply moved by their willingness to share their pain so that others would be encouraged to share their own pain with their families, or their therapists, or their close friends. I turned off the TV and began thinking about how Oprah used her personal trauma and the stage she had access to—her television show—to help others heal. And I began thinking *what do I have available to me that could provide help and healing to others?* Maybe I didn't have access to the same resources, but that didn't mean that my work couldn't be as powerful, maybe even more powerful, than the work done in regular psychotherapy. So what if I couldn't work every day? I could work at least one day a month. What if I had sexual abuse groups once a month, but for an extended period of time? And what if each all-day workshop focused on a specific aspect of healing the sexual abuse wound? By the end of that particular day in 1988, a personal miracle had occurred. Not only had I dashed off a letter to Oprah Winfrey and figured out a way to continue what I felt was my life's work, but even more importantly, I came up with what I thought was the right combination of time, participants, and subject matter to jumpstart a survivor's path to healing. I had found the format I had been searching for since my early days at the sexual abuse institute. Wow! I couldn't wait to begin.

And begin I did. In 1990 after another year of working with the material, gathering videos and other resources, and most importantly, getting feedback from other survivors and therapists, I launched Healing Steps. Each workshop was designed to be a catalyst to stir up memories, feelings, and unresolved issues.

This book, which grew out of those workshops, is also designed to be a catalyst, encouraging issues to surface so they can be dealt with and healed before they crawl back inside you, resurfacing at some unsuspecting time in your life, raising their ugly heads and taking you by surprise. They will—I can promise you that! And remember, memories return only when the individual has the ego strength and feels sufficiently safe in her life to remember.

Finally, I do want to add that this book is not solely my creation: it is the creation of all who have taken a Healing Steps workshop and all who have courageously reached out and shared their personal journey from victim to victor.

My hope is that women who read this book will be a part of the Silence Breakers, the women of courage who have stepped forward, each in her own way, to lay claim to her power and strength. She may not go public, she may not be in the public eye, but she recognizes that she was assaulted, abused, and used by another person in a more powerful position. We applaud the thousands of women (and the men who support them) who have come forth and said "Times Up," "Me Too," and enough is enough. Whether you were abused as a child or assaulted as an adult, it is time to stand up, to support others, and to learn how to heal your own wounds and strengthen your resolve to stop the abuse of the less powerful. It all begins with putting the blame and shame where it belongs. It begins with you and me.

One of the blessings of today's powerful cultural movement of honesty and truth-telling is learning that you are not alone. You are not alone in what you have experienced, and you are not alone in your struggles to heal and to find the strength to go forward with your head held high. We are all survivors; the difference is that we are no longer silent survivors carrying the perpetrator's secret; we are breaking the silence, we are shattering the myths, and we are standing tall in our shared reality. It's a great time to be a woman, and it's a perfect time for you to begin your own journey toward healing and power. May this book be a source of inspiration for you.

— *Sharyn Higdon Jones, San Jose, California*

P.S. At the end of 1989, I returned to full-time practice, my health has steadily improved, and now I am working less—by choice—so I can pursue writing and other long-delayed passions.

Introduction

Preparation for Your Healing Journey

*"We are healed of a suffering only
by experiencing it to the full."*
—Marcel Proust

*"You can't cross the sea merely by
standing and staring at the water."*
—Rabindranath Tagore

We all know the statistics: approximately one in every four women and one in every six men in the United States was molested as a child, and those numbers are also true worldwide. That means that in the United States, close to 63,000 children are molested every year, their median age being nine years old. It is estimated that 42 million survivors of childhood sexual abuse exist in America today. Knowing the numbers doesn't cure the problem, but it does help those of us who have been abused to know we are not alone. We're not alone in our suffering, not alone with our secrets, and not alone in the hope that we will be okay. Our hope has always been that what was done to us in the past will not color our choices, our decisions, or the quality of our lives in the present. But we are realists. We watch television, we read the news, and we go to the movies. We know the past haunts our present, and we know the past can influence our future. We also know that we have to move *through* the past and heal our wounds—not move on and forget about our abuse as others would like us to do.

I certainly do not believe that we have to live an experience in order to understand it. I do believe, however, that it is extremely difficult for those who have not suffered the humiliation, embarrassment, confusion, shame, anger, and loss to understand the complexity of the sexual abuse wound. Without treatment, the resulting emotional wreckage can continue for a lifetime. Since the perpetrator is generally someone the victim knows and trusts ninety percent of the time, and since the perpetrator is generally providing something of value to the victim when the abuse occurs, the repercussions are complex and confusing. We know that there are exceptions to this pattern. We know there is stranger abduction, stranger abuse, etc., and the effects are powerful and devastating in these situations as well, but we know that the majority of sexual abuse occurs in the context of an already-established relationship. No child is psychologically prepared to cope with repeated sexual stimulation. Even a two- or three-year-old, who cannot know that sexual activity is "wrong," will develop problems resulting from their inability to cope with the overstimulation that occurs during a sexual abuse.

As you embark on the process of healing, I want to remind you that this is *your* abuse and *your* process. You can decide with whom to share it, when to share it, or whether or not you even want to share it. There is one important exception to the "sharing" rule, however. If you have not shared your abuse with anyone, I strongly urge you to share it with at least one other person. As long as the secret is held between you and the perpetrator, the bond between you will be strengthened. I'll talk more about this in Step One – Breaking the Silence. Please note that I will use the pronoun "she" throughout this book. I have done this not to exclude the many men who have been molested, but because I am basing this workbook on my women-only Healing Steps workshops.

The Healing Steps process is one method for healing the abuse wound. The responsibility you have to yourself is to heal; it's not about your perpetrator now, it's about you and the actions you take on your own behalf. I hope the Healing Steps process will help you. If it doesn't seem right for you, fine. But keep looking and talking to others until you find a method that does fit for you, and *don't stop* pursuing possibilities until you embark on one of them. You are worth having a life that's lived in the present, not a life determined by your past. You are more than your molestation experience, and you deserve more than a life limited by the effects of your sexual abuse.

Once again, I want to remind you that you are not alone in your journey toward wholeness and recovery. Reclaiming yourself, your sexuality, your spirit, and your courage is possible for you. I believe it is possible. If I didn't believe in the reality of healing, I would have given up this work years ago. I have seen the difference one step makes, and the greater difference that the seven steps in this book make. A woman in one of the early Healing Steps workshops made refrigerator magnets for our group inscribed with the Chinese philosopher Lao-Tzu's words: "A journey of a thousand miles must begin with a single step," and this very important journey begins with the most important step of all—the first one. I congratulate you on your decision to take your life back, to explore your history, and to begin the process of self-empowerment and freedom.

Before we begin, let's look at some important guidelines.

Relationships Within an Abusive Family

Sexual abuse is defined as any sexual touch—by force, trickery, or bribery—between two people where there is an imbalance in age, size, power, or knowledge. Sexual abuse also includes voyeurism, exhibitionism, and inappropriate and age-inappropriate conversations or requests. If your molestation happened within your family and you are currently living with your family, this could be very difficult and confusing for you. Past blurs into present, present into past, and it's often difficult to stay centered without assistance. If you are working on past (or present day) molest experiences while still living with the perpetrator, I strongly urge you to seek professional help or to call a sexual abuse hotline

(800-656-HOPE). If you are not living with your family and the abuse happened within the family, then it is up to you whether you discuss your work with them or not. This is your experience, so you need to begin taking charge of it at this time. This includes taking responsibility for your own healing, setting boundaries for yourself and getting the help, support or guidance you may need.

Current Primary Relationships

If you are in a primary relationship, it is important to discuss with your partner the fact that you are embarking on a healing process which may be disruptive and which may create some tension within you. Take some time to let your partner know why you have decided to follow this process, and ask for support as you work through the steps. It is to the advantage of both of you that you succeed in completing your healing work. Your partner may not know you were sexually abused, you may worry that you will be judged for what someone did to you, maybe you don't want to be that vulnerable with someone else right now—that's fine. When one person in a relationship is molested, it becomes a relationship issue even if the abuse is unknown to the partner, or even if the abuse has never been discussed between the two of you. You don't have to discuss it with your partner. Right now, the main concern is that you are able to take the private time you need to do the exercises. You want that time to be respected. You don't have to share the content of your work, but it is important that you share that you are doing some very important personal healing. The way in which you honor your work will set the standard for others; hopefully your partner will recognize the importance of this step and support you. If not, seek out like-minded others in support groups, through your friendships, or through reading what other survivors have written. It's important to be reminded that even though you felt alone and isolated in the abuse you suffered, you are not alone at the present time. Thousands of other survivors are remembering, are sorting out their memories, are experiencing the same intensity of feeling, and are finding ways to heal their pasts—just like you.

A Word to Partners/Friends/Family

This paragraph is for you who love and care about someone who has been sexually abused and want healing for them, but who often feel impatient. You may find yourself showering them with comments such as "it happened years ago—just let it go," or "it's over now—you don't have to think about it anymore." You know the drill. It's painful for you to watch someone wrestle with the past, or to watch them repeat sabotaging patterns in order to avoid the past. They may self-medicate with drugs or alcohol, enter into the same bad relationship over and over again with the same predictable results, or live life under a cloud of depression. And if you're in an intimate relationship with someone molested as a child, then you know how their past can haunt not only their present, but yours as well. I strongly urge you to educate yourself and to find a specialist in your area to talk with, so you can understand your loved one and her struggles. You deserve the support, and just because your partner has a past darkened by abuse, it does not mean they do not have to be responsible to you and to the relationship. It is through relationships that the real healing can occur. All of us who are in a relationship know that our relationships provide the mirror through which we can see and know ourselves—if we choose to look. It's difficult to hold up that social persona day after day when we live with someone. Intimacy—or our attempts at intimacy—show us our limitations as well as our strengths. Be patient, be supportive, be interested if invited into the healing process, and respect your partner's boundaries if you are not. And, please do not pepper the survivor with questions. If someone tells you she was abused, let her know you are sorry she went through that experience and you'd be willing to hear about what happened if she would like to share the experience. Don't come back with "who abused you?" or "what did they do—what did you do?" Invite her to talk with you, but don't ask questions she may feel uncomfortable discussing with you at the present time. Respect her privacy while letting her know you are available should she want to talk about it. See also the section at the end of Step Six, which offers guidance and suggestions for you.

Therapy

If you are in therapy or plan to be in therapy, be sure to tell your therapist you are following the steps in this book so that he or she can assist you and integrate your Healing Steps work with the work you are doing together. This book is not meant to replace therapy, but rather to act as a guide or adjunct to your current work. If you are not currently in therapy, I suggest that you begin gathering referrals for therapists in your area who are experienced in working with survivors. I realize that therapy is a big commitment of time and money and may not be possible for you on a regular basis, but having a therapist available for some of the rocky times can be a big help. You can look to your local professional association for names of therapists; it is also quite common for therapists to have webpages that specify their specialties and their training, as well as their educational background, experience, and the kinds of licenses they have. You may even find a therapist who uses EMDR (eye movement desensitization and reprocessing), a technique that can be very powerful when used by a trained professional.

Also, ask for referrals from your physician or friends. Would you be more comfortable working with a male or female therapist, or does it matter? Once you have two or three names, interview these professionals by phone. Ask them about their experience and training in sexual abuse, their fee schedule, availability and how they handle emergencies. If you like what you hear, schedule an initial session to see how the two of you work together. If the chemistry seems right after the first session, schedule at least two more sessions and then evaluate how your work is progressing. If you don't feel comfortable with the therapist, or if you don't feel you are staying focused on your issues, speak to your therapist about what changes can be made. If you feel it's not a good fit for you, ask for a referral to another therapist. It's not necessary to feel comfortable in therapy, as it's rarely comfortable when you are working with abuse issues, but it is important to feel comfortable with your therapist.

If therapy is too costly, look for support groups that charge nominal fees: check with your local YWCA or with a county mental health center. Some therapists offer sliding scales, meaning they base their fees on what you are able to pay, so do ask when you are interviewing them. Local therapists may also know of support groups focusing on sexual abuse issues. Don't forget to check with your medical insurance company to see if they offer mental health coverage which can help offset the expense of individual therapy. Be persistent—you are worth the time and energy it may take to set up a support system for yourself.

Ten Guidelines for Taking Healing Steps

"We emerge into the light not by denying our pain,
but by walking through it."
— Joan Borysenko

1. Sexual Abuse is like a thumbprint—no two experiences are exactly alike, nor is one's healing experience just like another's experience. Yours is a unique path, so don't compare yourself or your healing journey with someone else's process.

2. The only way to healing and wholeness is through experiencing the feelings, the confusion, the darkness, and the remembering. There are no shortcuts.

3. You must be active in the healing process. There is no technique, person, book, workshop, or magic that can do it for you. There are only tools—and hopefully this book will be an effective tool for you. It has been designed to provide structure, support, and companionship as you travel along your healing path. You still have to do your individual work, such as the work you'll do through the exercises in this book: journaling, meditations, building personal power, etc. It's a bit like working in the garden. You can have the desire and good intention to have a lovely garden and excellent reference books that give you ideas—maybe even solutions, and certainly inspiration— but even the best of those manuals cannot plant, weed, and sow for you. Yep, the bottom line is that you have to do the work for yourself; no one else can do it for you. Remember, as the great poet Rabindranath Tagore said, "You can't cross the sea merely by standing and staring at the water."

4. Healing is best accomplished when not done in complete isolation. As you will see from the first Step – Breaking the Silence, secrecy is what binds us to the perpetrator and to the events that occurred. In order to break that bond and work through the shame, we must share with others either formally (in a support group or in therapy) or informally (with friends, other survivors, or those doing the work in this book along with you). I know many survivors have benefited from sharing on the Internet, which can be very helpful, but I feel strongly that personal, face-to-face interaction—if at all possible—is very powerful for healing. In *It's Never Too Late to Have a Happy Childhood,* Claudia Black writes, "Recovery is not a solitary journey. Even if you could do it alone, you don't deserve to do it alone."

Drawing by a sexual abuse survivor entering therapy

Private personal time is required, of course, to do your exercises. Private time also allows you to have contact with yourself, a skill not commonly well developed in survivors of abuse. Often much time has gone into staying out of contact and out of connection with one's "self." As you may know, a primary defense for abuse victims is "dissociation" which is simply disconnecting from feelings, from our bodies, and from our present experience. Dissociation is a survival tool, an adaptive response that's very common in abuse victims. The practice of staying in touch needs daily attention. I'll be giving you some exercises that can be done regularly so that you can learn that being in the present is really safe (and can be quite enjoyable).

5. When you are stuck processing a particular Step or when you are caught in a whirlwind of emotions, it is very important to have a guide (such as a therapist or a friend whom you've relied on in the past for counsel) to help you through the impasse. The reasoning here is different from that above: this is not just about isolation and secrecy, this is about the difficulty in moving forward when the going gets rough. There is a natural reluctance to look at certain aspects of the sexual abuse wound because they are too painful, uncomfortable, disgusting, repulsive, sad, or—you fill in the words. Since these are important steps, it's wonderful to have someone helping or encouraging you as you process them. Avoidance is very appealing, acting out becomes very seductive, and distracting yourself can become a way of life. This can be a difficult journey and having a coach, a therapist, or a friend who can be strong on your behalf is very important during this process. Many survivors don't complete the journey because they become overwhelmed. One of the later steps focuses on being there for yourself, but for now, do invite someone into your healing by letting them know what you are doing and asking them for encouragement so that you can stay on track.

6. Give yourself time to heal. Healing is about recognizing, dismantling and rebuilding a system of coping and managing. It's about past pain and current discouragement. There is no one timeline, and there are many levels of healing. Healing is about separating the past from the present and learning how to care for both. The Healing Steps process is designed to lead you through many of the issues associated with sexual abuse and allows you to repeat a step or parts of a step when needed.

7. A word of caution: keep life as simple as you can during the initial steps. This is not the time to take on extra work at the office, to increase your volunteer time, to remodel your house or to start a relationship—as tempting as all those things may be!

8. Pace yourself and remember, the Healing Steps workshops took place four to five weeks apart, so there was time to process the material. Give yourself the time and space to experience your feelings, to record your thoughts, and to complete the exercises.

9. Be aware of "flooding," which has nothing to do with El Niño. Well, actually it may be a kind of personal El Niño. Oftentimes, in an attempt to get through the healing process or to do it "right" with serious intent and enthusiasm, survivors will read stacks of books on the personal experiences of other abuse survivors, rent every movie dealing with an abuse theme, join several support groups, and live a life immersed in recovery. I believe strongly in pacing. Your own inner process will have an energy and pace of its own, and it's extremely important to stay attuned to that pace while you maintain a basic life structure. As you go through the healing process, it can also be very helpful to have a place in your home where you feel safe and comfortable, and where you have easy access to whatever helps you feel secure (music, a comforter, a favorite book). Create a sanctuary for yourself.

10. The exercises in each Step are designed to draw out your experiences and feelings as you move toward healing. I urge you to have supplies on hand before you begin Step One so that you will be ready to tackle the exercises when you are asked to do so. Make sure these supplies are handy so you won't have to scurry about trying to find them when the time is right for you to begin an exercise. These supplies include:

    • a journal or notebook reserved for Healing Steps

    • drawing pads – small and large

- marking pens

- crayons – fat ones, if you can find them

- access to relaxing music

- old magazines or catalogs

- a glue stick

- optional: a binder and lined paper (see exercises in Step One)

The abuse and your initial reactions to it have held you prisoner. Your long-held frustration and pain now lead a rebellion against your imprisonment and will eventually set you free. Let's begin.

*To wrench anything out of its accustomed course takes energy,
effort, and pain. It does great violence to the existing pattern.*

*Many people want change, but they are unwilling to undergo
the severe pain that must precede it. Rivers in extremely cold
climates freeze over in winter. In the spring, when they thaw,
the ice cracking produces an incredibly violent sound. The more
extensive and severe the freeze, the more thunderous the thaw.
Yet, at the end of the violent period of cracking and breaking,
the river is open, life-giving, life-carrying. No one says,
"Let's not suffer the thaw, let's keep the freeze."*

— Author Unknown

Step One
Breaking the Silence

"It takes two to tell the truth: one to say it and another to hear it."
— **Henry David Thoreau**

"And the day came when the risk it took to remain closed in a bud became more painful than the risk it took to blossom."
— **Anais Nin**

One of the most powerful moments in my Healing Steps workshops is the first minute of the very first day when each woman walks into the room. This is the moment when she has the courage to "show up," and by showing up, she lets us all know she was sexually abused. For some, this is the first time they have shared their secret with anyone. I am always impressed by this courageous move.

The power of breaking the silence is awesome. I don't believe real healing can occur until your memories of the molest are captured and the secret of being abused is shared. Keeping the secret may be as psychologically damaging as the abuse itself, because when you keep silent you remain isolated from others—and you feel somehow tainted and different. There is a freedom that comes with sharing your truth, a freedom that begins to change the isolation so often felt by survivors. Why revisit that awful scene or scenes? Why, after all the years of trying to forget, is it important to remember what can be remembered, and then to talk about it? And why share the details? Good questions. I wouldn't ask you to do anything that I didn't feel was essential for long-lasting recovery.

There are many ways to break the silence. One story I will always remember from the early nineties is a true story about an attorney who went a bit crazy in a courtroom during her first incest case. She was representing a 3-year-old girl. As her cross examination of the alleged perpetrator progressed, she completely lost control in the courtroom and began crying hysterically. Flooded with intense feelings, she rushed up to the defendant while he was on the witness stand and tried to strangle him! The judge immediately arrested her for contempt of court, and she spent the night in jail. The following day the judge gave her a choice of three sentences: serve two weeks in jail for contempt of court, be disbarred, or seek therapy. She was from a "perfect" family, she was Phi Beta Kappa in college, and she was in the top of her class in law school. How could anything possibly be wrong in her life? In spite of her doubts, she wisely chose therapy and uncovered a long-term molestation that she had repressed until that fateful day in court. She did her healing work and went on to work hard to reform laws regarding civil suits in the state of California. Sometimes we seek our therapeutic work, and sometimes it finds us when the time is right.

In 1995 the three remaining famous Dionne Quintuples decided to break a 45-year silence about their supposedly privileged lives: they gave an emotional interview about the sexual abuse perpetrated by their father. They stated how the abuse was "a part of our lives" and firmly advised other women *not* to keep it inside. They said they told a school chaplain about the fondling but were simply counseled to wear thicker coats!! Forty-five years is a long time to be silent, so I'm encouraging you *not* to wear thicker coats to protect yourself, but rather to shed the layers of secrecy, and to risk being vulnerable.

As I mentioned in the introduction to this book, as long as the secret is held, the bond between the perpetrator and the victim is strengthened. The *secret* is the tie that binds; it is the cornerstone of the sexual abuse wound. Often a perpetrator suggests to his victim that she will be blamed if the abuse is discovered, or that she will be removed from the home or separated from the family. Sometimes he threatens the child, or says he will hurt or sexually abuse other members of the family, or threatens to hurt himself. A perpetrator will sometimes tell his victim that it was the victim who seduced him, who started the abuse, and he will lay the shame and guilt on the innocent child. Some perpetrators provide something of great value to the child, which then sets up a real conflict within the child.

There are, of course, many reasons why the secret is held. I remember when Marilyn Van Derbur, Miss America of 1958 and an incest victim, was asked why she didn't tell anyone of the 13-year-long sexual abuse she endured from her father. In June of 1991, she explained in *People* magazine that it was "because I perceived there was no way out. A young child tells on her father and what happens? She's taken away from her family. Her father goes to jail. The family is destroyed, and the message is, 'It's all your fault.' " She certainly was and is not alone with her concerns. Children will tolerate a great deal to keep a family together.

Not knowing what to do or who to tell, not even having the words to explain what happened, fear of punishment and disclosure, feeling there is no one to tell, or at least, no one who we think will believe us—the list goes on and on. What is important here is for you to know what your experience was. Did you tell? Were you baffled and confused? Were you afraid? How did you make the decision to tell or not to tell? Did you find it difficult to find the words? One workshop participant who was initially very detached from her abuse experience wrote:

> *Words don't always mean anything. I can tell you anything you want to know and not have any feelings attached. Some people criticize me because they think I am too open about my past, but they don't understand that I'm simply reporting on someone else's life. The more I feel, the less able I am to use words.*

It's important to know that as soon as someone else knows about the abuse, the alliance between the perpetrator and victim is broken and the power-based relationship is over. In order for healing to occur, not only does the bond need to be broken, but someone else must be brought into what has occurred to help sort out the reality and meaning of your experience. There is a big difference between viewing what occurred through the eyes of an adult with the strength to heal (that's you—today!) and through the eyes of the child who was molested. It's that slippery slope where we lose our footing between childhood beliefs and adult knowledge that makes healing so difficult.

Having a third party to hold onto—so we can keep our footing—is important; having a trained person with us is vital in helping us sort out what our inner child has experienced and needs to express. The reality of what was done *to* us is difficult to comprehend. When you break the silence, you break through the denial and have the opportunity to shatter any erroneous beliefs that may surround your abuse. There can be as much damage to one's self-esteem, self-concept, sexuality, and capacity for intimate relationships from erroneous beliefs as from the actual abuse itself. The two most damaging erroneous beliefs held by survivors are "it was my fault—I allowed it to happen—and thus I'm not a victim, I'm a participant," and "I'm damaged goods not worthy of love or success in life." The power of these erroneous beliefs is that they often slip into the darkness of our unconscious and influence every aspect of our lives whether we are aware of them of not. They are the saboteurs who cut us off at the knees and cause havoc in our lives. We will discuss these Inner Perpetrators in Step Three—Confronting the Perpetrator.

Of course, the beliefs stemming from the abuse wound are many and varied; and they only serve to maintain the shame and secrecy that is so damaging. It's important to keep in mind that the *only* aspect of sexual abuse that a survivor is responsible for is her own healing. When you share your experience, you make it possible to receive understanding and support from others, and to create the beginnings of real intimacy with someone. As Henry David Thoreau once said, "It takes two to tell the truth: one to say it and another to hear it." Intimacy is difficult when abuse has occurred because intimacy is built on a foundation of trust. We will tackle this important issue when we look at Step Six, but for now just remember that you do not have to suffer in silence and you do not have to heal in isolation.

Who you decide to share your secret with is of great importance. It may be a family member, a trusted friend, a support group, a therapist—that's up to you. What I've found helpful is to begin by telling *yourself*. Yes, you heard me—telling *yourself*. The most important relationship in your life is the one you have with yourself—and certainly the one you have with the *one inside you who was molested*. You know the one I mean. Part of the work we are going to do in this section is to re-establish a relationship with her—the little one inside you who was hurt and confused by what was done to her. She may wreak a little havoc with you; she may show up when she is not invited with feelings you don't want, she may even momentarily overwhelm you with her feelings, or she may hide from you—not trusting that you will really take care of her. Expect the unexpected as you begin to establish a relationship with her.

There are several questions about remembering that come up repeatedly in workshops. "If I don't remember, how can I heal?" "If I don't remember the details, does that mean it didn't happen?" "Shouldn't I be undergoing hypnosis to force me to remember?" I say, take what you've got, work with it, and share it. If there is more for you to remember, you will. Stay open during this process, commit what you do remember to paper *and* share it verbally with one other person. That may just be enough. The assignments in this workbook will give you details about how to do this.

I'd like to discuss side effects for a moment. You may be entering unknown territory as you begin this process. There may be some landmines that surprise you and may be painful—landmines that may be confusing and leave you a bit dazed and off-kilter. That's normal and may indicate that you need to pace yourself in doing these exercises or may indicate that you need to be doing these exercises with a therapist experienced in working with the trauma of sexual abuse. Support and understanding are important companions on this journey. You survived the abuse, you will survive the healing, but you don't have to do it alone. There may be support groups in your area that can provide a wonderful community of fellow travelers who understand the struggles and challenges in the healing process.

One of the landmines that you may encounter is unwelcome memories. It's important that if unexpected breakthroughs occur, you have a safe place where you can let the memories emerge. In a sense, when you begin this process of healing, you're giving your unconscious the message that *you're ready—bring it on.* Sometimes uninvited memories and overwhelming feelings show up when you least expect them. Good. You're ready or they wouldn't show up at all. But you need to know how to manage those times. First, remember this is *just* a memory, *just* an intense feeling. This is not a continuation of the abuse or the presence of the abuser. Rather, it is an *aspect of the healing.* Be safe, don't use alcohol or drugs or self-defeating behaviors to alter your state. Experience it, so you can move through it. Remember, recovering your memories is a sign of health, not of craziness. You may want to call a supportive friend, your therapist, or someone who can just hang with you for a while. Expect to have reactions, feelings, some difficult moments as you move through the past on your way to a more balanced present. You really didn't expect it to be a smooth ride, did you?

Any truly life-threatening event, trauma, or major shock that you experience in your life needs to be dealt with, understood, and processed in order to set you free. If at the time of the trauma you were too young or too inexperienced to manage your experience, your mind will put it away until you are able to do so. As you do your healing work, it is normal to have breakthroughs or flashbacks; this generally happens when you are ready to manage the suppressed material.

It is also normal to have more than one flashback even though we all feel one is certainly enough! In order to move on, it's important to *feel* whatever feelings are evoked, to write them down, and to work with the content. It's important to keep in mind that the breakthrough is a *memory*, not an event happening in current time. Remember, you are ready for whatever is revealed, or it wouldn't be revealed. I'll be reminding you of that from time to time as we go through the Steps. It may take time to process the experience and sort it out, and it can certainly be confusing and overwhelming. This book is designed to be a catalyst, so don't be surprised when it stirs things up. It's difficult to work on material when it's deeply buried; much easier when it comes up to the surface and is available. Take advantage of all this archaeological work and grab onto what comes to the surface; work with it as it appears and before it slithers back into the unconscious.

Often there is an initial dark period or unexpected incident that kick-starts a woman's journey. (Remember the attorney I mentioned earlier?) I like to call these events "invitations" – invitations to begin a journey that we might not embark on willingly. Above all, take care of yourself during this process of self-discovery. Watch what you take on in your life and begin the practice of self-care, which I know is often difficult for survivors. You've suffered abuse, don't abuse yourself—you've had enough, right? So if you're ready, let's begin with Step One.

Making Contact with the Molested One

 In this and other sections of this book, we will use art and creative therapy as a tool for healing. When we do art therapy, we are creating a safe space where trauma-tized feelings can be brought out and processed in a way that can be more helpful than verbal processing. Trau-matic experiences are often first encoded in non-verbal images and feelings—without words. Capturing those feelings or images on paper can be a powerful tool to move us to the next level of our healing. To quote the great philosopher Goethe, "We talk too much; we should talk less and draw more."

Survivors have told me that these exercises sometimes cause their dreams to become more frequent and intense. Often dreams appear more like hellish nightmares than stories being spun in a coded language. Dreams however can be very healing in and of themselves. Pay close attention if they become repeti-tive or if you begin having nightmares – your dreams are simply trying to get you to pay attention to them. What are they telling you? Ask yourself for clari-fication before going to sleep the next night. You know how illusive dreams can be, so place a notebook and pen next to your bed before going to sleep and as soon as you awaken, write down your dream or dream fragments. Gather your dreams, take them into therapy with you, re-read them. At some point, their meaning may become clear to you. I had a client once who dreamt that a father figure appeared. He was a feeble and helpless old man. He put his arms around her, but when he tried to throw her down on the bed, she yelled at him, "Oh, no – *not* in my dreams – not even in my dreams!!" Clearly, she had internalized her power. She was strong, he was weak, and she was able to speak up and set her own limits: "Not even in my dreams!" A big step in the right direction.

Here is your first exercise. This one is designed to bring you in touch with your molested one.

EXERCISE: Visualization

Inside each sexual abuse survivor is a child who was hurt and confused by someone who took advantage of her. The child within is trapped with her hurt, her memories, her confusion; she needs to be released and healed. In this first exercise, we are going to get in touch with her, and hopefully forge a new bond and healing relationship with her.

Find a picture of yourself *at the age you were molested*—a photo that resonates with you. I recommend framing your photo (and thus honoring your inner child). Have the photo nearby when you do these exercises. (If this is too painful or upsetting, wait until the time feels right for you.) The point is to have a visual reference at hand—a reminder of just how young you were at the time you were molested.

In this exercise you will be asked to do some visualizations. (Some people have difficulty visualizing, and that's fine. I'll present another option for achieving the same results.) I recommend you either record yourself reading the instructions below, or find someone to read them to you. Either way will be helpful.

Put on some soothing music—no words, just relaxing instrumentals or sounds of nature. My longtime favorites are "Deep Breakfast" by Ray Lynch, "The Fairy Ring" by Mike Rowland, and a CD called *Desert Flower*. Get comfortable in a chair, on your bed, or on the floor. Turn off all your electronics—the phone, iPads, TV, etc. Do whatever you need to do to make your environment quiet and secure.

Now close your eyes and take several deep, cleansing, relaxing breaths. Breathe deeply into your diaphragm and slowly release your breath, letting go of any thoughts of the day or any concerns about doing this exercise the "right way." There is no right or wrong way. Just let yourself *be* for a moment. And then follow these directions:

I'd like you to imagine a very lovely and protective "safe place" in your imagination—a place you find restful and peaceful. This may be a garden, a particular place that you have visited in the past, a lovely cove next to the ocean, a favorite quiet room—whatever speaks to you of quiet and safety. Look through your mind's eye at the beauty there—smell any scents that may be present, feel the warmth or coolness of the day, notice the light. Is it morning, or noon? Or is it late in the day—is it night? And when you're comfortable with the scene you have created, imagine a bench or chair placed in your scene, and on the bench you see the child within you—the child who was abused. Notice how old she is. Do her feet touch the floor or ground? What is she wearing, how does she wear her hair? Notice the look on her face—see if you can tell what she might be feeling or thinking by the expression on her face. Just be with her for a minute or two.

Now I want you to introduce yourself to her. Let her know you are a safe person in her life, strong enough to stick up for her and protect her. You are here to help her heal and to tell the story of what happened to her that hurt her. Tell her you will take care of her and guide her healing. Tell her it is okay, that she is safe, and that you are someone she can trust. Ask her if she would be willing to take the first step and that you will show her how. You may ask her what she would like to be called. You may ask her what she would like you to do for her at the moment. If she asks, respond. If she is silent, just sit with her.

Take your time with this process. It may take you several times to do this before you feel satisfied that you've made contact with her or that she feels ready to tell her story. Repeat this exercise once a day until you feel ready to go on to the second part of this exercise—the art projects. It's very important that each time you leave her to conclude this exercise, you tell her you will be back. After doing so, "shrink" your image of her and symbolically tuck her into your heart before opening your eyes.

If you do not have an image, just let her know with your words that you will always be close by, and that she is not alone anymore. I recommend doing this visualization or meditation daily, spending intimate time with her as you go through all the Steps. Research shows that meditating five minutes a day, five days a week, is enough to lower stress levels and enhance the connection you feel with others, as well as with yourself. You don't have to spend more than five minutes a day with your little girl, your Inner Child, but there is a great deal of neglect in her history, and I think five minutes a day is well-deserved.

It takes time to develop a relationship with this part of yourself. Remember, the intent here is to imagine the child whose pain you can feel. It's about seeing her, touching her first with your words of support and then enveloping her with your words of comfort and understanding. It's about inviting her to express herself and committing to protect her. Eventually, of course, it's about healing her and becoming one with her. And it's at this magical place of integration where we can rediscover the wonder and the playfulness and the creativity that she can offer us. As Alice Miller, author and Jungian analyst, writes, "Only when I make room for the voice of the child within me do I feel myself to be genuine and creative." A goal worth reaching for.

If visualization is difficult or impossible for you, as it is for many people, just sit quietly, close your eyes, and say to yourself, "The part of me that was hurt and needs to be healed is ready to help me in this process with her openness, her willingness, and her strength." Take five minutes to repeat this over and over with deep breaths in between each repetition. You will know when you are ready to do the second part of this exercise.

If you would like a recorded alternative to this visualization, the best CD or mp3 I know of for healing is Emmett Miller's *Inner Child Healing*. It includes a beautiful guided imagery, led by Dr. Miller and his daughter, designed for women who were abused as children. On the same CD is a powerful interview with Margot Silk Forrest, the founder and creator of *The Healing Woman* newsletter. Two of the people I most respect in the healing arts on one CD designed for women like us—perfect! The information for this resource is at the end of this chapter.

✔ *EXERCISE:* Art Projects

Materials needed: Large drawing pad, large crayons or marking pens, magazines or catalogs, relaxing music.

Turn off all electronics so you will not be disturbed or distracted. Put on your soothing background music, and take several deep breaths, at least six, until you find yourself ready to begin this exercise. Choose one of the following options:

- **Draw a picture** of your molest with your non-dominate hand (if you're right-handed, use your left hand; if your left-handed, use your right hand), incorporating as much detail as you want to include. If you feel too overwhelmed, wait and pick another time. If there is more than one picture that wants to be drawn, draw it—and keep drawing until you feel finished. Take your time. There is nothing more important for you to do right now.

- **Create a map** of the house or place where you were molested. Include all the details you can remember.

- **Make a collage** about your abuse. Cut out words from magazines or catalogs, or write/draw them yourself. Glue images to a large poster board or something that has some substance to it. Feel free to embellish your collage in any way you choose. Create a "composite" of your molest that makes intuitive sense to you.

When you are finished, do whatever feels right with the drawing or collage. Put it away in a safe place, rip it up, put it aside until later, hang it up. You decide. It's your experience and your picture. Appreciate yourself for your willingness to bring your experience forward, instead of keeping it inside.

A Survivor's Drawing

Writing: If drawing feels too uncomfortable for you, write as much as you can remember about your abuse, including as much detail as you can. I suggest you do so on lined paper which you can put into a binder later. You are certainly welcome to do both writing and drawing, and to do them as often as you like. If you are describing different incidents, then write the age you were during each incident at the top of the paper. Write, write, write—don't worry about details, don't be concerned with the language you use. This is for your eyes only. I personally like a combination of writing and drawing on a large drawing pad. My own experiences were big; I wanted my drawing pad to be big as well. I used a black Sharpie for writing.

If possible, keep your drawing and writing supplies out and available. When thoughts, feelings, memories, or ideas pop up, keep them moving by capturing them on paper. Not only do you keep them from being buried once again, but you open the space for whatever was beneath the emerging material. As one of my important teachers once told me, "The only way *to* is *through*."

EXERCISE: Self-Soothing

If you are like most survivors of sexual abuse, taking care of yourself is probably not one of your strong points. You may be quite good at taking care of others, but self-neglect is a common residual effect of having been abused. We'll discuss this in greater detail in following chapters but for now, it is important to honor yourself as you begin this healing process. Self-soothing means the ability to take care of yourself in simple, nurturing ways when you are in emotional pain.

You may want to have a "soothing object" selected by your Inner Child who is stepping out of the darkness to be healed. The object could be a symbol of beginning a new chapter in your life, or perhaps a cuddly object that your Inner Child is drawn to. This should be an intuitive choice, so look around your home, go to a shop, or peruse a toy store—and let your "gut" make a selection for you. You will know it when you see it. Keep it close by when you do the exercises throughout this book.

Also, enjoy your Inner Child: take her to the park, the zoo, the boardwalk. Play with paints, clay, and don't forget to smell the Play-Doh! Laugh with her by watching the movie *Big* with Tom Hanks, or Disney's *Inside Out*. If you have been caught up in the wonderful coloring book resurgence that's going on right now, this is a perfect time to treat yourself. There are adult coloring books available everywhere. What a wonderful way for you to merge your Inner Child and your adult self.

Learning to self-soothe is a tough one for most people and certainly a challenge for survivors, but this is a good place to start. Learn that during this process, you need to take breaks, and not push yourself to a place where you are overwhelmed and under-equipped. Make a list of relaxing distractions that give you a break and soothe your soul, and keep that list close by. Warm, relaxing baths, a walk in nature, a TV show that tickles your funny bone, a book about a courageous person you admire, a cup of tea with a friend, yoga, a mystery novel—make your list right now. And I recommend you put at least ten things on it to give you plenty of options.

Breaking the Silence with Others

Now you have broken the silence with *your-self*. You have admitted that, yes, you were sexually abused; and yes, you are strong enough to remember what occurred to the best of your ability; and yes, you believe that to be healed you must now break the silence by telling one other person if you have not already done so. You see the importance of breaking that bond that ties you to the perpetrator and your past. You also recognize the importance of no longer remaining in the dark, which only perpetuates the shame that is *theirs*, not yours. As was so accurately stated in *The Healing Woman* newsletter, "Victims of child molestation become the guardians of silence and the architects of deception."

Telling Someone in Person

This is your experience, so you decide what you want to share, with whom you want to share it, and what you want in response to your sharing. It is up to you to know when you are ready to share, although I'm guessing if you are reading this book, you are ready. It is important to tell a friend or family member only if it appears that they can deal with the information. Be selective. People with experience or training in the area of sexual abuse can provide the best support, as others may have good intentions but may err by minimizing your experience in order to protect you from hurting. You can also choose someone with whom you have shared information in the past and who you know cares about you. If you are disclosing incest, I recommend telling someone other than your family in the first go-round.

This brings up the issue of telling your partner or significant other. Whether to tell a partner always instigates a lively debate, often strong opinions, and usually confusion about the "right" thing to do. If the molest occurred within the family, the survivor or her partner may have a current relationship with the perpetrator. As one workshop member told the group, "I don't want my husband to confront my uncle at a family gathering—and he would. That would be worse for me than keeping the secret." Another survivor, when asked if she would discuss her abuse with her husband, emphatically stated, "I can't think of a good reason to share the experience. I am perfectly able to deal with it alone. I need to be independent and strong on my own; I see no reason to include my partner. There are some things in my life that I feel are mine alone; he doesn't need to know everything about me!" She had clearly decided the best option for herself.

Many other women, however, have reported that sharing their past has strengthened their relationship, and they have found their partner to be empathetic and supportive. Shelley said her husband was at first "shocked and couldn't deal with it," but the knowledge "brought us closer together, and he became more sensitive to my needs during lovemaking." She went on to write, "I wanted to share with him who I am and why I'm so afraid to get close to him—and why I behave in such a teasing sexual manner and then push him away. I wanted him to know that I wasn't rejecting *him,* that it was a pattern of mine that I am working on. I thought it would help him to understand me better." Shari admitted, "I was ashamed, uncomfortable, afraid of what he might think of me and doubted that he would believe me. He was stunned. He said it made some things between us make more sense. I was married for nineteen years before he knew anything about my background! I felt I was betraying a long-held secret, and I had a lot of really mixed feelings. The most difficult feeling of all was the guilt I felt in telling: I hadn't kept the secret." Another survivor remembered telling her partner and how much fear she felt wondering if he would think she was responsible for the abuse. "Telling him caused me to relive the molest with much sadness and pain," she recalled. "At the end I was relieved I could discuss it with him. He was very supportive, empathetic and accepting. He asked for more information but never pushed or pressured me for details. I just gave him general information— the number of times, who, their relationship to me. In the beginning I wasn't sure how much information about the molest I wanted to divulge. I felt my sharing with him helped him understand me on a deeper level."

And here was the common thread of the women who wanted their partners to know of their sexual abuse: they wanted to be *understood,* especially as they came to understand themselves better through their own therapy or self-reflection. They were also willing to be vulnerable, and they felt ready to trust their partners with this sensitive information. Sharing a molest experience with a significant other is an individual choice ranging on a continuum from mentioning it to your partner to sharing intimate details of your experience. This is *your* molest experience and *your* choice as to whether you want to share it with your partner.

A word of caution: regardless of who you decide to tell, don't set yourself up for unrealistic expectations of what the listener will do or say. Just hope to be heard. Most people don't know what to say or do when they hear a story about abuse that happened to someone they care about, so build that into your disclosure. Once you have decided whom to tell and when you are ready to speak up, practice what you will say. Write it down, say it out loud to the mirror, or tell your dog or cat. For example, you might say:

> *Mary, I'd like to share something with you about myself that I have not talked about before. Since this is my experience, I'm asking you to not share it with anyone else. It's my story to tell. I'm telling you because I'm starting a process of healing and this is an important part of my journey. I'd like you to just listen—you don't have to do anything or solve anything—just be my friend and listen. Would you be willing to do that?*

Remember that this step is about disclosure, not about confrontation, so don't let your first step be telling the perpetrator that you know what he did to you. The results of that kind of confrontation will probably be unfortunate and painful—unless you are well-prepared. We'll talk more about that in a later chapter.

This is also an opportunity to write about the feelings evoked when you *think* about telling someone else what happened to you. You may want to write an imaginary dialogue—or "script"—of what and how you would tell someone, including what you fear they may say. Write how you would respond if they said, "It was a long time ago—time to move on," or "I know him. He would never do that!" or "I'm so glad that it's over and you are just fine now," or "How do you know that happened? Maybe you got it all wrong." You get the picture. Listen to that imaginary dialogue of your friend expressing doubt, and practice your responses *which will always have the strength of your truth.*

Telling Someone in a Letter

Letter writing (and this does *not* necessarily include mailing the letter) is an excellent way to record your thoughts. Doing this on a computer can be helpful because it allows you to easily change, correct, and capture exactly what you want to say. But if you do choose to write your letter on the computer, copy it in longhand in your journal. There is a closer connection between you and the experience when you write the words on paper with a pen.

By the way, I found a "Do Not Disturb" sign in a gift shop that I keep on my home office door. I've found it invaluable when I'm writing, thinking, doing my own healing work, or just needing quiet time. I shut the door and hang it on the doorknob. This was useful especially when I had two children at home and didn't have my own home office. I would hang it on the bedroom or bathroom doorknob, and I would take private time in whatever increments were appropriate for the age of my children. I would set a timer outside the door and let them know that this was "my time" and they were to wait until the timer went off before knocking on the door. I told them unless the house was on fire or someone was wounded, I was not to be disturbed! I had to practice honoring myself by setting boundaries. (More about the important issue of boundaries in a later chapter.) I had to learn that I deserved to not always be "on call" for my children. I also had to believe that my needs for privacy were important, as were the needs for privacy and personal space for my children. Oh, and remember libraries? A wonderful place to do your writing and not be disturbed!

EXERCISE: Write a Letter

It doesn't matter which letter you write. What is important is that you have the courage to choose the one you responded to when you first read through the choices. This assignment may take several sittings. Don't give up. Complete it through to the *appropriate signature* at the end.

- Write a letter to someone you feel close to, and share your secret with that person. If you have trouble getting started, take another look at the suggested dialogue in "Telling Someone in Person."

- Have your Inner Child—the young part of you who experienced the sexual abuse—write a letter to your adult self, explaining what she has always wanted someone to know and understand about her experience.

- Write a letter to the young one inside you who has kept the secret. Let her know that you know what happened and you are always there to support her. Tell her what she needs to hear from you right now. There is no one who knows her needs like you do.

Telling Your Story in Court

One of the most stunning and disturbing revelations of sexual abuse came in 2016 when allegations were made against Larry Nassar, the doctor who served the USA Gymnastics team through four Olympic Games. Nassar was an associate professor at Michigan State University from 1997 to 2016, where he was also the physician for the women's crew and gymnastics teams. Many of our well-known and gifted Olympic athletes were sexually abused by Nassar, and they were courageous enough to come forward and confront him. They also expressed their anger at USA Gymnastics and the University of Michigan for "enabling" the abuse to continue. As of this writing, debate is still going on as to who knew what and when—and who was responsible for the continued abuse, but one thing remains clear and indisputable: Larry Nassar was a serial predator who took advantage of girls as young as six years old, and his abusive behavior continued for years. He pled guilty in November 2017 to a total of ten counts of criminal sexual conduct (digitally penetrating girls between 1998 and 2015 for no legitimate medical purpose and without consent), and he admitted that he used his position of power and trust to abuse young girls entrusted to his care. Several days were set aside in a Michigan courtroom in January 2018 to give the 125 victims who filed police reports of abuse the opportunity to give victim impact statements. As it turned out 160 young women, and their parents, came forward to confront Larry Nassar. The number of victims violated and emotionally traumatized by the former sports medicine doctor makes this the biggest sexual abuse scandal in the history of sports.

As of this writing, the 54-year-old Nassar has been sentenced to 60 years in prison on federal child pornography charges, and a minimum of 40 years for systemic sexual abuse. He will be eligible for parole in 99 years—in the year 2117. In her statement, Olympian Aly Raisman, said, "Let this sentence strike fear in anyone who thinks it is okay to hurt another person. Abusers, your time is up. The survivors are here standing tall and we are not going anywhere."

The court process is a long one. After a secret is revealed, the investigation begins, the attorneys prepare, court dates are set, and the anxiety builds for the victim. The opportunity to speak up during the trial can be emotional and traumatizing, which is why some survivors don't wish to speak up in this setting. But telling your truth can also be cathartic and freeing. For some victims it provides the only opportunity to tell their story in their own words in front of the perpetrator. There is power in truth, there is freedom in truth, there is strength in relieving yourself of a secret long kept. Is that enough? No, but it is an important step toward health and healing. I applaud the bravery and tenacity of the many women who did come forth, who did break the silence of their lengthy abuse, who did confront the institutions that allowed the abuse to continue, and who helped all of us take a step forward in moving sexual abuse out of the shadows and into the light. Such action is indeed worthy of a gold medal.

On Valentine's Day, 2018, President Donald Trump signed a bill into law aimed at protecting athletes from sexual abuse. This legislation requires the reporting of all sexual abuse allegations to the police within 24 hours and extends the statute of limitations to up to 10 years after the victim realizes he or she was abused. Diane Feinstein, the Senator from California who sponsored the bill, issued a statement saying, "The days of turning a blind eye to abuse are over. This vital reform was possible only because of the incredibly courageous women who decided to come forward, share their pain, and do all they could to make sure this dark chapter is never repeated." A positive step after the brave disclosures by so many young athletes.

EXERCISE: Setting up an Autobiographical Binder

One of the tools that has been the most helpful to many of my clients is the "All About Me" binder. Buy a binder with lined paper and dividers, and label the sections by ages—such as 0–5, 6–10, 7–12, 13–18, 18–25, 25+, etc. When you complete your writing assignments, such as those in the previous exercises, put your pages in the appropriate section. I encourage you to write or journal as much as possible as you continue through these Steps. By capturing the memories and events that have occurred in your life and putting them in chronological order, you will develop a better understanding of your life. If you have pictures of yourself at various ages, insert them. This journey is all about getting reacquainted with yourself—with no secrets to hide, nothing edited, and with the purpose of creating the kind of life you envision for yourself without the chains that bind you to the past.

Women Write about Breaking the Silence

I want to share the reflections of three women who went through my "Breaking the Silence" workshop. The first is a letter.

Dear Sharyn,

I had no idea what I wanted to get out of your workshop. I had some vague ideas about healing the shame and working with my "kid," but your session was a real eye-opener. I knew there were other women, like myself, who had experienced the same horrors as I, but when I came face to face with it, it really blew me away. I felt like a composite of all the other women, and many times it felt as if there weren't eight separate people, but rather, one being who was going through all the hurt and pain we were all feeling. I left the workshop in a strangely elated mood, considering the emotional climate we had just waded through.

When I got home, I couldn't believe it! I sat down with my two teenage girls and told them all about the workshop and the sexual abuse I had suffered as a child. After I was finished [and this is the hard part], my 19-year-old daughter got tears in her eyes and reluc-

tantly told me of an incident between her and her older brother. She said she had carried the guilt and shame around all this time. There was a lot of loving and sharing between us that night, and I haven't been closer to my kids since they were babies.

If I ever had any doubt that getting the truth out and talking about it was the right thing to do, this incident decided it for me. Now I'm going around, thinking who can I tell next. So tell all the women you work with that telling is healing—not only for yourself but for someone else who may be suffering in silence. I feel good and strong right now, although I might not always feel this way. I'm enjoying it while it lasts.

Thanks again, Sharyn, for helping me on my journey to health.

With love,

B.

And from another woman:

This poem is dedicated to the wonderfully courageous women of the Healing Steps workshop and their caring leader, Sharyn. The title refers to the common bond we all share, and the little child that each of us carries inside.

Between You and Me

Between you and me,
There are secrets we share
Between you and me,
It will always be there
The shadowy faces
The fears, the dark places
The things that were done
The tears and the pain
A part of that hurt
Will always remain
Between you and me.

Between you and me
No one can know
The guilt and the shame
We feel, as we go
Back to that time
When we were a kid
And a memory from which
We will never be rid.

Between you and me
It's our wish to deny
Those unspeakable acts
That made us want to die
For how could an adult
Do that to a child
And the rage deep inside us
Just makes us feel wild
But it's between you and me.

Between you and me
Don't you think that it's time
For the one who's responsible
To take blame for the crime?
We have carried it with us
For so many years
Now's the time to let go
And shed healing tears.

Let's start being good
to you and me
Take care of us, nurture us,
So we can feel free.
But most of all, take the time to tell

The whole world about your private hell.
And by Breaking the Silence
You ensure there will be
No children who feel
Like you and me.

And more wisdom, just as a group member wrote it:

Two years ago, when I envisioned what it would be like to be in a group working through the effects of childhood sexual abuse, a less than attractive image of a bunch of bitter women commiserating about their lives stuck in my head. I didn't particularly like the idea—I preferred to do my personal work personally, and I had no desire to participate in what I imagined would amount to no more than a structured bitch session.

While I admit that I attended my first Healing Steps with little room to be disappointed, that in no way accounts for the tremendous treasure I found in the participants who were there that day and the facilitator, Sharyn Higdon Jones. In the beginning, the participants were strangers who immediately earned my respect by telling their stories, working through challenging exercises, and even by refusing to participate when it was too much for them. Now they are a cherished part of my life—friends within a narrow but profoundly important area of who I am. I will always credit these women with providing me the support and agitation I have needed to revive important qualities of my character, which as an act of survival were forced into the shadows so many years ago.

Healing Steps has made a difference for me between "knowing" what I needed to do, and "getting" how I needed to do it. I always knew I needed to be angry, but until I sat in a group getting incredibly angry at a man who had the audacity to hurt the woman next to me, I didn't get that the men who perpetrated against me deserved the same anger. By getting angry for the women I valued so highly in my group, I learned to value myself and be angry on my own behalf. By supporting the women in my group as they pursue their own healing, I find within myself the capacity to heal also.

I used to believe the capacity to heal meant the ability to put the past behind me, go on as if the abuse never happened. Through highly focused exercises and meditations led by Sharyn, good cries and better laughs, the women in my group have taught me otherwise. Though initially I was hoping for a quick fix, a finite number of steps that would make it all better, I have come to appreciate that every choice I make is a potentially healing Step, and every day is not only an opportunity to build on the healthy choices I make but also a fresh start when taking care of myself.

Healing Steps has taught me that to heal means to acknowledge my experiences and grow not as a victim who is afraid to see the truth, but as a survivor who is stronger for having come through it all with dignity.

I cannot end this chapter without a caution. Breaking the silence is not a minor step: it may be the biggest step of all. And like any major movement, there can be repercussions. You have given yourself permission to open up, to go "public," to put down the burden of shame, to start or continue a journey of healing. For some, this step opens up painful memories, interrupts relationships, unleashes intense feelings, and wreaks havoc in your daily life. Prepare for this. I cannot stress enough how important it is to have a support system, a good friend, a therapist, a group who can be there for you and bring clarity to what can be a confusing and murky time. There is hope, there is healing, there is an end to the intensity of feelings evoked by every Step in this process.

A participant in Healing Steps wrote a short article under the pen name of Lily Storm and published it in *The Healing Woman* newsletter. She explains the process.

Accepting the Inner Child's Pain as Our Own

With dry mouth and churning stomach, I climbed the steps of the gray concrete building where the Healing Steps workshop was being held. For the first time, I would be talking with others about the childhood sexual abuse I suffered—and I had never felt so scared or so alone. I walked into a brightly carpeted room with throw pillows scattered about, inviting a cozy intimacy.

However, the nine women in the room were anything but cozy or intimate. Some were trying to make polite conversation, while others sat quietly, clasping and unclasping nervous hands. One woman sat alone, shoulders hunched, staring vacantly ahead, while keeping a death grip on her styrofoam cup. Mostly, we played "eye tag" because none of us wanted to see our own abuse reflected in another's eyes.

We were all on our separate islands of pain, waiting to plunge into the icy waters of telling and bridge the gap of isolation we had put between ourselves and the rest of the world. It was a brave thing we were doing, but none of us felt very brave. Our inner children were very much in evidence that day. I know mine was squirming uncomfortably in my lap.

With the encouragement of our therapist, and as the workshop progressed, each of us, like timid flowers, opened up and told our stories. The flood of emotions was so intense that many women fell apart. Some had flashbacks they refused to believe, while others were still shaming and blaming themselves for their own abuse. I was surprised and pleased to see that after just six months in therapy, I was able to empathize with the other women and yet remain strong in my own healing process. I was sure that my therapist would be very proud of the way I had handled myself in the workshop. These same thoughts would return later to slap me in the face.

("Lily" goes on to say how she had an intense flashback that evening with new information about her molest. Her memories came crashing through her consciousness, leaving her stunned. I'm not giving those details because this is her molest and her story to tell. I will go on with what she shares about the meaning of this experience.)

> *I realized that the pain I was experiencing was my Inner Child's pain; that the Inner Child was really me and that I was experiencing my own pain. In my therapy, I had always stood beside my Inner Child, nurturing and comforting her, but I never shared her pain. I realized that as long as I continued to look upon her as a separate being, I could deny that the abuse really happened to me.*
>
> *As the reality of the abuse hit home, it became almost more than I could bear. I was disoriented and unable to get my emotions under control. Finally, in despair and sobbing hysterically, I called a friend. I told her I was going crazy and I was afraid of being devoured by those painful memories, losing the real me, forever. She assured me that feeling all this pain was a necessary part of the healing process. At the time, I wanted to tell her to go jump in a lake. But she was right. The craziness did get better as I held my Inner Child close, letting her know how loved and protected she was, as I surrounded myself with people who were giving me the same message.*
>
> *I learned that unless I share the pain of my Inner Child and accept it as my own, I can't finish healing. It is as simple, and as difficult as that, with no shortcuts. But I know I will get though the pain, and then both my Inner Child and I will be stronger and healthier.*

By telling your story, by breaking the silence, you will join a community of men and women who are no longer willing to be silent, who are courageous enough to break the bond with their perpetrator and who will no longer keep the secret in which sexual abuse thrives. I've heard it said that owning our story can be hard, but not nearly as difficult as spending our lives running from it. We remember, we open all the wounded places within us, and then we heal.

As you take this journey, you may find strength in this beautiful prayer by Michael Leunig, in his book *A Common Prayer*:

Let us pray for wisdom. Let us pause from thinking and empty our mind. Let us stop the noise. In the silence, let us listen to our heart— the heart which is buried alive. Let us be still and wait and listen carefully. A sound from the deep, from below. A faint cry. A weak tapping. Distant muffled from within. The cry for help.

We shall rescue the entombed heart. We shall bring it to the surface, to the light and the air. We shall nurse it and listen respectfully to its story. The heart's story of pain and suffocation, of darkness and yearning. We shall help our feelings to live in the sun. Together again we shall find relief and joy.

# Suggested Reading

Your Inner Child of the Past, by Hugh Missildine

Recovery of Your Inner Child: The Highly Acclaimed Method of Liberating Your Inner Self, by Lucia Capacchione PhD

Healing the Child Within, by Charles L. Whitfield MD

Outgrowing the Pain: A Book for and About Adults Abused as Children, by Eliana Gil

I Know Why the Caged Bird Sings, by Maya Angelou

The Courage to Heal: A Guide for Women Survivors of Child Sexual Abuse, by Ellen Bass and Laura Davis

Betrayal of Innocence: Incest and Its Devastation, by Susan Forward and Craig Buck

I Never Told Anyone: Writings by Women Survivors of Child Sexual Abuse, by Ellen Bass

A Common Prayer, by Michael Leunig

I strongly recommend the relaxation CD *Inner Child Healing,* by Emmett Miller, MD, with his 11-year-old daughter, Aeron. The CD includes an interview with Margot Silk Forrest, founder of *The Healing Woman.*

If you know of a man who was sexually abused, I highly recommend *Victims No Longer,* by Mike Lew, and *Beyond Betrayal,* by Richard B. Gartner, PhD.

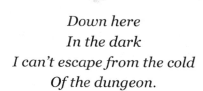

Down here
In the dark
I can't escape from the cold
Of the dungeon.

It chills me
The cold filled with pain.
Won't someone
Turn on the lights.

I can't see
Like everyone else.
I just can't see through
The pitch blackness.

It's like being outside
In a thick fog at night
With no streetlights
Nothing to keep me warm.

Not even a friend.

— a survivor, age 16

Step Two
Where Was the Loving Protector?

"The arms of the 'divine' Mother are always around you.
You have only to lay your head on her shoulder."
— **Ondrea Levine**

Webster defines "protect" as *to cover or shield from injury or destruction; the support of one who is smaller or weaker*. It is often said that the best antidote to child abuse is a close relationship with your mother. In her 1981 book *Father-Daughter Incest*, Judith Herman states, "Only a strong alliance with a healthy mother offers a girl a modicum of protection from sexual abuse." Why do you think she made that statement?

I always started the second Step workshop with these questions:

- Did you feel protected as a child?

- Did you feel that someone in your home was aware of what was happening or had happened to you?

- Did you feel that person could or would take action to shield you from injury or further abuse?

- Did you have someone in your life who was connected to you and could see your "clues," at least at some level?

- Where was the protector in your life?

And I always had the following quote on a large board in the front of the room:

When I was a child, I had a recurring fantasy that was so powerful, it was almost hallucinatory. I would imagine that I heard someone crying, and this crying was so poignant, so compelling, that I would leap up from my bed each time to try to find that person and take care of her. I had no idea until much later in life that the crying was part of myself.

— Kathie Carlson, In Her Image:
The Unhealed Daughter's Search for Her Mother

Stop reading for a moment and answer these questions for yourself:

- Where was your protector?

- Did s/he know?

- Was s/he capable of stepping up to protect and support you?

In most of my cases—either in individual therapy or in my workshops—the designated protector is the mother. (If you have another "protector"—a grand-mother, foster mother, etc.—just substitute the name of your protector when I use the word "mother.") Generally, Mother is the one responsible for our feeling of security, and that means that she assumes four major roles in our lives: she is our protector, our nurturer, our role model, and our biggest cheerleader. She is also the one who (hopefully) accepts us for who we are. Because we are so deeply dependent on our mothers for survival, the most frequently asked questions *and* the issue that weaves itself in and out of our lives relentlessly until we learn the lessons presented here are:

- How could the one person we counted on, the one who was supposed to protect us from harm, the one who was expected to shield us from pain and betrayal, how could she let this happen?

- How could she not understand what we were going through? How could she not do something to end our suffering? How could she not see how alone and overwhelmed we were?

In my experience with sexual abuse survivors, the most intense and longest lasting anger—as well as the deepest pain—is *not* around the behavior of the perpetrator; it's around the perceived or actual betrayal of the Mother. Even when delving into multi-layered issues around their mothers, survivors remain haunted by these unanswered questions. The sense of betrayal is because we expect Mother to be the nurturer who protects her daughter or son at all costs. We expect Mother to be a bear who rears up and ferociously protects us. We expect her to see all, know all, and to have eyes in the back of her head. The archetype of the Mother is firmly imprinted on our psyche: our expectations are in place and our disappointments are visceral. Mothers are the Jupiters of the familial Universe; they are the ones who shield us from harm and destruction. If it were not for Jupiter, the Earth would be destroyed by renegade matter in space. And we expect the same sort of protection from our mothers.

It's important as we do the work in this Step that we don't blame our mother for the actual molestation unless she was the perpetrator or the co-perpetrator. Blame her *only for her part.* She may have known and didn't act, she may have been neglectful, she may have denied that anything happened—but don't displace onto her what belongs to the perpetrator. The abuser deserves the full blame for the abuse, and she deserves the blame for what she did or didn't do that resulted in the abuse wound that was inflicted on you.

A Survivor's Drawing

When I worked with molesters as part of a sexual abuse treatment program, I found that not only did perpetrators minimized their actions (if they admitted them at all), they were also quick to blame someone or something else. And if they weren't blaming, they were rationalizing: "the child initiated…"; "she liked it because she didn't stop me…"; "I was drunk… ." The rationalizations were all predictable and tired. The most outrageous and creative excuse I ever heard was from a man from California's Central Valley who said his wife must have added something to her homemade spaghetti sauce because every time he ate it, he molested his daughters. Clearly, he couldn't be held accountable when it was his wife's sauce that caused the molestation, right? Of course, he didn't have an answer when I asked him why he didn't just stop eating the spaghetti.

Put the blame for lack of protection or support on the designated protector *if* she didn't protect you or support you once she did know. Keep the blame for the abuse on the abuser.

Common Types of Mothers in Abusive Families

It's clear that it is the sexual abuse itself *plus* the lack of protection and support that leads to the deepest wound. It is this wound that contains not only the painful experience of the abuse itself from which we need to heal, but also a shadow that colors or darkens much of our life. When we don't have someone to protect us when we're young, we not only feel anxious, we are also more vulnerable to a sexual predator. There are countless circumstances where we can feel abandoned and unprotected as children.

The Absent Mother: Sins of Omission

Mentally Absent: There are many ways a mother can be mentally absent from her role as the protective parent. She can be otherwise preoccupied, she can be mentally ill, she can be an alcoholic or addicted to prescription or recreational drugs. Other addictions come into play here as well—work, exercise, shopping, Internet, television etc. She may be a "workaholic" mom, with a closer relationship to her work life than to her family life. Her mental energy may be focused on a disabled sibling, or on financial struggles.

Physically Absent: A mother can be struggling with a long-term illness, episodic illnesses, hospitalizations. She may have permanently left the home, she may have taken frequent or extended business trips, or she may have been out of town caring for another family member. She could be physically incapacitated. She may be a single mom having to work several jobs in order to provide for her family.

Emotionally Absent: A protector can feel powerless, be depressed, or view herself as a dependent "little girl." Often such women are themselves victims of a husband's dominance or abuse and have never learned to speak up for themselves, let alone for their child. She may have been sexually abused as a child and has never done her healing work. Mothers often shut off the pain of their own abuse by ignoring signs and clues coming from their abused children.

Studies have shown that approximately half the mothers of sexually abused girls are incapacitated by physical and/or mental illness, including drug addiction. These mothers are often unavailable physically because of multiple hospitalizations, and emotionally because of their physical challenges. This kind of abandonment of the child by the mother, whether intentional or not, is often associated with molestation. As you can imagine (or have experienced), an absent mother produces strong feelings of separation and neglect in the child. Developmentally, a girl yearns to be deeply understood by her mother, and when that doesn't happen, she is left with a deep scar. As one woman described it: "It's like a pit of loneliness that seems to always be there."

You Turned Your Head

Mother, I wanted you to save me.
You turned your head.
He says if I tell, you will die, Mother.
I sever myself from my body.
My tongue is a glass bowl, underwater.

I want to hear your comfort.
Paste your voice to my skin
Like velvet China nights.
Kiss the power of your beautiful face.
I wanted you to love me.
Mother, you turned your head.

— *Excerpted from "You Turned Your Head," by Janice Mirikitani*

Hand in hand with the pain of the unavailability of the protector is the anger that grips you—and doesn't let go. You are pissed at what you didn't get—and never will get—from your mother, and angry that you always had to take care of yourself—and still do. Two ultimately self-defeating but understandable declarations usually attach to these devastating feelings: "When is it my turn? I want my turn!" and "I won't give it to myself until it is given to me!" The unhealed child wants what she never had and often insists on it throughout her entire life. In the article "The Mother Wound" (*The Healing Woman*, 1994), I was quoted as saying that "if your mother is physically present but unavailable, it is sometimes only your anger that keeps you connected in a relationship with her. Your anger is the only way to hold onto her." The thread of connection may not be healthy, but it is a thread. And it explains why it can be so difficult to let go of our anger and move to what lies beneath—the even more painful possibility of emotional abandonment.

Among women who have been abused as children, two diametrically opposed struggles often present themselves in adulthood: an ongoing "neediness," and the attitude that "I can do it myself—I don't need anyone." A deep pit of loneliness and disconnection lies beneath the inflated independence and sense of responsibility, a lifelong yearning for connection. Needing someone or something makes a survivor feel exquisitely vulnerable—and consequently, vulnerability is generally avoided by the adult survivor.

Another result of mother abandonment in all its forms is a loss of respect for our mother, a view that she has "sold out," that she is invisible, or that she did not do all she could have done because of her "limited" role as a woman. We see her as not taking care of business, or not speaking up on her own behalf, or on behalf of her children. We see her as being avoidant, weak or fearful. And we sometimes generalize what we experience with our mothers, applying it to "women" as a whole and incorporating this "passive woman" into our definition of ourselves as women. These women—our role models—leave us with limited possibilities and silent voices, limitations that may be internalized as we grow up, creating self-imposed barriers and faulty belief systems about being a woman in today's world.

Just before my father died of a heart attack, he purchased two tickets for an anniversary trip to Paris. After he passed away, my mother felt she could never use the tickets, because a woman "could not travel without a man." Her lifelong dream was to see Paris, but she never went because of her own belief system. She had the means, she had the desire, she had a daughter willing to accompany her, and she outlived my father by twenty years—but she never could move beyond her own self-imposed limitations.

What do I think is the *most* devastating result of an absentee protector? It's that we use our mothers as models for how to nurture and care for us—and we learn well. We continue a dysfunctional pattern of self-abandonment and self-neglect into our adulthood. I'm guessing that most readers of this workbook can relate to this and will agree with me that self-care is a major and continuing struggle in your life.

The Co-Conspirator Mother: Sins of Commission

Sexual abuse by women is rare (5 percent), but maybe not as rare as once thought. Of course, we're all familiar with the teacher-student abuses that have grabbed the headlines in the last decades, but there are other occurrences. Mathews, Mathews, and Speltz, in a 1992 exploratory study of women perpetrators, wrote about three types of mothers who molest. One type is the "predisposed woman" who has been a victim of sexual abuse herself; she often has low self-esteem and has not healed her abuse wound. The second type is the "teacher/lover" who sees herself as a peer and teaches her young victim about sexuality; she sees herself not as an offender, but rather as a "lover." The third type is the "male-coerced" woman who is pressured either emotionally or physically into the abuse of her children. She tends to be passive, does not feel cared for, and acts powerless in her life; these are the mothers who prioritize their relationship with the abuser over their relationship with their children. She may be insecure, dependent on her abuser financially, or afraid of being alone if she says "no." She may use her daughter as bait either to attract a man or to secure a relationship.

These "co-conspirator mother/protectors" generally don't initiate abuse, but consciously or unconsciously, they consent to the abuse. In some cases, they collude with the actual abuser and in other cases, they agree to look the other way.

The betrayal by these co-conspirator mothers results in deep-seated trust issues for their victims. If you can't trust your mother with your boundaries and can't trust her to look out for your best interests, who can you trust? The pain can be doubled and the healing long and intense. One of the women on the Healing Steps journey reflects this in the powerful story of her mother's betrayal and how it affected her:

> *My mom started bringing me into her sex life by bringing a chair to my bedroom and having sex with a man in front of me on the chair. She then met a man who would be her second husband who was a co-conspirator of the abuse. On my ninth birthday, he picked me up from under a table where I was hiding. He carried me into their bedroom where they had sex with me in the bed next to them. This was the start of many episodes where I was put into the bed while they had sex, including their wedding night. While my stepfather would try to include me more in the act, my mother just wanted me to watch.*
>
> *I had a physical and emotional breakdown when I was twenty-five. I asked for my mother's help since I couldn't work, and she said she would give me money under the condition that I attend therapy. Ironically, when the therapist heard how she was still touching me inappropriately, we worked together to have me cut off communication with her. This break from my mom lasted four years. For the*

*next twenty years I was continuously in individual or group ther-
apy, dealing with the fallout from my childhood.*

*Healing Steps was an important part of my healing. I saw that
other women had been through a lot and that they were seriously
impacted by the abuse, just as I had been. All the defenses that I had
formed from the sexual abuse slowly dissipated, and I was able to
process my grief. In group, I saw people being vulnerable, and that
helped me open up to process the pain in an intimate and safe way.*

*I never got the mother I dreamed of having. The loss is still with
me, and the hope never dies that somehow she will realize what she's
done and magically be a wonderful mom. One of the hard parts for
me is that the abuse affected the way I am able to trust women. I have
difficulty having female friends. I experience conflict when I have a
female boss. I can be passive-aggressive in situations where I feel
powerless with a female. I use the defense mechanisms I learned from
the abuse to deal with other women. I project my lack of trust onto
them which makes it more difficult for me to see them as they are.*

*I still struggle to be my own person because she has so infiltrated
my own psyche that it's hard for me to feel she is not a part of me. Sometimes I feel that I am melding into her or that I am her. I still struggle
to be free from the omnipresence she had over my body and sexuality.*

The wound of sexual abuse goes deep; when it involves the one person whom
you count on to understand you and protect you, it is heartbreaking. As the
previous survivor so poignantly writes, her mother's violation weaves through
many aspects of her life to this day. It affects her relationship with others and
certainly her relationship with herself. Like so many other women, she is still
waiting and hoping to have that mother that every little girl deserves.

Another example of the co-conspirator mother is the mother who overtly or
covertly supports the abuse of the child because there is something to be gained,
but the mother is not physically involved. The mother may want to hang onto a
relationship she has, or childcare she needs, or financial security. I remember a
case where the mother was afraid of losing her new husband. When she discov-

ered that he was spending intimate time with her 11-year-old daughter, she did not speak up out of fear of losing him. The abuse was finally uncovered, and all members of the family entered therapy. In the mother's therapy, she revealed she had been sexually abused as a child. She told me, "It didn't hurt me any, so I figured she (the daughter) could deal with it like I did." The pattern of repetition continues when there has been little or no healing.

The Narcissistic Mother

The Narcissistic Mother/Protector uses her child for her own emotional needs, rather than focusing on the well-being of the child. She sees the child as an extension of herself and as a mirror to reflect what she wants to see. Sometimes she is unaware of the molestation, but often she is aware of the special relationship between the offender and the child. If this is the husband or boyfriend of the mother, this will evoke jealousy and competitive instincts, and she either devalues the daughter or sets up a peer relationship with her, as the mother of the woman in the example above went on to do. There are as many possibilities here as there are stories, but one thing is always the same: the mother's needs are important, while the daughter's needs are ignored or minimized.

The results are somewhat predictable in that when the daughter's needs have been ignored for so long, she either loses sight of what her needs are, or her life becomes centered around getting those neglected needs met. Often she chooses a partner who is unable or unwilling to address her needs, and she is once again left with that hole in her soul. This is a prime example of repetition compulsion. The patterns of an unhealed childhood are destined to be repeated throughout adulthood; the survivor seeks out relationships that recreate the same painful patterns she experienced as a child. The search continues for that ideal person who will deeply understand her and see her for who she really is.

I'm not sure which is more difficult—the strong need to be understood and "seen" to the depth of one's being, or the denial of one's own needs stemming from not even knowing what the needs are. Both are difficult paths. One of the dangers of not being aware as an adult of one's own feelings, needs, impulses, etc. is that often this survivor does not see her own role in things and thus loses the ability to create change for herself. These abuse victims leave themselves out of the equation because *they were left out of the equation*! Their mantra is "things just seem to happen to me." They are totally unaware of their part in an interaction; they are aware only of their response to it. Mantras can be invaluable tools for healing—but this one isn't.

When you have not been allowed to be who you are, or are not seen for who you are, a lifelong search for identity ensues. You may become a "drama queen" in a desperate attempt to get the attention that was withheld from you for so many years. Or you may find that you can define your identity only *through others,* one in which your accomplishments can be enjoyed only by being "the wife of…" or "the mother of…" or "the one who… ."

Narcissistic mothers often blame their sexually abused daughters for the abuse, or for the adaptive behaviors that stem from the abuse, especially if they inconvenience her. For example, the child is blamed if she has to participate in court-ordered therapy that costs the family money, or if restrictions are imposed on seeing the offender when he's someone important to *the mother.* Often these mothers turn their backs to what is happening to their daughters because they are aware of what the outcome of a confrontation or police report would do to *them*. They may be talked about or shunned, the offender may have to leave the home, the community may blame the mother, there could be financial repercussions, etc. Being a "bad mother" may be devastating if this is the only identity a woman has; a daughter's welfare may be a small price to pay in comparison to being seen as a failure. Remember, a narcissistic mother is self-absorbed and is never wrong about anything.

One of the Healing Steps women told me:

I always felt like an orphan, raised by "this person" who was too needy emotionally to be able to do anything beyond trying to get her own needs met. She could never see beyond herself. Now I think I'm going to be able to let go of Mom as being a parent—she is just a person in my life. But she is a given, and if I don't expect any "mother-type" behavior from her, then I won't be so disappointed when I don't get any.

If this section resonates with you, *The Drama of the Gifted Child* by Alice Miller may be a good book to pick up at this time, as it addresses many of the issues we have touched upon.

The Abusive Mother

 Abuse comes in many forms, but all abuse creates a major breach in the relationship between mother and daughter. Your mother may not have been sexually abusive, nor overtly complicit in your molest, but her abuse of you may have kept you from going to her for protection or support. Often the abusive mother becomes the opponent, and the potential perpetrator becomes the child's advocate—a perfect setup for sexual abuse. As one deeply scarred woman told me, "My molester was the only one in the family nice to me. He was the only one who was not hitting or beating on me."

There are basically four types of abuse in families—sexual abuse, physical abuse, neglect, and emotional/psychological abuse. There are over 7,000 cases of abuse and neglect reported every day with 3.6 million referrals to Child Protective Services a year; this is the worst record among all the industrialized nations.

Let's define these types of abuse further. If you are reading this book, you are clear what sexual abuse is, but be aware that sexual abuse also includes voyeurism, exhibitionism, exposure to pornography, and communicating in a sexual manner in person, on the phone, or over the Internet.

A physically abusive mother is one who injures her child, either intentionally or unintentionally, by acts of physical aggression. Included here are beating, slapping, punching, shaking, throwing, pinching, biting, choking and hair pulling, burning with cigarettes, splashing with scalding water, or the use of other hot objects. Any severe physical punishment is included in this category, such as "using the belt," hitting with objects, etc. *The emotional scars are always more profound that the physical scars and the deepest scars do not just disappear with time.*

Neglect statistically occurs twice as often as sexual and physical abuse put together. Neglect is an act of omission rather than commission, so it is often tough to pinpoint and elusive to deal with. There are obvious signs of neglect—not having enough food, not having clean or appropriate shelter or clothing, not being enrolled in school, neglect of medical needs. Neglect also means not keeping a child out of harm's way or protecting the child from real or *potential* abusive situations.

Emotional/psychological neglect—difficult to spot from outside the family—is tragic in its consequences when experienced firsthand. Obviously, if your mother or caretaker knew about your sexual abuse and did nothing, or did the minimum, that is neglect. But what about knowing of sexual abuse within the family and not tending to the effects on you? Would that constitute "neglect"?

Sally was a woman in my practice who was sharing details of a cousin who had molested her when she was 10 years old. Then—almost as an afterthought—she casually mentioned that when she was 18 and still living at home, her father had been found guilty of molesting another girl and was sentenced to county jail. This latter incident was never discussed at home. Her mother never asked Sally if her father had molested *her,* and no one offered her counseling for this unsettling situation: her mother simply never brought the subject up. Her father returned home to the family after his incarceration, and life went on as usual. For years, her father would make inappropriate comments to Sally's girlfriends when they visited, causing Sally extreme anxiety. Her mother did nothing.

Emotional, or psychological, abuse is defined by Healthy Place, the largest consumer online mental health site, as *an attitude, behavior, or failure to act that interferes with a child's psychological health or social development*; in other words, any treatment of the child *that may diminish her sense of identity, dignity, and self-worth.* It often takes the form of verbal insults or ridicule, often vicious and toxic, or ongoing critical judgments. It destroys self-esteem and lasts into adulthood. What is said becomes part of who the child is, part of her own self-definition. Making threats, placing undeserved blame on a child, and negative labeling are all examples of emotional abuse. Also damaging is non-verbal communication such as "the silent treatment," physical rejection, looks of scorn or disgust, locking children out of the house, invading privacy. Most parents do not intend to become emotionally abusive, but many have been emotionally abused by their own parents; they swear they will not do to their children what was done to them, but they don't know what to do instead.

Can a "good" mother sometimes be emotionally abusive? Yes. What is important, however, is looking at your own relationship with your mother and the *overall* nature of your relationship with her. There is a difference between an "incident" and a pattern of behavior. Making Daughters Safe Again, an online support site for information on mother-daughter sexual abuse, states:

> *If a woman did not feel adequately loved, safe, secure, protected, valued, and respected before giving birth, she will, in all likelihood, attempt to use the child (and later the teen) to fill those needs. If she did not feel adequately in control of her own life as a child and a teen, she can be expected to try to control her sons or daughters as compensation. This is the recipe for emotional abuse.*

This is worth thinking about in terms of our mothers—and certainly for ourselves, if we are mothers or hope to be mothers in the future.

When your mother is abusive, your protector becomes your enemy in the only possible sanctuary you have—your home. There is no respite for you; no place to feel safe. Your external circumstances are stressful, and your internal sense of well-being is being undermined. Your value is reflected in the eyes and behavior of the person you look to for unconditional love, acceptance, and protection. When there is abuse by the person we inherently look to for love and security, we take a "heart bruising" that haunts us into adulthood.

The Innocent Mother

Yes, there are innocent protectors: evidence that a child has been abused is not always obvious. Mothers may not have a clue; we must remember that 85 percent of children never report their abuse to anyone. We also have to remember that sexual predators are very clever, often forming an alliance with the protective parent in order to win her trust. Offenders go to great lengths to make sure the protector does not know. Also, and I'm sure every reader knows this, there is a shield that people hold up to ward off that which does not feel tolerable to us. I close my eyes if a spider is shown on TV or in the movies. I don't go to movies focused on war. I protect my psyche from that which creates a negative reaction in me. It's human nature. Does that excuse someone from not protecting a child? Absolutely not! But we do have to accept the fact that some protectors did not know—did not see the clues that seemed so obvious to us. We also must remember that most offenders, especially in the case of molestation within the home, go to great lengths to make sure that the protector does not know, and they are very skilled at this. And because your mother didn't know, that does not mean that you—the survivor—did not feel abandoned and enraged. It may even mean that you felt more vulnerable because no one was picking up on the clues that things were not right with you, or they knew that "something" was not right, not okay, but didn't pursue it so you could be taken care of. As one woman questioned, "If we were supposed to be such a happy family, why didn't anyone notice how sad I always was? Where was my mother?"

There is a voluntary organization called Mothers of Sexually Abused Children (MOSAC) that helps educate and support non-abusive mothers and other caregivers. If your mother is just learning of your abuse and is supportive, or has been supportive in the past, this may be a helpful resource for her.

I will always remember the powerful scene in a documentary on abuse where two adult women confronted their mother about their long-term incest. They asked, "How could Dad be using vibrators on us in the bathroom while you were in the living room—and you didn't hear it?" The mother had learned of the abuse only through a letter written by one of the daughters on the day she left home. This story had a disturbing ending. While the mother made the father leave the home, he eventually went on to molest two of his grandchildren: no one was watching him with the next generation. His daughter finally reported him to the police, and this time he was arrested. Molesting behavior does not generally "self-correct," so when deciding whether or not to take action, keep this example in mind.

The question is often asked, "Do mothers really *not* know? Or are they simply in denial?" It is true that there is a built-in need to disbelieve sexual abuse or incest has occurred in *your own* family. Many of us don't see what we don't want to see, and yes, there are mothers who don't want to see because then action would need to be taken, and either they don't know what to do, or they believe that what needs to be done could have potentially devastating results for the family. Many partners feel strongly about "till death do us part" and have a high tolerance for dysfunction in a family. Others fear not being able to support their families financially, or being rejected, or losing their security. So, are there mothers who deny? Yes. And are there mothers who really don't know what is occurring whether it's inside or outside the family? Yes, there are. The good news is that the numbers of quiet sufferers are decreasing since the silence is finally being shattered by the courage of all the survivors—adults and children—who come forth and tell their truth.

On the other hand, it's important to pay homage to all those mothers who did know, who did see the clues, and *who did take action* to protect their daughters or sons. I have witnessed many mothers take difficult steps to ensure the safety of their children—in many cases, ending long marriages, and in some cases, risking their own lives. These women face their worst nightmare, and their own journey often becomes incredibly painful. A mother who discovered her daughter was being molested writes, "To be the mother of a sexual abuse victim has been very painful—a journey filled with loneliness and confusion—but I now consider it a privilege to have been called to support such a brave and beautiful young woman."

As I mentioned earlier, the intense anger a survivor feels is often placed entirely on the protector: it's easier to focus on the protector, since the raw anger that is felt toward the perpetrator may arouse other undesirable and painful emotions. Those emotions run deep, and as survivors we tend to displace them or skirt around them. Hopefully, by doing the exercises in this book, you will be able to separate the feelings you have toward the perpetrator from those you may have toward the protector who wasn't there for you. Just don't confuse one with the other.

Steps to Healing Your Mother/Protector Wound

Simply writing about your feelings surrounding your mother/protector is in itself a healing act. It allows you to synthesize and make sense of your experiences, thus decreasing the traumatic effect of those experiences. Research has shown that writing about a traumatic experience positively affects medical and psychological conditions you may be struggling with. Not bad, right? Writing also allows thoughts to shift and change, rather than to solidify in familiar first responses. And it's important to move your initial memories or feelings from your mind to your journal so you can make room for anything else that may surface from your subconscious. Often the piece of your experience that could be transforming is buried under familiar layers of recall.

EXERCISE: Write About Your Own Mother

Now that you're motivated to do some writing, carve out some private time for yourself to address the questions below. Don't just to answer the questions in your mind: write them in your journal or binder.

I know this is a lengthy list. But if you skim over this Step, you will be "stuck" here like so many victims—and I know you want to move on to the next Step in your recovery. If you have a photo of your mother/ protector, you may want to position it in your line of sight as you answer the questions.

1. Face the Reality of Your Mother's Role in the Abuse

- Did she really know when the abuse was occurring?

  Face this honestly. A child often expects her protector to be all-seeing and all-knowing because it gives her the illusion of safety and protection. We have a right to certain expectations, but expecting a protector to have eyes in the back of her head is magical thinking.

- Did you leave "clues" or hints for your mother and want her to understand?

- Did she just look the other way?

- Does she know now? If not, do you want her to know?

- Was she a co-conspirator in the abuse, either covertly or overtly?

- Was she also a victim of the perpetrator's dominance or abuse?

- Was there ever a time when you felt your mother knew but did nothing?

- What did you expect of her at the time? What do you expect now?

- Did she meet your expectations? If not, how did she let you down?

- If she did meet your expectations, how did she take care of you?

2. **Remember Your Feelings About Your Mother as Protector**

- Do you remember what your feelings were about your mother during the time of the molest?

   Begin by considering your feelings of anger, blame and resentment. This is about the release of feelings, so write freely using the language that feels in alignment with the feelings. Ex: "I am so pissed that you were so damn selfish..."

- What do you remember about feelings of sadness, hurt, neediness and disappointment?

   These feelings are often under the anger. When anger has been expressed, there is a shift—and hurt and pain can surface. Is that your experience?

- Did you experience fear or insecurity?

- Don't forget the three R's: remorse, regret, responsibility. Were they present?

- Are love and/or forgiveness part of the equation for you?

3. Face Your Feelings Now

- Are your feelings the same or have they changed over the years?

- Do you hold your protector accountable *for her part* in the abuse?

- Do you still feel dependent on her for approval and validation?

- Does she still have the power to wound you? How do you give her this power?

- How have you carried your "mother-daughter" experiences out into the world?

There are probably many different aspects to your mother's personality, just as there are many different aspects to your own; and that makes for a great deal of complexity in your relationship. However, it is essential that you accept the truth about your mother/protector, and the truth is this:

You were not protected, and the past cannot be changed. Your wounded child will never *get from your mother what you wanted in your childhood when you were being hurt and victimized.*

This statement can evoke significant disappointment. It is a *very* painful reality to hold onto. The hurt and anger are often only a backdrop to the ever-present longing for the understanding that we have talked about. Yes, there is suffering, but that suffering will lead you to the next healing Step. Continuing with the following writing exercises will assist you.

4. Describe the Feelings You Have About Not Being Protected

Write about what it was like for you to be left to handle your abuse by yourself. Be as detailed as possible.

5. Create a Dialogue Between the "Today You" and the "Past You"

If the past you had a nickname, use it in your dialogue. For example, I was called "Sheri" as a little girl, so I use that name in my dialogue. Your dialogue, which can be as long as you like, might go like this:

> **Today you:** I'm sorry that you had to go through what you did. It breaks my heart. Who could have been there for you to help you?
>
> **Past you:** *Writes or draws the answer.*
>
> **Today you:** What could this person have done or said to help you?
>
> **Past you:** *Writes or draws the answer.*
>
> **Today you:** It makes me feel _____ that no one was there. How did it make you feel to know that you had to go it alone?
>
> **Past you:** *Writes or draws the answer.*
>
> **Today you:** I want you to know that from now on, I'm here with you. You will never be alone; I have your back. You now have an adult who will take care of you and stand up for you. And I'm going to practice doing that beginning now!

6. If There Are No Words, Draw or Make a Collage

Pick images that capture your feelings, and glue them onto a poster board of whatever size and color seems right to you. The theme here is Protection. What images are evoked when you experience yourself as that little one being molested when there was no one to stop it and protect you? Let your "past you" assist you in selecting images from magazines, words from newspapers, your own drawings, etc. Put them together in a collage that speaks to you. Do you feel anger? Sadness? Fear? Or something else? How did you take care of yourself?

Drawing by a Survivor

Before we can expect the Inner Child, the "past you" to come forward, she must know that you are there for her, can manage the intensity of her feelings, and allow her this freedom of expression. As you open the door to your abuse, you will find not only painful memories, but also belief systems created at the time of the abuse. Truths are waiting to be uncovered, myths to be dispelled, and your sense of who you are may begin to fall apart. Proceed slowly and gently. The experience is similar to opening a jigsaw puzzle: you see the image on the top of the box, but once you open the box, rather than seeing the whole picture you see only a myriad of pieces to dump out on the table.

The process of healing is like the process of putting a puzzle together. Some areas will be easy—while others will be more difficult than you imagined. And when the picture does come together—and it will—it never looks exactly like the image on the box, does it?

I do want to mention the importance of meditation techniques and mindfulness work at this time. There are many age-old techniques available, as well as workshops, classes, and therapists who teach mindfulness. Mindfulness is defined as the awareness that arises from paying attention *on purpose* in the present moment, without judgment. Taking the time to be with yourself in silence, learning the importance of calming your racing brain, and having the ability to self-soothe are all wonderful by-products of learning to meditate. One of my favorite sayings is, "Do you have the patience to let the mud settle and the water clear?" This can be a wonderful result of meditation or mindfulness.

Meditation may also help you realize that you don't have to crash through the walls of your resentment: you may be able to simply walk around them. It may bring you closer to "settling in" rather than "acting out." I'll be giving you some information about mindfulness in a later Step, but if being quiet and silencing your racing brain sounds good to you, search online for some additional techniques to get you started.

Developing an Inner Protector/Nurturer for Your Inner Child

The next section of exercises is designed to help you develop what you didn't receive growing up: a custom-designed nurturer for your Inner Child—a supportive listener who is on call 24/7. Believe me, there is no one who can give you what you truly need better than you, and the best part is that you can *always* be there for yourself, right? This is the beginning of trusting yourself to make good decisions; trusting yourself to listen to your intuition (that little voice within you that "knows"); trusting that if someone betrays you or abandons you in some way, you will not only survive, but you will be okay.

In "How to Be Your Own Good Mother," an article by Pam Tablok published in *The Healing Woman*, I was quoted as saying that it's your little girl inside who needs that mother/protector— not the adult. The needs are different. Your past self needs to express her feelings, to be accepted for her truth, and to be listened to. She also needs to know that you will not neglect her, and that she can count on you. One of the things I found in my own healing was even though I did learn how to take care of my little girl, I would still get tripped up by my own expectations when I spent time with my mother or spoke to her on the phone. My little girl would get hooked by unfulfilled expectations that would creep in, and I would deflate in a matter of seconds. With the help of my therapist, I decided to "fire" my mother from her role as Mother and reassign her the role of "quirky relative," which she was really good at! I actually would post sticky notes on the phone (days of the landline) to remind myself what the relationship was: "This is not your mother so don't expect her to act like one—this is a quirky relative." It worked.

Kathie Carlson, author of *In Her Image*, said it well when she wrote:

Taking the unhealed child's needs seriously but letting go of our daughterhood; suffering the pain of what we didn't get, without becoming masochistic; and letting go of the wish/demand that our mother "mother" us is not easy. It means accepting our past as it was, while carrying the legitimacy of our needs. It means accepting the limits of what we experienced with our actual mothers and bearing the pain of realizing that the childhood experience with her is over.

In a sense, it means letting go of the claims of the "daughter" role and allowing our mothers to let go of the role of "mother" as well. One woman in a Healing Step workshop recalled that it was a very freeing day when she realized that her mother had done the best she could and that she would never get what she wanted and needed from her; it was simply beyond her mother's capacity to give her that. That's when her healing began because she recognized she had to turn to the one in the mirror—herself.

Teresa had long-struggled with not having a mother who would or could rescue her. She endured years of cruel abuse with no protection from anyone in her world. As she started Healing Steps for the second time, she wrote:

I feel less helpless that I used to, but I still don't think I want to accept responsibility for my life now, even though I believe that is the only healthy choice I have. My guess is that the part of me that is angry and really wants to blame my perpetrators for my pain and the losses I've suffered is still waiting for "someone" to rescue me and transform me into a happy, healthy, loving and loved person. And this will happen magically, of course—I won't have to do the work. Maybe I'm ready to climb the Steps of healing now. This time I plan to consciously give more time and effort to each Step.

Teresa wanted to receive the gift of transformation through the mythical powers of the mother. I'm not sure that's possible, but I certainly think she deserved to be rescued from the grips of her sadistic family member when the abuse was occurring.

If, like Teresa, you are still struggling with the anger and disappointments of not having that protective mother and this keeps you from taking the next step in your recovery, here are two questions for you to ponder:

- Can I see my mother's life in context and recognize her limitations?

- Can I let go of the demand that she be the one to care for me in a deep way just because she is my mother?

Learning to Nurture Your Inner Child

Here are some ways to help your Inner Child—the one who didn't have a protective Mother. The more of these activities you do, the stronger you will feel within yourself.

EXERCISE: Teach Your Inner Child What She Was Never Taught

Take her to a bookstore or anywhere where there are children's books and let her select one. Several that I use in workshops are *It's O.K. to Say No, Your Body is Your Own, Sometimes It's OK To Tell Secrets,* and *I Can't Talk About It: A Child's Book About Sexual Abuse.* Maybe no one has given her permission to draw a line for herself yet! Let her pick the book that she needs, and read it to her. It's the Inner Child who needs to get the message—on her level, by someone who cares—finally!! This was a favorite exercise of the Healing Steps women.

EXERCISE: Find Someone For a Role Model— Someone Whom You Think Would Be a Strong, Loving Protector

It may be someone you know, a character from a book, someone you admire from a TV show or movie. Bring that energy into your relationship with your Inner Child.

A friend of mine said she would pick Whoopi Goldberg because Whoopi appears to be a fierce defender of the injured, as well as a person who holds people accountable for their actions. She appears to execute with strength, balance, and humor. Another said she would choose Meryl Streep because she shows such commitment to her work and her family and seems to be so centered—with a quiet strength. She is not afraid to speak up or speak out. I would choose my friend Susan who doggedly kept me on track until I saw what she understood, and I entered therapy in 1972. Who would you choose?

Oprah Winfrey searched for a good Mother for herself and found one in Maya Angelou. I heard an interview with Maya Angelou where she talked about not allowing swearing or denigrating words to be used in her home. Regardless of how rich or powerful the guests, she would actually escort those guests out her front door if they broke this rule. She didn't hesitate to protect her space from negative energy, regardless of who the offender was. She is such a wonderful example of a fierce, spiritually-grounded woman.

If you can't come up with a role model to help you grow into that position for yourself, then come up with a symbol or object that symbolizes strength, protection, and comfort. I have a rock on my desk that has naturally been formed into the shape of a heart. A gift from Divine Mother? A gift of nature? A random gift found by me? It doesn't matter—the meaning and symbol remain mine, and it reminds me that I'm never alone in my journey.

As I was writing this book, I reconnected with many Steppers. One brought me a gift: it was a copy of a small poster that I'd given to members of my initial Healing Steps group to remind them that it was up to them to protect their Inner Child. She'd framed the poster in 1991 and hung it in her entry hall; it still hangs there today reminding her that she is never without protection. The poster shows a protective figure standing in front of a smaller figure while looking at herself in the mirror and declaring, "Mess with my kid and you mess with me!" Exactly.

EXERCISE: Write the Letter to Your Inner Child That She Has Always Wanted to Receive

Offer her the kind of protection she needs—a letter that nurtures and comforts her. She's been waiting a long time to hear these words; please don't make her wait any longer.

For example, let her know how sorry you are that the abuse happened, and tell her that if you could have, you would have stopped it. Let her know you know it was not her fault. Let her know you can handle whatever feelings she has and can manage anything she has to tell you. Most of all, let her know you are committed to this process and will not leave her, will always protect her, and will walk hand in hand with her as you both take the next step.

A Healing Steps woman who was repeatedly physically and sexually assaulted by her father wrote that she would not be defeated by what her father did to her. In order to protect herself, she said her "...little girl was put away in a safe room (inside of herself). She doesn't really believe I can protect her, but she is willing to let me leave her in the safe room. I feel sorry for her because she is such a worn out little thing. When I look in her face, I see an old woman's eyes looking out at me." She was very reluctant to open the door and make contact with the part of herself that was so wounded, but she finally wrote a letter to that little girl. The following is an excerpt from that letter:

Letter of Truth to my little one,

It is not our fault the scum hurt you so much. He did not deserve to have such a sweet little girl. You have to remember that you were just a little girl...how could you stand up to such a big, mean man? There is nothing you could have done to stop what he did to you. You should not have had to be so quiet, so still, so perfect. You should not have had to hide your fear, your hurt, your terror.

He had no right to rape you. He had no right to sodomize you. He had no right to make you take his penis in your mouth. He had no right to beat you up. He had no right to say things to make you feel like a failure. He had no right to make you feel so afraid all the time. He had no right to blame you and make you feel responsible for his abuse. He was wrong. He lied. He lied about just about everything.

I know you did nothing to deserve what happened to you. I also know how he manipulated you and told you over and over that it was your fault. Try not to believe his lies. I wish I could change what happened to you. I know you felt all alone and very little and very scared. I am with you now. I will not leave you alone. I will do everything I can to keep you safe. I know it must be very hard to trust me, too. I am trying to protect you now. I don't blame you for not believing you can trust anyone. I think you're pretty smart not to trust anyone—why should you? You don't have to trust anyone if you don't want to. I want you to do whatever it takes to feel safe. I will do whatever it takes to help you feel safe. I honestly don't know if there is anyone else we can trust to protect us. We will take this thing slowly. You do not have to remember more than you want to. But I want you to think about accepting the truth that we were horribly, terribly abused. I know those words don't touch the reality—but let's at least accept that as the truth. We will take however long it takes to make you feel safe and loved.

You are a good, loving, spiritual child. You know you can trust God. I can feel that you know that. YOU ARE OK. And I love you. YOU DESERVE TO BE LOVED. YOU ARE WORTHY OF BEING LOVED. YOU ARE LOVABLE. I LOVE YOU.

You are not alone anymore.

— May

EXERCISE: Visualization

Sit in your comfortable and secure place either in silence or with soft music in the background. Take several of those deep, relaxing breaths and let them go, bringing yourself quietly into yourself. Then:

Picture your need to be nurtured and protected as an umbilical cord coming out of your body. Included in this cord are the needs for love, acceptance, nurturing, and protection—maybe the need for understanding as well. Notice the size of the cord, the shape of it, the length of it. Bring your childhood mother/protector into view, and feel your cord reaching out to her. Feel the yearning, the desire you've had for her to really know, to understand, to be compassionate, to protect you. Let yourself experience all that pent-up yearning and longing as the cord reaches out to her—and you see that the cord just misses her: it can't quite touch her. She backs away, turns and walks away. Feel that loss. She is not there for you to plug into.

Where have you tried to plug in that cord to get what you need in your life? Into a person? Into that mother/protector? Into a relationship? An addiction? Food? A career? Take a moment to visualize yourself trying to "plug in."

Now try to plug that cord back into yourself—perhaps into your head, or into your heart—and see if you can turn back to yourself, to that one person who does know, who can understand. Does the plug fit? What do you have to do to get it to fit?

If you can't plug it into yourself at this time, can you plug it into a symbol of a Higher Power or Higher Consciousness or Higher Understanding? Into a spiritual figure who has meaning for you—or a spirit guide or guardian angel—or something that represents love and nurturance to you. Just plug it in and the feel the flow of energy. Whether you plugged into yourself or into a higher power, begin the flow of love, acceptance, and nurturing. Let yourself experience the fullness of feeling loved for exactly who you are—and for being accepted at this very moment.

Remember there is no one who knows or understands your Inner Child better than you do; there is no one who can always be with her when she needs someone like you can; there is no one who can hear and understand her like you can; and there is no one—*no one*—whose acceptance means more to her than yours.

I *insist* that you listen to Shaina Noll's song "How Could Anyone" on YouTube. I always played this at the end of this workshop. It's so important for all of us to hear these powerful words sung to us.

And last but certainly not least, here is an affirmation to be repeated every day:

I carry my own Inner Protector and my own Inner Mother within me. Their energies and abilities are always available to me to nurture me, to protect me, to accept me and to guide me.

Healing the Child Within

In sum, here are the six steps to healing your Inner Child. This is the foundation for your healing, and every other Step depends on the strength of this particular Step.

- Identify the Inner Child's needs and claim them as legitimate.

- Share the childhood pain with a friend, therapist, a fellow "Stepper."

- Recognize that something really has been lost. The child's need can never be met in its original context.

- Ask deeper questions: What does it mean for my life that I had this mother? Who or what did I have to become because of this experience? What have I had to develop in myself that might not have been developed had my experience been different?

- Care for the child within. What are her needs? Does she need some play-time, or does she take too much playtime? Does she want to spend more time in nature? Listening to music? Does she want to fingerpaint? Fly a kite? Chase a wave? Does she need time to "show off" her skills or enthusiasm?

- Ask: can I let go of the demand that my mother be the one to care for me now when she couldn't take care of me then? *Can I be the one I've been longing for?*

Forming A Mother/Protector for the Adult Woman

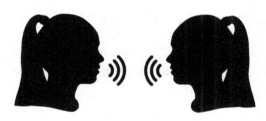 Your adult self needs some basic life skills—such as how to set boundaries, how to say "no" *and mean it*, how to ask for help from appropriate others, how to be vulnerable with trusted others, how to differentiate between what is another's issue and what is yours. In this next section and in subsequent chapters, we will focus on these issues.

Speaking Up

Let's begin with setting boundaries and speaking up. If you are like most survivors, setting limits and boundaries in your personal life is a struggle. "Yes" comes easily and immediately when you are asked to do something. You may not want to, you may know you don't want to, but there is a barrier to saying "no." Have you noticed this in your life?

Some survivors never say "yes" because they have learned that saying "no" is a way of protecting themselves from harm. These are the women who say "no" even when they want to say "yes": they say no to relationships, no to their own creativity, no to taking chances, no to reaching for what they really want in life. They don't take the time to figure out what they really want to do.

When we feel "safe," we handle life differently. If we are in touch with ourselves, if feeling empowered is an integral part of our personhood, if we knew how to express ourselves, our lives would probably be different than they are today.

In some families, we are encouraged to speak up and speak out. We are positively reinforced for having ideas, thoughts, and desires that differ from others in our family. In other families, we are criticized for our individuality. The key here is to know what it is you want to say "yes" to, what it is you want to say "no" to—and to practice giving your answer out loud until you are comfortable with speaking up for yourself.

Here is an exercise on this issue. Choose the variation that fits from the three choices below.

EXERCISE: What Will You Say "Yes" or "No" To?

- **Choice One:** If you are a "yes-sayer," say "'no" *one time* each week when you are asked to do something. If you are a "no-sayer," say "yes" *one time* each week when you are asked to do something. These incidents can center around going to lunch, donating money, staying late at the office, driving your daughter to soccer practice—you pick. What's important here is that you practice the opposite of your normal response for four weeks.

- **Choice Two**: Whenever you are asked to do something, respond with "let me think about it" and wait 24 hours before saying yes or no. During that time, decide what your answer truly is and then respond with your authentic wishes.

- **Choice Three:** Do both.

There's a wonderful Ted Talk in which Shonda Rhimes speaks about "my year of saying 'yes' to everything." As you may know, Shonda is the titan behind *Grey's Anatomy, Scandal, How to Get Away with Murder,* and *The Catch.* She did what was foreign to her in order to regain what she had lost. Check it out.

Learning Self-Care and Self-Nurturing

The most important time to learn to self-nurture is right now while you are taking the most important step you will ever take—healing from your sexual abuse wound. Make the commitment to do what is necessary to break the silence, repair the damage, and strengthen all the wonderful qualities that already live inside of you. This is not a path for the faint of heart, and I applaud you! So, the first nurturing gift you can give yourself is a pat on the back for going on this journey and making an agreement with yourself to cross the finish line—no matter what.

As you may know, there is a difference between self-care and self-nurturing. Self-care is really about the basics, such as eating well, getting enough restorative sleep, having a supportive physical environment, having physical exams on a regular basis—including gynecological exams and dental care—and having healthy supportive relationships. Although taking care of ourselves in these ways is very nurturing, when I talk about *self-nurturing* I'm talking about *supporting and comforting ourselves when needed*. Self-nurturing is often difficult because it involves accepting the fact that *we deserve it*.

Do not confuse true nurturing with "negative nurturing"—by which I mean those compulsive behaviors we convince ourselves are "okay" because we "deserve" them. These behaviors include decisions or actions that don't have any lasting value for us, such as extravagant shopping, overeating, drinking too much, and risky sexual stuff. In the end, they make us feel worse the next morning.

For many survivors, it's either about "too much" of what's not helpful, or "too little" of what's nurturing and comforting. Either end of the continuum can get activated when we are stressed, out of our comfort zone, or avoiding our feelings or needs. If you struggle with negative ways of blowing off steam, just know that opportunities for genuine self-nurturing will increase as you do your healing work. If you don't pay attention, you will slip into your old, "negative nurturing" patterns.

***EXERCISE:* Examine Your Self-Nurturing Behaviors**

Don't let avoidance be your buddy and temptation your companion whenever you are confronted with a stressful situation in your life.

- **List your current go-to activities when you need comfort, distraction, or nurturing.**

  Do these choices work for you without any negative feedback—either physically, psychologically, emotionally, or financially? Be honest with yourself.

- **Make a new self-nurturing list—or expand your current one.** Stretch your imagination and creativity. Find options that do not cost money or take a great deal of effort. And try to avoid food rewards. I'm aware that food abuse can be a real struggle for abuse survivors. Often, the problem is either too much food, too little intake, or the wrong choices— so hopefully compiling a non-food list will be helpful.

  Make sure this list is easily accessible so that it's available when your spirits need a lift. Be sure to include a few support people to call, along with their phone numbers. I suggest you put the list in the front of your binder or journal, if you are using those methods of tracking your writing exercises; otherwise put it on a bulletin board, in your phone, or any place where it is readily available.

  Here are a few self-nurturing activities from my own list:

- take a walk when the leaves are falling
- pet my kitties
- read a mystery novel by a favorite author
- go to an estate sale
- cut out recipes for meals I'll probably never make
- take a warm bath with Philosophy's vanilla-scented bubble bath
- make photo albums that capture good memories—or revisit some that I've already made

In discussing her own work with her Inner Child, Sandy Flaherty—incest survivor, teacher and author—writes in *The Healing Woman*:

> *I had experienced my Inner Child before, but this was very, very different. ... I was able to be both individuals simultaneously—the abandoned child and the caretaking adult. Through the experience of the child, I could remember my abuse and feel it. As the adult, I heard her cries, and I could whisper words of comfort and bring her home to safety and love. When she was in deep pain, I could hold her, ask her what she needed, and give it to her. Often, she'd asked me to listen while she told stories about the abuse. She asked me to hold her and to keep her safe from violence. And again and again, I promised her that this time I would protect her.*

As one of the Healing Steps women shared, "If I hadn't learned to parent my Inner Child, I would not have been able to parent my daughter."

So listen deeply. Hear the feelings behind her words, see the plea behind her eyes, and embrace the needs that reside in her heart. She's your child now. Bring her home, stop handing her over to others. You're the one she needs; her healing is in your hands.

Seek guidance, seek support, ask questions of others, reach out to those who have walked this path before or who are joining you in their own healing. I remember when I had my first child. I was young, and to say I was inexperienced would be understating it! But I read, I educated myself, and I reached out to other new moms and a mother-in-law who would make me tea while I walked the floor, reassuring me that we would get through this. *You will get through this*. It's not about going it alone or suffering in isolation. It's about accepting that the child within really needs you at this time, and *you are now committed to growing into that important role for her*. This is one of the most empowering Steps you will ever take. It may even change your life.

 Suggested Reading

Mothering Ourselves: Help and Healing for Adult Daughters, by Evelyn Bassoff, PhD

Motherless Daughters: The Legacy of Loss, by Hope Edelman

My Mother, Myself, by Nancy Friday

Reclaiming Our Days: Meditations for Incest Survivors, by Helena See

The Woman's Comfort Book, by Jennifer Louden

Overdoing It: How to Slow Down and Take Care of Yourself, by Bryan Robinson, PhD

In Her Image: The Unhealed Daughter's Search for Her Mother, by Kathie Carlson

The Drama of the Gifted Child, by Alice Miller

Trapped in the Mirror: Adult Children of Narcissists in Their Struggle for Self, by Elan Golomb, PhD

If you are currently in an abusive situation:

The Verbally Abusive Relationship, by Patricia Evans

The Battered Woman, by Lenore Walker

Before Taking the Next Step

As you know, the Healing Steps journey is designed to take you on a trip through your past, circling around to spend time in your present, with an eye always on winding up in a future that reflects what is important to you. The goal is a stronger, clearer, empowered *you* living a life that is no longer in someone else's hands.

The journey is a tough one, which is why I recommend that you find fellow travelers for support and encouragement, as well as a guide who is familiar with the terrain. I'm glad you've packed both determination to take each Step, and courage to complete every Step to the best of your ability. We've discussed taking breaks, going at your own pace, occasionally setting your baggage down and enjoying some healthy distractions. Remember to give yourself enough time to process each Step: the opportunity to take the next Step can wait until you're ready.

You have also packed your tools and have them at the ready: your support expert, who is only a phone call away; your journal, pens, drawing pads, etc.; and of course, your willingness to engage in this process. You also have your favorite ways of self-soothing and nurturing, and your comfort list is made and easily available, right?

Now I must warn you that there are three travelers who may unexpectedly jump on board as you continue on this journey—Memories, Breakthroughs, and Flashbacks. Memories may be startling, disturbing, confusing—and they can enter through your mind, your body, or your emotions. Most people are bothered if memories *don't* show up during this process, so you may want to make sure you leave the opportunity open for them to slip in when appropriate.

Memories are like messengers: you should try to remember what they have told you by writing down the information they bring to you. You don't have to make sense of the content: just consider the messages "clues" to solving the puzzle of you.

Breakthroughs arrive with a bit more commotion. They startle us. They shout "aha!" They shake us up when we feel their presence. If Memories are like puzzle pieces, Breakthroughs are the universal puzzle-solvers. Breakthroughs put the pieces together in ways that we had not thought of before or sometimes not even imagined. They are ultimately postive experiences that move us even faster along our journey. After a Breakthrough, we absolutely must jot down our thoughts, and then take time to sit down and catch our breath. Breakthroughs require contemplation before we continue on to the next step; we need to integrate these pieces into the whole of our experience. Breakthroughs are the special guests on the Healing Steps journey. They *will* show up; we just don't know when that time will be. Please welcome them with respect and gratitude as they may fill in a missing piece or rearrange the pieces of your experience, thus making some of the more difficult Steps a bit easier.

Flashbacks always arrive uninvited and unexpected. They generally come in two ways—with a lot of clamor and drama (a bit like a Kiss performance); or quietly, tiptoeing into our minds and taking us to another time and place (more like a seductive Sinatra song). Flashbacks pick us up and toss us back into an experience we've already had when we least expect it. They make us feel as if we're in a scene from our own Lifetime Movie. We *become* that five-year-old or that twelve-year-old—with the same point of view and the same feelings. Sometimes it feels like we get caught in the web of that experience and can't get free. Sometimes it feels as if that past experience is so "here" that we can easily slip into it if we so much as think about it. Flashbacks sometimes indicate that we are moving too fast without enough protection or preparation. They may indicate we need to have an experienced guide with us to help us work our way through a dark passage. Sometimes we need to learn how *not* to go there; sometimes we need to learn how to find our way *through* by going there; sometimes we need someone who has also traveled there to help us make the best decision for ourselves.

Flashbacks are powerful and intrusive, but our focus needs to be not on bolting the door, but rather on being prepared should one occur. I live in California earthquake country and have experienced some major shakes and quakes, including the Loma Prieta 7.1 in 1989. I've felt the aftershocks and watched the rebuilding and retrofitting needed for future strength and protection. I think there are similarities here. In California, we know that the question is not *if* we have an earthquake, but rather *when* the next big one will hit. We are all familiar with geological maps, seismographic readings, and emergency procedures. We educate ourselves, we retrofit our homes, and we have earthquake preparedness kits assembled in our cars. Flashbacks are your earthquakes, so you do the same: educate, prepare, and if necessary, be ready to rebuild. Remember if you withstood the actual traumatic events, you can and will survive the Memories, Breakthroughs, and Flashbacks on your way to healing.

Step Three

Confronting the Perpetrator:

the One Outside and the One Inside

> *"The Jewish tradition understands that the punishment the killer most fears is the victim's memory of his deed."*
> — **Elie Wiesel**

Before you start reading this next Step, get out your large pad of paper and your fat crayons, marking pen, or sharpie. Now write the name of your Perpetrators on the page. Please don't be tempted to skip this step.

Okay. Now step back, read the names, and take note of what is going on in your mind.

- Thoughts?

- Feelings as you write each name?

- Body sensations?

It's probably difficult to feel "neutral" after writing down the name of someone who has created such havoc in your life.

It's important that we confront the two perpetrators you are struggling with—the one who sexually abused you, and the one *inside you* who sabotages your recovery and good intentions. We'll get to your Inner Perpetrator at the end of this chapter, but first let's take a look at the Outer Perpetrators.

As you come upon an exercise in this chapter, I strongly recommend that you stop and complete it before moving on. The exercises are designed to give meaning to what you are reading as well as to personalize the experience for you.

Who Are the Perpetrators?

A child molester is defined simply by his or her behavior. Rare is the offender who molests once and then self-corrects. According to a study by the New York Psychiatric Institute's Sexual Behavior Clinic, the average molester has abused an appalling 73 victims. Since most offenders are male (only 5 percent are women), I will use the pronoun "he" in this discussion.

There are two categories of perpetrators—the "situational" perpetrator and the pedophile. Situational predators generally differ in characteristics from pedophiles: they are attracted primarily to adult women and can often respond to interventions and therapeutic help. The situational offender practices self-deception and minimizes the harm he causes. He generally projects the blame for the abuse onto the victim, his partner, his drinking, or any convenient excuse he happens to think up. He employs defense mechanisms such as denial and minimization to relieve the cognitive dissonance between how he sees himself and what he does or has done in the past. Unlike the pedophile, he does not see himself as having a predilection for being sexually attracted to children.

We generally think of child molesters as domineering and controlling, which is often the case among repeat offenders. But situational molesters are often shy, passive, and unassertive. These men don't have the ability to meet their needs appropriately and often lack intimate relationships in their lives. Hank Giaretto, a pioneer in the treatment of both offenders and victims, says it well: "These are not the flirtatious men at the water cooler—they don't have the self-esteem to seek a woman of their own age." He explains they are too afraid to look at themselves, because the truth of who they are would be devastating, and they could not confront the ramifications of their behavior. If you ask these men why they molested (*if* they have the capacity for self-awareness), they would likely say: for love and acceptance, because of difficulties being intimate with an adult woman, and because of opportunity and convenience. They are what Robert A. Nass, PhD, calls "quasi-adult sex offenders"—men who yearn for a loving relationship with another adult, but who are unable to have one because of their own immaturity. And so, they turn to a child.

Similarly, A. Nicholas Groth, PhD, who has extensively researched the "typology" of offenders, concludes there are two categories of offenders—fixated and regressed. "Regressed" are the ones I call "situational" and Nass calls "quasi-adult." They are attracted to their peers, but when confronted with a stressor such as illness, loss of a job, or breakup of a relationship, turn to a child as a substitute.

I worked with regressed or quasi-adult perpetrators in the early 1980s. They were considered treatable through a very rigorous regimen of individual, couples, family, and group therapy that took two to two-and-a-half years. Therapists who work with these offenders agree that in order for rehabilitation to occur, two elements are essential—*the perpetrator must take responsibility for what he has done, and he must be able to develop and express empathy for his victim.*

In her poem "Where Bodies Are Buried," Janice Mirikitani paints a powerful picture of a broken man who uses his victimization of a vulnerable young girl as a bandaid to cover his own wounds:

> *There is always danger, I tell*
> *you who know about our vulnerability,*
> *about men who want to hurt us.*
>> *They are incomplete, broken in places*
>> *they want to hide. They carry weapons*
>> *to imitate body parts,*
>> *and damage things, throw us against walls*
>> *then paste our pieces*
>> *onto their wounds.*
>
> — excerpted from "Where Bodies are Buried,"
> graciously shared by author Janice Mirikitani

A true pedophile, on the other hand, is someone who is both sexually aroused by children and sees nothing wrong with gratifying himself at the child's expense. He has little regard for society's taboos and no moral qualms about hurting a child to get what he wants. Pedophilia is thus a specific combination of deviant arousal and a character disorder. Groth calls these men "fixated"— meaning they continue to have an exclusive or nearly exclusive sexual attraction to children. Their predilection does not respond to therapy, and their behavior is repetitive and compulsive.

A pedophile does not consciously choose to be attracted to children. Sexual *preference* (not to be confused with sexual *orientation*) is not something an individual decides, but rather something that is discovered or learned, usually during puberty. Acting on sexual preferences generally begins in adolescence and is reinforced through fantasy or action. More than half of all offenders start in their teen years. When a pedophile has sex with a child or masturbates to fantasies of children, his deviant urges are reinforced. That behavior, which often becomes compulsive, does not respond to traditional therapy or rehabilitative intervention.

The causes of pedophilia have been studied at Johns Hopkins University for well over thirty years. Some biological, hormonal, or brain abnormalities may be involved, but the results are not conclusive. What we do know is that treatment is not about cure, but rather about "management." The best protection against repeat offenders is still caution and prevention. If you have children in your life, be sure to read the last chapter of this book for tips and tools on how to protect them.

Pedophiles come from every walk of life, every social class, every ethnic and religious background; and there is a strong correlation between sexual abuse and religiosity. Some offenders prefer girls; others, boys. Some abuse both. The offenders range in age from 13 to 94 and are very adept at gaining access to children and covering their tracks. They are cunning and manipulative and are skillful at hiding their deviant behavior from their wives, their colleagues, and their friends. They are practiced liars. They don't have the capacity for empathy, for remorse, for guilt, or for concern as to how their behavior affects their victims. Victims are only objects to these offenders.

Pedophiles often look for passive, quiet, lonely children, building trusting relationships with them and often with their parents. This "grooming process" is timed, calculated, and methodical. It is also gradual. After gaining the potential victim's trust, the offender sees how far he can go until he hits resistance from the victim. At that point, he may stop; or he may threaten, cajole, or continue with the molest and take his chances. One molester likened this to putting a frog in a pot of water and slowly turning up the heat. The warming of the water is so gradual that the frog gets used to it and tolerates the increase in heat until he finds himself in very hot water. So it is with the pedophile's victim.

On a February morning during the 2018 Winter Olympics, former Olympic swimmer Ariana Kukos Smith appeared on *CBS This Morning* and shared her story of alleged sexual abuse by her Olympic coach. After beginning therapy a few months before, Ariana had realized how important it was to her healing that she "put words to what happened to me." In a tearful interview, she stressed the importance of spreading the message about this *grooming process* which she experienced as manipulation, control, and isolation. She recounted how difficult it was when the alleged perpetrator was someone respected and supported by her parents and her community, which in her case left her feeling even more powerless. "As an innocent, young individual who saw this man as a mentor, as a father figure," Smith said, "it was very confusing. ... It's been a complicated journey to really understand what happened, and how somebody you trust, who's gained your family's entire trust, can do something so horrific."

The Internet has also become a hunting ground for these predators. Hardly a week goes by that we don't read of how a young girl or boy was conned by a predator. The Internet has also provided pedophiles the opportunity to share information and resources as well as to see themselves as part of a group bonding over shared experiences.

 Contrary to myth, pedophiles are not strangers lurking in the shadows. Rather, they tend to be "respectable" and otherwise law-abiding people who know their victim, and usually the victim's family. They are masters at ingratiating themselves into the lives of their victims and are trusted by—and with—the children of the family. They are coaches, boyfriends, camp counselors, pastors, and town leaders. The majority of sexual abuse occurs in neighborhoods and households that look very normal from the outside. A powerful example of the grooming process is depicted in *The Tale*, an HBO movie written and directed by survivor Jennifer Fox.

As we all know, there are exceptions to every rule—and these are the perpetrators who generally make the news. Who can forget the well-known cases of Elizabeth Smart in 2002; or of Jaycee Dugard, whose abuse began when she was abducted at the age of 11 in 1991 and lasted for 18 years? Both women have called attention to stranger-danger and the importance of never giving up in the worst of circumstances. All of us admire their strength, their tenacity, and their willingness to share their stories so that we may all learn from the nightmares they lived.

In the Healing Steps workshop, we viewed the PBS video *Men Who Molest,* which highlights a treatment program focused on modifying a perpetrator's inappropriate and damaging sexual behavior. The interviews with molesters, their young victims, the mothers, and mental health professionals are powerful. The story of one father who began molesting his daughter at the age of six is heartbreaking. His story fit the model described earlier in this Step. He molested a young girl when he was 12 years old, continuing to fantasize about the molestation and becoming sexually stimulated by the thoughts of his first victim and her younger sister throughout his marriage. When his daughter was just a baby, he began to feel aroused by seeing her naked body and ended up molesting her on a regular basis just a few years later.

Seeing and hearing perpetrators talk about their thoughts, their behaviors, and their feelings is always unsettling; it's impossible to hear a molester talk about his abuses without having strong reactions. Talking, listening, and reporting, however, is the key to prevention. Some experts say that as soon as the media began presenting television shows about sexual abuse, reporting increased by 35 percent—and those numbers included reporting by children themselves. Since secrecy is the cloak of the molester, we must keep awareness front and center.

There are many different theories about the roots of this predilection. Why children? Some say perpetrators are repeating their own abuse as children, although research tells us that only 40 percent of abusers were abused as children. Is there a difference in perpetrators of incest and perpetrators of other types of sexual abuse? Once again, research shows there are many paths to incestuous behavior, and that sexual abuse is committed by more than one kind of predator. But those discussions are too broad and complex, and not for this book. This chapter is about *you*, for *you*, to help *you* uncover your experience with your perpetrator and to break the ties that bind you to the past.

We'll start with the person or persons who abused you. You may never confront the perpetrator(s) in real life, or you may not have the ability to do so, but they do have to be confronted *within* you in order to move forward. The deeper they are buried within you, the more layers of secrecy you have shrouded them with, the more control they will have over your decisions, your belief systems, and your behavior today. The effects of the molest depend on a wide variety of variables, as we will discuss in Step Four—but *who the abuser was to you* is certainly significant.

We need to begin this Step with a writing exercise, even though the material is clearly uncomfortable and unpleasant to think about. In order to heal, it is absolutely essential to break the bond with the perpetrator—and we do that by exercising our willingness to do the work in this Step.

EXERCISE: Answer the Following Questions in Your Binder or Journal

• Was the perpetrator a designated protector in your life? Was he someone you thought you could trust?

• Did this person live in your home or have access to your home? (Significant because often our home is the one place where we feel safe from outside harm; if the perpetrator is in the home, there is no sanctuary.)

• Did he play an important role in your life—that is, was he a parental figure, a teacher, a spiritual figure, a coach?

• How did the particular relationship you had with the abuser affect you?

• Have you generalized your feelings about your abuser to others in the same category? (Based on your early experiences, you may believe that "all priests are child molesters" or "all blue-eyed men can't be trusted," etc. We actually do this to feel safe: "Aha! I know who the bad guys are, so I can protect myself!")

• Is the perpetrator in your life today? If so, how do you deal with that?

The Inner Child and the Abuser

When I ask adult survivors what they want from their perpetrators, they generally answer:

> *I want an apology, an acknowledgment of what he did to me, and especially an acknowledgment of how his behavior has affected my life. I want him to get it, to understand how much suffering his abuse has caused me!*

In some cases, survivors want to take the perpetrator to court so there will be restitution for their pain and suffering, preferably followed by a public flogging! Sound familiar? Just to let you know, I have supported many survivors through the court process—and never once did it bring the healing and peace of mind the victim initially hoped for.

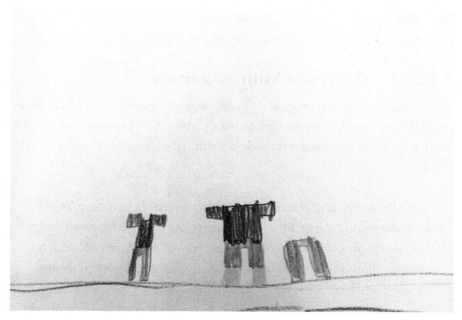

A young survivor's drawing of his perpetrators

When I worked with children and adolescents and would ask them what they wanted to have happen to their molester, they would say, "I want him to be eaten by lions, or devoured by sharks, or cut up in small pieces" or something equally colorful and grotesque. I remember doing sand tray therapy with one little boy. He took a good-sized figure of a "bad guy" and made his way to the sand tray, intending to put the figure in the tray. He hesitated for a moment, and then hit the side of the tray with the "bad guy"—gingerly at first, and then with more force. He hit again and again, energetically banging the figure against the side of the tray for about ten minutes. Finally, one of the hands broke free from the figure. Only then did he put the figure down and quietly say, "Now I'm safe."

I have always kept that broken hand in my desk drawer as a reminder of how important it is to finally feel safe from harm.

Children often want to see their perpetrator victimized: they want to see him being mastered by something bigger or stronger that he is. They want to see him disarmed, or in the case of the boy, dis-handed. They want to know the perpetrator is unable to hurt them, and their methods to that end are instinctual and primitive. That's why this next exercise is so important; an important part of the healing is *with the little child who was abused*—not with the adult you.

EXERCISE: Draw Your Experience

If this exercise seems too much to do alone, do it with the support of your therapist, a trusted friend, or if appropriate, your partner. You'll need a large pad, fat crayons, marking pens, and if possible a picture of yourself at the age you were molested.

> *Visualize yourself at the age you were molested. Take a deep breath and imagine yourself at a time when you were being molested. Now envision your perpetrator. Take note of the difference in size between you and the perpetrator. Using whatever image comes to mind—there is no right or wrong here—draw your perpetrator through your eyes as a child.*
>
> *Tell your little one that she can do anything she wants—on paper—to the one who hurt her. Draw on the pad as many pictures as your Inner Child wants to draw. When you are finished, take time to thank her for completing this exercise.*

How was this exercise for you? Did it bring up any feelings, thoughts, memories? Did you learn something about your experience you may not have known or thought of before?

EXERCISE: **Write a Letter to Your Perpetrator From Your Inner Child**

 If you have difficulty visualizing, the next exercise can be very helpful as it is a writing exercise. You do not have to stay within the confines of the letter suggested below; you can write the letter using your own format. It is important, however, that you address the key issues that are important to your Inner Child. Of course, if you can visualize, it is helpful to do both exercises. Once again, pace yourself; and if you feel overwhelmed, stop the exercise and continue at another time.

Invite your Inner Child to complete this letter to your perpetrator:

Date: _____

To: _____

There are many things I want to say to you. At first, I thought _____

_____

and then you _____

_____.

Things changed when _____

_____.

When I think of _____

_____,

I feel _____

_____.

Sometimes when I remember what you did, I _____

_____.

I would like to _____

and _____.

[Take as much space as you would like with this part.]

Signed: _____

P.S._____

_____

At the end of this exercise, close your eyes and see your little one safe inside your inner sanctuary, the safe place you created in Step One. Be sure to take several deep, cleansing breaths. This is very important as you want to bring yourself back to a place of calm after initiating some sharp emotions. Give this as much time as you need.

If you are in individual or group therapy, you may want to take your picture[s] and letter to your next session to share and process. Congratulate yourself for having the courage and willingness to do a very difficult exercise. It takes strength and determination to break a web of deceit. You are indeed stronger than you imagined yourself to be.

The Issue of Confrontation

This brings up the subject of actual *confrontation*. Should you confront your perpetrator or perpetrators in reality? Ask yourself the following questions: Is confrontation necessary in order for you to heal and regain your power? Do you remain a victim if you don't muster up your courage to face him and let him know that you *remember*—and you are *pissed*? Are you chickening out if you don't let him know how he's ruined your life, poisoned your relationships, shattered your self-esteem? Are you aching to hear the words, "I'm sorry. I know what I did and the damage it created"?

Some Steppers have responded with this set of questions: "My perpetrator is dead. Does that mean I won't be able to heal?" The reality is there is only one person who can heal you—*only one*—and you saw her face in the mirror when you brushed your teeth this morning. There are no words you can hear, no words you can say, that will fast-track you to healing. Would it be wonderful to hear words of acknowledgment and remorse from your perpetrator? Absolutely. Is it *probable* that you will hear such words if you confront your perpetrator? *No.* It's not impossible, but *it's certainly not probable.*

Our instinct tells us that if we were to get to a place where we could courageously confront our perpetrator with all the clarity and communication skills we have now, we might evoke an apology that would free us. We would be validated, our pain would be over, our wounds healed. Or we might imagine that an expression of our justified anger would free us from the victim-perpetrator bond. We would be the victor, our words would slice our connection to the past, and it would finally be over. I wish it were so.

I'm not saying: *Don't confront.* I'm saying: *Be prepared, and don't have unrealistic expectations about what may occur.* I also want to say: *There's no evidence to suggest that confronting someone in person leads to healing any more than* symbolic confrontation. Examples of symbolic confrontation are letter-writing, role-playing in therapy, art therapy, writing and then reading aloud your feelings to a supportive person. In other words, doing many of the exercises in Step Three of this book.

Face-to-face confrontation can actually lead to additional abuse and wounding. I have seen cases where the victim becomes the villain in the eyes of her family, a situation that created yet more pain. If, after careful consideration, you decide that confrontation is what you want to pursue, it is *imperative* that you prepare yourself—preferably with a therapist skilled in working with sexual abuse. Here are the suggestions and guidelines I go over with my clients:

Preparation for a confrontation with your perpetrator

- Do you truly believe that *you did not cause the abuse*? Your perpetrator is likely to deny the action or to blame you. *Self-blame* is common, and it must be worked through *before* meeting with your offender. Are you crystal clear about who was responsible for the abuse, and have you worked through any self-blame? *The abuse is a statement about him, not you.*

- Do you have a *plan*? First and foremost, will you be safe? Are you emotionally ready for what could be a devastating experience?

- Do you have *support*? Will someone be accompanying you? Will there be someone to help you debrief after the confrontation?

- Are you prepared for the "*aftermath*"? This confrontation is sure to evoke strong feelings within you. You may feel abused again. Friends or family may blame you for stirring up trouble. You may feel disappointed or angry with yourself for how you handled the confrontation. It is not over with a confrontation.

The choice is always yours, but I do think it would be helpful to complete all seven of the Healing Steps before confronting your perpetrator. I've facilitated many confrontations between a victim and her perpetrator, and each one has been intense and unexpected in some way. I strongly suggest that you have a third party present, preferably someone trained in sexual abuse, whom you trust. It's very difficult to stay close to yourself and your feelings while managing the confrontation. Self-care is of primary importance whenever you are considering any manner of confrontation.

EXERCISE: Write a Letter to Your Perpetrator from Your Adult Self

Rather than a face-to-face confrontation, it may be helpful for you to write a letter to your perpetrator from the *adult* part of you—the one who has taken on your healing. In this exercise, I want you to write that letter confronting your perpetrator. Let him know how his behavior affected you. If you have any questions, ask them. If you have some things you've always wanted to say to him, hold nothing back: say them in your letter. You will know when you have finished the letter.

Now you have several choices: you can mail the letter, you can share the letter with a trusted person, you can imagine the perpetrator sitting in a chair opposite you while you read him the letter. Or you can hang onto the letter and simply feel the release of "getting it out." You can put the letter away in a safe place, or you can destroy it. It doesn't matter. I'm guessing you will intuitively know what the right choice is for you at the present time.

Ellen was referred to me by a friend of hers after suffering several panic attacks and a long battle with anxiety. During her intake history, she mentioned she had not talked to her father for many years—and that he lived in Europe. She had no relationship with him and didn't expect to ever see him again. As the story unfolded, she divulged that he had molested her, and she expressed her relief at having him so far away. She felt stuck in all the fear, anxiety, and perpetual vigilance resulting from the abuse. She would grow pale when I brought up her father, and building up of her sense of safety and ability to take care of herself was a slow process.

Ellen completed many of the exercises in this chapter—writing letters; role playing; practicing confronting her father with her memories, her anger, and her fear—even though she knew she would never see him again. After about two years, the panic attacks disappeared, her anxiety significantly decreased, and she felt free for the first time in her life.

About six months after she terminated therapy, I received a call from her. Her father's company had sent him to San Francisco on an unexpected business trip and he wanted to see her. She called me—not because she was having a panic attack, but rather to tell me she had decided to meet him for lunch.

Later, she called to let me know that even though it was a difficult and emotional experience, she did confront him—and she was okay. She felt ready and seized the moment when it was unexpectedly presented to her.

Do you suffer from the hyper-vigilance associated with abuse? Do you sometimes anxiously wonder: *what if I run into my molester?* If so, you may find the exercises in this chapter particularly helpful. And remember Ellen. She did the work—and so, when the opportunity presented itself, she was prepared to make a decision about meeting with her perpetrator, and she was clear about her intent in doing so. The point is not that she confronted her father. The point is that she developed enough security and empowerment to know what she wanted to do and to follow through for herself.

After so many years of doing this work, I know that every experience is as unique as a thumbprint. I've also learned to be careful about any assumptions I may make. That being said, I'd like to introduce you to Lily Palazzi, who as a teenager had a completely different point of view regarding her perpetrator.

When she began therapy at the age of 23, she did not see her perpetrator as an abuser, but rather as her lover and rescuer. She had previously suffered severe emotional and physical abuse from her mother after her parents' divorce, and her journey was long and complex. Her story is her own, and I will let her tell it:

When I was sixteen, I ran away from my abusive mother and found my father. It had been nine long years since I'd last seen him. My father and I spent a lot of time together, catching up on lost time. I loved the way he listened so attentively to me, hanging onto my every word when no one else seemed to care much about what I had to say. His eyes could see right through me, to my very core. At first, I felt very exposed and vulnerable, unable to hide from him because he knew exactly what I was thinking and feeling. But that soon changed when I found that I really liked being seen and understood like that. It was like he instantly knew who I was and what I needed, and even on my bad days, my bitchy days, he didn't judge me or yell at me or beat me like my mother had. He just loved me.

I know it sounds crazy, but the more time I spent with my father, the more I fell madly in love with him, and before long we started to have an affair. When my father told me "no one will ever love you more," I believed him. I loved him. He was my lover, my protector, my hero, my best friend. I'd never been happier.

As you can see from Lily's story, some incest victims struggle with the ambivalence between hating and loving their offender. He may be the most nurturing person in the victim's life. As we discussed in the previous chapter, having an abusive mother is a perfect set-up for aligning with, and seeking solace from, a perpetrator. Certainly, this was the situation for Lily, and I'm sure she's not alone. By rejecting the perpetrator or expressing her confusion, or even questioning the relationship, she was in danger of breaking the most important—and possibly the only—tie in her life. You can read the intimate story of Lily's abuse, and her courageous road to recovery, in her book *My Daddy the Pedophile: A Memoir.*

The Victim–Perpetrator–Rescuer Triangle

How could Lily be so confused over whether her father was a Perpetrator? Who was there as a Rescuer or protector for Lily? Did she ever feel like a Victim? The Victim–Perpetrator–Rescuer triangle is important for us to understand because it is a complex dynamic so powerful that it can play out in our lives without our conscious knowledge—sometimes in the most destructive ways.

Here's a writing and drawing exercise that will hopefully help you understand the importance of this triangle to your recovery.

EXERCISE: Explore the Victim–Perpetrator–Rescuer Triangle

Draw a big triangle on your drawing pad. In one corner, write Victim; in another, Perpetrator; in the third, Rescuer. Under Victim, write your name (*Step One: Breaking the Silence*); under Rescuer, write the name of the person who either rescued you from the Perpetrator, or should have (*Step Two: Where Was the Protector*); and under Perpetrator, write the name of your Offender (*Step Three: Facing the Perpetrator*). Your triangle will look something like this:

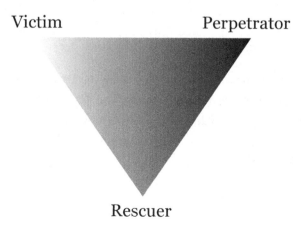

V-P-R
The Victim-Perpetrator-Rescue Triangle

Victim   Perpetrator

Rescuer

Take a moment and look at what you've written. Have you included each name that needs to be on the sheet? If possible, post your diagram on a wall or somewhere easily available to you so you can look at it over the next several days.

In your journal, answer the following questions: Does looking at the V-P-R triangle evoke any feelings for you? If so, what? What thoughts? Did looking at this model add anything to your perception of your abuse? Were there other ways you were victimized, aside from being sexually abused?

The powerful dynamic between Victim, Perpetrator, and Rescuer was imprinted on our psyche when we were abused, and it soon became an inner struggle that begged for resolution. A healthy resolution can occur when we have a certain degree of awareness, healing, and balance in our lives. *However, problems develop, and self-defeating behaviors occur, when we overidentify with any one aspect of the triangle in a negative way.*

The Inner Perpetrator

"That I feed the hungry, forgive an insult, and love my enemy ... these are great virtues! But what if I should discover that the poorest of the beggars and the most prudent of offenders are all within me, and that I stand in need of the alms of my own kindness; that I myself am the enemy who must be loved? What then?"
— Carl Jung

It is not uncommon for a Victim to internalize the Perpetrator's role. Sometimes, we ourselves become a Perpetrator or "bad ass." Sometimes, we become a Bounty Hunter—always looking for the Perpetrator. And sometimes we internalize our Perpetrator's messages and perpetrate against ourselves. Let's take a closer look at these behaviors.

• We become a Perpetrator or "bad ass"

As children, we weren't stupid. If we were abused, we noted there was a Perpetrator and a Victim and we figured it was probably less painful to be a Perpetrator. The decision not to be a Victim is certainly understandable, but the decision to *have power*—rather than to be truly empowered—is often made when we are not equipped to know the difference between aggression and assertion. Our intent is to keep ourselves from being victimized, but we send out an undeveloped part of ourselves to take care of that business. The masculine side of a woman generally develops within her psyche to protect her; but when there is childhood trauma, there is not enough time for this aspect of her psyche to develop naturally within her. We send out a boy to do a man's job—and the results are various primitive characteristics of aggression.

For example, when we overidentify with the Inner Perpetrator, we sometimes develop black-and-white thinking: things are either all right or all wrong, and we have no ability to consider the gray. We may lack impulse control for what comes out of our mouth: we "tell it like it is" with no regard for how our words hurt or wound someone else. We become practiced at being self-righteous, sarcastic or judgmental in relationships. We believe that strength and control are the only important characteristics of our being, and this sometimes leads to ignoring our moral conscience and breaking the law. An irritability or moodiness often develops in our demeanor, creating distance in relationships. It's a little like the demeanor of a sleeping giant who was awakened too soon—because he was! Remember that we identify with the Perpetrator so as not to be victimized ourselves, and we hold tight to this position. We want to remain safe and not be "penetrated" in any way. Does this sound familiar to you?

- **We become a Bounty Hunter—always searching "out there" for the Perpetrator**

 When we get stuck in this role, we are sure that protection comes from "getting him before he gets me." We become hyper-vigilant—watching for whoever is causing difficulty or creating chaos or pain in our lives. There is comfort in identifying who the Perpetrator is: the nightmare comes out of the closet and into the room, and he is no longer a menacing shadow. "Knowing" brings relief even when there is no evidence that the identified Perpetrator poses a threat. Aspects of the actual Perpetrator in our past may be generalized: thus, all men become suspect because we all know they "only want one thing" and "will use you, then abuse you, or leave you, or cheat on you"—or whatever your story may be.

Over the years, I have seen many victims who feel more comfortable with a known Perpetrator in their lives. And if there is none, they will create one. Often, they create a pattern of broken relationships with a litany of abusive partners, nasty bosses, mean-spirited neighbors, and so forth. Many therapy sessions are spent figuring out if survivors are reliving their victimization (overidentifying with that role in the triangle) by picking abusive partners to reenact their unhealed past, or if they are finding or creating offensive partners to bring relief from the exhaustion of being vigilant (or being a Bounty Hunter).

A tragic example of this dynamic was a woman in Healing Steps who experienced long-term, brutal incest as a child. As we all know, when the abuse occurs within the home, there is no place to feel safe. The vulnerability is on-going and the vigilance is nonstop. When she became an adult and had her own home, she understandably felt fearful and on guard in her own house. She didn't know why; she didn't associate it with her growing up because she was no longer in "that crazy house." She had her own home with a very gentle mountain of a man who cared deeply for her. It didn't make sense—until she had a child. She reported that her son was always troublesome, always a handful, evoking feelings in her of not knowing what to do, of being helpless. She couldn't control his crying, his sleep patterns, or his behavior as he got older. He became the cause of her anxiety, her bouts of depression, her inability to get a good night's sleep—and eventually he became her enemy. She became convinced he was a sociopath, malicious, and out to hurt her just as her father had done: he was evil incarnate, and he had to be removed from her home, and eventually her life. And her husband's life, as well. I wish I could tell you this story had a happy ending, but it didn't: it resulted in a broken family and a great deal of heartbreak. As we know, unhealed abuse leaves its own legacy in the next generation.

The obvious problem here: we make erroneous assumptions about others; we feel comfortable only when we know, or think we know who the Perpetrator is; we are continually suspicious of others' motives and behaviors; and, worst of all, we end up hurting ourselves deeply.

- **We perpetrate against ourselves**

This may be the saddest response of all: we identify with the devaluing that often occurs with molestation. As we endure the actions of the Perpetrator, we come to see ourselves as bad, a piece of shit, worthless, shame-filled, etc., and we develop a self-concept based on this negative view. We don't need to find someone else to perpetrate against us; we can do it ourselves. As a matter of fact, we are sure to do it before someone else gets a chance to do it.

Complete this sentence: "I must be _____ because I was molested." Fill in the blank as many times as you need to until you feel there are no more possibilities for yourself.

Every time you define yourself in a way that reflects your abuse, you are abusing yourself. If you say, "I'm damaged," "I'm less of a woman," "I'm bad," "I'm stupid because I didn't tell," "I don't count," "It was my fault," you continue the abuse. How do you perpetrate against yourself? Do you demean, diminish, devalue yourself? As one Healing Steps woman said, "There is something ugly about me that I wear. I put it out there ahead of me—it's like an energy." Is that true for you? Do you treat yourself like a sexual object who is readily available to fill requests? Do you treat yourself as inferior or unworthy, or like your feelings don't matter? Do you harm yourself with addictive behaviors? How about drugs, alcohol, pain killers?

Our self-esteem and well-being need to be rescued from the Perpetrator who is us! We need to turn up the volume on this repetitive, negative talk. Listen to yourself. Better yet, write down in your journal every negative thing you say to yourself in a 48-hour period. At the end of the 48 hours, look at each item you've listed and ask yourself with the clarity you now have: "Is that really true for me today? Does that really define who I am now or how I behave?" If not, self-correct. If so, ask yourself, "Is this something I want to change? If so, how would I go about doing that?" If you're not sure, ask someone close to you whom you can trust to tell you the truth. For example, ask, "I see myself as socially awkward and stupid when I talk to people. Do you see me like that?"

The other way we perpetrate against ourselves is with self-sabotage. We undermine ourselves and our growth. We avoid intimacy even when we crave it. We set our intentions and then come up with multiple excuses why we "can't." We overeat or under-eat; we never treat ourselves; or we compulsively shop, running up our credit cards. We make dates and appointments and don't show up; complain about our relationships and verbally berate our partners; suffer with body issues but don't go to a doctor or body worker; and so on. We break agreements that would challenge us and help us grow.

We all have the one inside who sabotages us and stops us from taking that next healthy step. And most of us can tell when that Inner Saboteur is at work. She is all too familiar to us as she creates havoc in our lives. Excuses slip off her tongue with ease. Reasons not to _____ are just a breath away. Sometimes the Inner Saboteur even fools us into thinking that we deserve to devour that quart of ice cream, or that we have a right to have that unaffordable piece of jewelry because of how we have suffered. One of the Healing Step women expressed a point that resonated with many other women in the workshop when she said that because she didn't get what she needed as a neglected child, she felt "entitled." And who could blame her? The wounded child deserves this, right? Tricky.

I believe the Inner Saboteur has a real purpose in our lives: she always shows us how we don't go forward. She shines a light on our failures and our challenges. The whole job of the Saboteur is to point out to us our challenges so that we can rise to the occasion and grow beyond where we already are. It's up to us to pay attention and to ask ourselves, "What is getting in the way of my being healthy, vital, empowered, challenged, in a good relationship, etc.?" And "why did I set myself up to stop growing at a certain point?" Our psyche is always pushing toward growth, and it compulsively attracts situations to us that challenge us to grow. When we say, "Oh, no, not again! I always seem to become involved with an alcoholic," or "I always get the worst managers," or "this is always happening to me," pay attention. The word "always" is a clue. It's also important to remember that the Inner Saboteur usually appears around issues of money, career, love relationships, sex, and health. Forewarned is forearmed.

EXERCISE: Get to Know Your Inner Saboteur

The Inner Saboteur—also known as the Shadow—is definitely a part of ourselves that we have to get to know. There is power in the Saboteur being in the shadows, so let's bring her into the light and give her some form:

- Make a list of adjectives that fit the Inner Saboteur. For example, is she cold, judgmental, emotionless, fiery, competitive, ruthless, slothful, lazy, uncaring, seductive, scared?

- Can you give her an image? Look through magazines, look around you, look at TV characters, movie roles.

- Give her a name so you can have a discussion or dialogue with her the next time she shows up in your life. For example, someone in Healing Steps claimed she had an inner John Wayne—tall, strong, just plows through life, no emotion or empathy, just "gets the job done with spurs spinning." Another had a menacing Dragon who lashed out with a fiery tongue, scorching everyone and everything around her. One petite woman shared her Inner Saboteur—a huge, slouchy bean-bag self who never wanted to put forth effort and yet complained that nothing ever changed in her life. One of my personal favorites was Sleeping Beauty, who remained clearly under a spell—so unconscious that she had *no choice in the matter*: "I forgot...," "I was daydreaming...," "I just closed my eyes and—I don't know what happened!!" Be imaginative with this exercise and see what you come up with for your own Inner Saboteur.

- Ask yourself, "Why am I sabotaging this idea, this relationship, this opportunity? What part of me is this? Is it about fear?"

- What would you do if you could silence the part of yourself who sabotages? What would be the first three things you'd do?

- How do you perpetrate against yourself? How do you perpetrate against others?

Everything around us in the outer world casts a shadow. Likewise, the identities we hold onto inside cast a shadow in our psyches. Our Inner Saboteur—our Shadow—hides in our secret shames, disguises herself in our projections, lurks in our addictions and blurts out in slips of the tongue—those "Freudian slips" we are familiar with. She erupts in sarcasm and sees humor in cruel jokes at another's expense. "I was just kidding," she says. "Can't you take a little joke?" She often rears her head at midlife when we feel time is running out. She reminds us of the work undone and shakes us out of our complacency. In her book *Romancing the Shadow*, Connie Zweig reminds us:

The Shadow, or Inner Saboteur, is a demanding taskmaster. [She]
requires endless patience, keen instinct, fine discrimination, and

the compassion of Buddha. [She] requires one eye to be turned out toward the light, while the other eye is turned in toward the world of darkness.

So we need to honor her. In fact, our Shadow may come bearing gifts; she often shows herself in our creativity as she builds a bridge between our conscious and unconscious worlds. But the opposite is also true. If we ignore her, she will only become more dangerous.

The Inner Victim

When a wound remains unhealed, we unconsciously select players in our individual dramas who will help us recreate a situation so we have a chance to undo or redo the result. Remember the movie *Sliding Door* with Gwyneth Paltrow? There's always another chance to say "no," to recognize the slightly "off behavior" of the person we're in relationship with, or to set a stronger boundary to take care of ourselves. Until we have learned to care for ourselves, there will always be someone on our front doorstep who will test us to see how far they can go with their own hurtful agendas before we say "stop!"

However, it's not about them at this point; it's about us. And while the learning is painful, we don't have to go it alone. If you have way too many stories about the people in your life who have used you, hurt you, stayed too long, or remind you of the main character in a country western song, then it's time to call that therapist your friend has been telling you about. You deserve more. You deserve better. You know it's time.

In order not to get stuck in this aspect of the triangle, we have to challenge that inner voice—the one who is meant to inspire us, not limit us. We have to confront the illusion that everyone else has the authority and that we have none. It's about taking back our power, instead of giving it away. As my daughter used to say, "I am the boss of me." The tricky part here is that we have to do this through action in order to really feel the empowerment; we cannot find it in a theoretical idea. The only way we can feel the power is to make a choice that ignites our courage so that we can go forth and actualize a change. We must take action to challenge the victim within. Sexual abuse is not categorized by how severe it is; the damage is determined by the victim's reaction to the abuse. This idea is actually empowering because healing is placed back into our own hands. Being a Victim is about fear: "I can't take care of myself financially," "I don't know where to get my car fixed," "I can't do my taxes," "I can't say no," etc. I know these concerns are real, but there is a difference between being immobilized by "I can't" and being mobilized with "I can find the help I need." When you have a grip on your identification with the Victim, you'll be in better charge of your fear, and then you can recreate your reality in a whole new way. The dynamics of life won't scare you as much anymore.

We can learn some powerful life lessons from simple life experiences. One of the most powerful lessons I learned about being a Victim happened a number of years ago when a close friend was getting a divorce. She moved out of her home and into an apartment where she had created a lovely, healing nest for herself. There was a place for everything—except her books. She had a huge collection— they were her soul mates—and the boxes cluttered up her apartment. Finally, she decided to take action: she was going to find a wall of bookshelves and unpack her books. So off to Ikea she went, measurements in hand. She found the bookcases, the folks at Ikea helped her load up her car, and she returned home about seven o'clock that night excited to start her project. She got out of her car, took one look at the pile of boxes in her minivan—and broke into tears. There was no way she could haul all those boxes to her second-floor apartment. She simply wasn't physically strong enough. After about ten minutes of a good pity cry, two men from her complex saw her and asked if they could help. She told them her dilemma. They said "no problem" and carried the boxes up to her apartment. She felt great. She opened the boxes, pulled out the instructions, and went, "Holy crap—what in the world is a Phillips screwdriver and who the hell is Phillip?" She decided that someone must know who Phillip was and could help her. (She was a fast learner!) She grabbed the instructions and headed for the closest home improvement store. She bought what she needed and wound up staying up all night building those bookcases and unpacking her books. When I talked to her the next day, she told me she learned the most valuable lesson about being a Victim: as long as there was someone to ask, there would be someone to help. I've never forgotten that story. In that moment, she moved from Victim to Victor.

The Inner Rescuer

Saints, I'm going to address you here. One of the ways to escape from the tension of the Victim-Perpetrator dynamic is to hide out in the role of the Rescuer. And it's so safe there. Such a respected place to be, so selfless. You try to hold all the wounds of the world in your own two hands. Here, in the safety of the Rescuer role, you can distance yourself from your own pain of being a Victim, and you don't have to look at how you hurt others or sabotage yourself with your Inner Perpetrator. You're much too busy looking after others, becoming so "other-directed" that you don't become the Rescuer of your own inner Victim. You may deny your own need for protection, and overwhelm yourself by helping, supporting, and tending to others. You may exhaust yourself, give away what you don't have, and remain out of touch with the one within you who may need some of that tenderness for herself. One Stepper, V, wrote in her journal:

> If I am needed and can make a difference, then I take care of everyone else. That makes me a "good person" so that's what I do. I don't know how to say no! I feel guilt and pressure; I am "selfish" if I put myself first. If I can help, I will, but a lot of times I resent it and a lot of times, my mouth goes off before I realize what I've done—a lot of times! I need to be needed because I am not wanted. I perfected the ability to run to the rescue.

We all see the challenges in V's situation; she has difficulty setting boundaries, she wants to be a good person, and she hides out in her selfless role. Some of us have even gone into the healing professions—to hide, or perhaps to share our understanding with others. Many women who have gone through Healing Steps have gone back to school to become therapists, body workers, or child advocates. The good news is that we bring rich life experience and a knowing kind of empathy to our work, but the bad news is that we sometimes give at the office and not at home—and not to ourselves. Balance is, of course, what is needed here so that we don't abandon ourselves as we have been abandoned. A major part of healing is giving back, extending our hands and experience to others on the path. That being said, we also have to be aware of the seductiveness of *reaching out* when we need to be *looking in* to see what we are needing right now.

Here are a few quotes from survivors struggling to give up victimhood. From Suzanne Simon's article "Don't Play the Blame Game," in *Healing Woman*:

The truth is, yes, we were sexually abused, and yes, the responsibility for that abuse lies on the shoulders of our abuser, but the responsibility for our lives lies directly on our own shoulders. We have the responsibility for creating our lives now. If I hold him/her responsible for my life today, then I have given over my power to him/her. Once again, I claim my power, and I claim my life.

From Iyanla Vanzant, on Oprah's *Super Soul Sunday* television show:

There is no greater battle in life than the battle between the parts of you that want to be healed and the parts of you that are comfortable and content remaining broken.

And here's a dream related by a Stepper who was molested by her father:

I was in a large house with very spacious rooms, lots of wood wainscoting, paneling on the walls. There was a wide staircase in the center of the house reminiscent of the one in Gone with the Wind. It was nighttime and the house was very silent. I was downstairs and was aware that my father was in the house. I was scared and had that familiar feeling that something ominous was about to happen and that my only hope was to be very quiet—to be invisible—and to go upstairs to bed. I was very young—perhaps three or four—and I was aware of my size and vulnerability as I walked up the stairs, reaching up to hold onto the railing. My bedroom was at the head of the stairs. I slowly made my way up to my room and quietly crawled into bed, snuggling down very deliberately so as not to be noticed. I breathed a big sigh of relief: "Phew, I made it."

Then I heard my father coming up the stairs. I began to feel trapped and frightened. I got out of bed and tiptoed to the edge of the stairs and watched him—one slow step after the other. All of a sudden, I felt this energy in my legs and arms; I felt strong and alive, powerful, and the fear left my body. I stood up straight, put my little arms out, and I flew—FLEW right over his head, right over the staircase and off to safety. With my newfound ability, I realized that I was the one with the power—and I said to myself, "Fly, Sweetheart, fly..." and I flew.

Remember this Healing Steps woman and her newfound power when you hear Alicia Keyes' song *I Am a Superwoman*. Listen carefully to her lyrics and feel your own strength and ability to be a superwoman. And fly, sweetheart, fly.

 ## *EXERCISE:* Facing Your Inner Victim-Perpetrator-Rescuer

Here's an exercise to help you better understand the makeup of your Inner Perpetrator. Study the graphic and answer the questions in your binder/journal.

Facing Your Inner
Victim-Perpetrator-Rescuer

Victim
Sensitive self
Overidentifying with this role:
- recreates being abused
- sees self as powerless

Perpetrator
Assertive self
Overidentifying with this role:
- perpetrates on others
- perpetrates on self

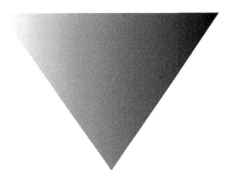

Rescuer
Nurturing self
Overidentifying with this role:
- distances self from Victim feelings
- projects needs for protection, help and support onto others
- never becomes Rescuer for own Inner Victim

- Do you over identify with the Victim? The Perpetrator? The Rescuer? If so, in what ways? Be specific.

- Do you allow yourself to be victimized? To be taken advantage of? When do you say "yes" when you want to say "no"?

- How do you perpetrate against yourself? How do you demean, diminish, devalue yourself; treat yourself like an object, treat yourself as inferior or unworthy, or treat yourself as though you don't matter or that your feelings don't matter? Past and Present. Examples?

- How do you perpetrate against others? Past and Present. Give examples.

- How do you sabotage yourself? Give examples.

- How do you "do unto others" and neglect yourself? Give examples.

EXERCISE: Visualization

Imagine an inner Board of Directors seated around a large conference table. Put your molested Inner Child at the table, and if you have identified with your Inner Perpetrator, Inner Victim, or Inner Rescuer, put them at the table, too. Include whatever parts of yourself you're aware of at this time. Know that you are the CEO: this is your company, and you are in charge. Now put your adult self at the head of the table in the power position.

First on the agenda: tell your molested Inner Child that she is no longer running your life. Release her from her management job; she can let you know about her limits and boundaries, she can share her feelings and be heard, she can let you know when something is scary, she can provide fun in your life and times to play—but that's all. Her job is to be a kid.

Invite your Inner Saboteur to come into the room. Picture her in the image you came up with earlier; if you don't have an image, that's okay. Tell your Inner Saboteur, "You've been doing a good job for me, but from now on you have to check in with me first before taking action in the outer world. I've been giving you free reign, but that's going to change." Also tell her from now on you are not going to accept her abuse of you. No putting you down. Make that clear. When you have done so, excuse her from the room. Make an announcement to those sitting around the conference table that from now on you are taking responsibility for protecting those of your inner family in a manner that is adult and sane. You may have to bring in outside consultants on how to do that, and this may take some practice, but you are telling them that you are committed to new beginnings and a new relationship with yourself. Ask if there are any questions, and if not: "The meeting is adjourned."

 Suggested Reading

Father-Daughter Incest, by Judith Herman, PhD

Co-Dependence No More and Beyond Co-Dependence, by Melody Beattie

Awakening the Warrior Within: Secrets of Personal Safety and Inner Security, by Dawn Callan

Women and Self-Esteem: Understanding and Improving the Way We Think about Ourselves, by Linda Tschirhart Sanford

My Daddy the Pedophile: A Memoir, by Lily Palazzi

A Tale, an autobiographical film written and directed by Jennifer Fox

Break the Chain

Chain reaction
Chained to you
Chain of command

Captain of my sea
Shepherd of the flock
Yet, I walk in the valley, still wanting

Wanting love
Wanting hope
Wanting peace

But all the pieces are scattered
Some destroyed, some lost
I can't put it back the way it was

And in this way I see
You're letting go, I'm free
But still the chain leads back to me

Twisted and tangled
My body's in knots
I long for the stretch of release

And hope that when the last link breaks
I'll find myself underneath
Battered and broken, but still breathing

And when I gasp that first breath
And finally cut this rotting cord
I'll be born

    — "Jean"

Step Four

Then and Now:
How the Ghosts of Your Past
Seem to Haunt Your Present

*"A life of reaction is a life of slavery, intellectually and spiritually.
One must fight for a life of action, not reaction."*
— Rita Mae Brown

*"It's not the wound that shapes our lives, it's the choice we make as
adults between embracing our wounds or raging against them."*
— Geneen Roth

Every Healing Step is important, but healing actually comes from the completion and integration of all the Steps. In my years of working with survivors, I have found that they often do not do the next three Steps in their regular therapy. Rather, they focus on "what happened" and deal with the obvious symptoms and feelings stemming from the molest itself. Certainly, anger at the perpetrator and failure of the mother figure to protect and understand are addressed. But the struggles that continue as time goes on often do not get addressed or connected to the abuse wound. The normalization of the belief systems that arise from the experience, the limiting self-definitions, the sexual or physical struggles, the relationship issues that show up in indirect ways—these are often ignored. As one woman told me, "I have gone through therapy and I have been to support groups—and everyone focuses on how I handled it then. No one asks me, 'How are you doing now?'" When I asked her how she was doing now, she told me with a great deal of emotion in her voice, "I struggle with relationships, I struggle with being touched, I have issues with intimacy, I don't know how to trust or who to trust. I feel my healing is stuck somewhere between the past and the present." This is an all too common and frustrating pattern with which many survivors struggle.

Years ago I had a dream in which I was trying to seduce a man—quite unsuccessfully I might add. No matter what I did, my seduction failed. In desperation, I went to someone else, a woman I trusted to be honest with me, and I asked her, "Why? Why couldn't I seduce him? What's the matter with me?" My friend looked me in the eye and reminded me, "You are only ten years old!" I was shocked when I awakened. I was obviously an overly sexualized little girl in the dream and perhaps in real life as well. Where did this energy come from?

Becoming pseudo-mature or erotized is one of the most common aftereffects of being sexually abused. In Step Four we will look at the effects that molestation has had and may continue to have in our lives. The aftereffects are often linked to how we got through the molest, what we learned (or didn't learn), and how we adapted. It's also important to understand that we may share many of the same aftereffects, but differences arise based on a number of variables, such as how old we were when the abuse took place, how long the molestation lasted, whether violence was involved, whether there was anyone who provided a safe haven, our relationship to the perpetrator, our own inherent resilience, etc. We will look at these variables throughout this Step.

But before we do, it is important to understand that we need to move through four levels of acceptance in order to proceed:

1. We must accept that the abuse really happened. (Put denial to rest.)
2. We must accept that the abuse has had a profound impact on our life, on who we are, on our belief systems, on our relationships and partnerships,

on our relation to the world and to ourselves, and perhaps on our careers and our dreams for the future.

3. We must accept the responsibility for recognizing and cleaning up the aftereffects of the abuse. The power is no longer in the hands of the perpetrator, nor is it in the hands of the parent who wasn't there.

4. We must accept ourselves as a whole person as opposed to a fragmented self and see our potential for growth and for healing. *Molestation is an event, not an identity.* Our wonderful Spiritual Self was not touched by the sexual abuse.

Who Was Impacted by the Abuse?

Your age when you were molested is an important factor in looking at the effects of the molest. We have certain developmental tasks to complete during different stages of our life, and if those tasks are disrupted or interrupted, then there is work to be done later in life. There will be commonalities in the effects of abuse on 4-year-olds, but there will be differences in the effects of abuse on a 4-year-old and a 12-year-old because the developmental tasks associated with each age are different. Of course, there will also be differences stemming from individual personality traits, resilience, relationship to the perpetrator, support system, etc., so be careful not to compare yourself to others when it comes to the aftereffects of your molest. For example, Lily, a member of one of the early Healing Steps workshops remembers:

During my early therapy work, I joined Healing Steps, my first women's group for survivors of child sexual abuse. I had never heard another woman speak about her abuse before. Sitting in a circle, I listened as a woman told her story of being molested one time. She was 10 years old when it happened. The experience had left her totally devastated. As I looked around the circle, everyone seemed to be very sad for her. I wasn't. I thought, "Lady, you were molested only once. Get over it, already. That's not devastating." In comparison, my story was far worse. I couldn't count the times I'd been molested by my stepfather, nor could I guess at the extent of the abuse by my father. Besides, if she really wanted to know what it felt like to be totally devastated, she should try throwing her dad, who was once her lover, in prison. But as I sat there, impatiently waiting for her to finish her story so that I could tell mine, I heard her cry of pain, a cry I knew all too well. At that moment I realized it didn't matter if she had been molested once or a thousand times, her little girl's pain was no different from mine. We had both gone to that same dark and lonely place where no child should ever have to go. In fact, as we went around the circle and shared our stories, each one was as unique as our fingerprints. Every cry of pain sounded exactly the same as mine, and I knew we had all gone there. We all knew how it felt to be abused and broken. I felt a real connection with each brave and beautiful woman sitting in the circle around me. They all felt like my sisters. I felt like I was home.

Share, don't compare. The bottom line is it's really about the way it makes you feel inside; the only yardstick to assess the damage created by abuse is the pain experienced by the victim.

The Three Developmental Stages Impacted by Sexual Abuse

"Every part of our personality that we do not love will become hostile to us."
— Robert Bly

Inner Child

Our Inner Child, who develops from birth to age 11 or 12, develops trust in the world, and learns autonomy and competency. She also holds our spontaneity, creativity, and imagination in her hands. The steps in the ongoing development of our Inner Child build on one another just like building blocks.

The danger, of course, is that when a trauma occurs, blocks can be knocked out—and often we return to the first block in our developmental tasks: trust versus mistrust. This foundational block is developed between birth and age two when we learn (hopefully) that the world is a safe place, and someone is there to take care of our primary needs. When we are betrayed by sexual abuse at an early age, we often return to this primary stage of development and come to believe the world is not a safe place and there is no one "out there" to take care of us. This often evolves into a continuous need to be taken care of. Many women I've worked with become stuck and can't, or won't, move forward until that caretaker comes along to take care of them. (Remember the stories in Step Two?) For others, it's continually searching for the perpetrator in every relationship and overlaying the "mistrust" on him, thus further victimizing ourselves.

As the developmental stages continue, other tasks need to be mastered: gaining competency and control, taking initiative, controlling impulsivity, building self-esteem, and, of course, handling peer relationships. You can see how being sexually abused at this vulnerable and strength-building time can influence us. Competency starts to develop between the ages of three and five, and that's when we start saying "I can"— or sometimes "I can't" or "I'm not good enough."

At the same time, we are developing our feelings of shame and guilt. It's important for you to know the difference between these two concepts. Shame is a statement about who you are and your lack of self-worth. Guilt is a feeling resulting from a certain behavior or feeling that is counter to your personal value system. "I don't deserve to have a successful relationship because I am damaged goods" is a shame statement; "I should have told someone about the abuse and then maybe my sister wouldn't have been abused" is a guilt statement. It is our feelings of shame that tend to give us the most trouble and are the hardest to self-correct.

Examples of other issues that you may struggle with if violated during your childhood or preadolescent years are a lack of playfulness, no defense against the intensity of your emotions, a primitive quality to your emotions, and, of course, dependency. You may not have been allowed to individuate, to have your own feelings or a sense of yourself. This may be reflected in an inability to say "no" or to stand up for yourself. You may feel trapped or scared, or you may have difficulty operating in the world with a sense of competence and self-esteem. You may have a fear of abandonment if you do act on your own behalf. You may believe "the world is not safe," "I can't trust anyone," "I can't take care of myself," "I can't go on because I've never been loved." Often, we stay a "good little girl" or at least a "little girl," and the subsequent developmental tasks of adolescence don't have a foundation to build on. Someone stuck in this stage of development often gets tangled in the "blame game" of being a perpetual victim; power is lost and quality of life depends how others see you and treat you. Since we tend to hold onto a belief system like a tenacious bulldog, we self-select people in our life who will continue to demean or abuse us or keep us in a position that is familiar, and painful. Remember that repetition compulsion we mentioned in the last Step?

A look at social psychologist Erik Erickson's developmental stages can be helpful here. (Research the Eight Stages of Psychosocial Development online.) *Knowing what your developmental tasks and challenges were at the age you were molested, and how the interruption caused by your abuse may have affected you, can shed some light on your current struggles.* When you were being abused, your world revolved around that fact and how you could deal with it. *That* was your major challenge, often to the exclusion of the traditional developmental challenges of childhood.

When we feel scared, immobilized, trapped or abandoned, we are in our Inner Child state *now*. When we feel powerless, helpless, less than, or incapable, we are in our Inner Child state *now*. As children we didn't have the physical freedom to take ourselves out of our negative situations even momentarily, much less to manage the complexities of what was occurring. Of course, we felt helpless. We *were* helpless. *Then*.

Inner Adolescent

This brings us to the difficult period of the Inner Adolescent, ages 12–18; this is a time for identity formation and the development of proactive responses to the world. As an adolescent, this is the first time we may see a way out—some kind of escape—because we have become physically independent: we may be able to drive a car, to spend the night with friends, to spend time away from home. We may have a few dollars in our pocket and an inflated sense of who we are. We begin to feel empowered to make choices and take risks.

The major task during our teen years is the development of an identity. We are all familiar with the identities we assumed in high school, right? The Stoners, the Jocks, the Brainiacs, etc. Different generations have different names for these groups, but that sense of who we were, who we were seen as, with whom we associated, and how we measured up, were very powerful. The developmental challenge here is what we do with the conflicts, the hormonal changes, the challenges in our peer group, the stresses that we experience during this very significant time of our lives. How do we establish who we are? Do we "act out" (destructively) or do we "take action" (constructively)?

You can imagine how this process gets disrupted if sexual abuse takes place between the ages of 12 and 18. The choices teens are faced with are tough enough in the best of circumstances, but if there is abuse in the mix, extremes can become normalized. We know that the three normal reactions to sexual abuse are flight, fight, or freeze, and we can see how those choices play out in adolescence. Outward-facing choices include destructive, risk-taking behaviors designed to help us zone out of our situation: they include alcohol, drugs, sexual promiscuity, running away, creating another dysfunctional relationship, shoplifting, and letting our impulses take over (including having anonymous or unprotected sex, cutting, etc.) Inward-facing choices for dealing with our difficult life situations often result in depression, low self-esteem, withdrawal, social isolation, numbing out, fantasy and daydreaming to the exclusion of healthy outlets, moodiness, suicidal ideation or attempts, non-participation ("I won't—you can't make me"), passive-aggressive behavior ("I can't be angry with you, but I can make you angry"), eating disorders, etc. The list is as long and creative as there are adolescents suffering from abuse. An abused teen is forced to concentrate on survival and adaptation issues, rather than on individuation issues. Survival mode thus become a large part of who we are—and we become defensive and vigilant creatures.

Let me introduce you to Jean, who discovered her Inner Adolescent and liked her lifestyle so much that she decided to spend most of her time there. Over the years, she has had an occasional visit to adulthood, but she always returns to booze, drugs, and bad decisions. Jean's original abuse by a sibling led her through all the "right" treatments. Other family members had been abused so there was counseling for all, reporting of incidents to the authorities, and interventions according to appropriate treatment plans. Except for one thing. When Jean's stepfather learned of the abuse, he began sexually abusing her on those weekends she spent with him and her mother. She was betrayed again when she was at her most vulnerable. She didn't tell her parents or her counselor at the time. It was only years later when she entered therapy with me that she told me what had happened. She was full of shame, and deeply angry at her stepfather for taking advantage of her when she was so raw and confused. I notified her parents and made a report to the authorities who responded right away. Her confidence began to return, and she believed justice would prevail. She was relieved to think the perpetrator, who was by this time divorced from her mom, would be taken off the streets. She bravely agreed to participate in a sting, all was arranged—and then the case fell through the cracks. An arrest was never made. As of the last sighting, her abuser was seen enjoying coffee at a neighborhood Starbucks.

Jean had done it the "right" way: she'd followed all the protocols and the rules. And where did it get her? So she decided to live life her way. She began using drugs and alcohol to numb her pain, and she had a child with a very abusive man. I had lost touch with her over the past couple of years, but I wanted to use a poem she had written (the powerful poem at the end of the previous chapter). When I contacted her to ask her permission, she told me she was exactly thirty days clean and sober—and feeling very confident about what lies ahead for her. She is one of the brightest stars I know; she shines with intelligence, creativity, and a laugh that is infectious. Not all stories of recovery are neat and tidy: they, too, are as individual as thumbprints.

Some teens react by continuing the *good girl* syndrome; these are the high achievers, the perfectionists, the ones who identify with what they do, not with who they are. They distract their families by becoming the "shiny object." Often, they are also the ones who develop anorexia, bulimia or other physical ailments. One of the most delightful Steppers I know was a woman who suffered from eating issues and was the very personification of the Inner Adolescent—full of suspicion, resistance, and avoidance. She was very clear on her registration form what she would and would not do in my workshops. Keeping in mind this is California, she wrote, "I am very wary of group situations where we are being told things and can't disengage when we need or want to. I won't chant anything with the group, and I will leave if we have to chant. I have to be able to get out when I want to. I won't do any 'affirmations' and I hate all that New Age crap. I would like to check in as much as possible, so we can see if anyone in the group is feeling weird." She was clear about her limits, and initially she used every ounce of her charm and brilliance to avoid doing her own deep work. "Danielle" grew into herself during the workshop series, and she attended additional workshops while doing individual therapy. We all cheered her on when she decided to return to school. She applied for and was awarded a full scholarship to Stanford University and then continued on to earn her PhD in childhood development from Harvard University. This woman graduated on many different levels because of her tenacity and willingness to show up, even though each step was so uncomfortable for her.

Besides eating disorders (which are four times more likely in women who have been abused than women who have not), other physical effects often arise from sexual abuse. In the study "Unhealed Wounds," published in the *Journal of the American Medical Association*, researchers at Johns Hopkins found a strong correlation between child abuse and physical problems later in life. For many, the physical symptoms were *as strong as* those suffered by women experiencing *current* abuse. Physical problems in the 1,931 women surveyed included back pain, chronic headaches, chest pain and abdominal pain. The study, completed in 1997, also found that women abused as children were nearly four times as likely to attempt suicide, and more than three times as likely to have been hospitalized for an emotional or mental problem. They had more anxiety, depression, and stress than never-abused women; and they were more likely to have problems with alcohol and drugs. According to Dr. Jeanne McCauley, principle researcher, it made little difference whether the abuse was physical or sexual, in the past or ongoing.

Psychologist Jacqueline Golding, a researcher at the University of California, San Francisco, writes that women who have been sexually abused are more likely to report physical ailments and physical limitations. In seven different population studies done throughout the country spanning more than a decade, Dr. Golding found that 362 of the 3,419 women (ages 18-96) surveyed had a history of sexual abuse, and these women were more likely to have such medically unexplained symptoms as painful menstruation, irregular periods, lack of sexual pleasure, and pain during intercourse.

Medical studies have shown that survivors of sexual abuse report more physical symptoms, such as gastrointestinal disorders, chronic back and pelvic pain, and a wide range of reproductive and sexual health complaints. Survivors also suffer from a high incidence of irritable bowel syndrome [IBS] and fibromyalgia, and they make more physician visits than women without a history of abuse. It's interesting to note that there are ethnic differences in symptoms. For example, black women have a higher number of reproductive symptoms and report more trauma resulting from incest than do white women. Sexually abused Hispanic women have the highest rate of unexplained sexual symptoms, including sexual indifference. Perhaps because the Hispanic culture places such an importance of virginity, the abused women may feel both culpable and tainted by sexual assault.

Sexual abuse in childhood can also impair the brain's physical development and leave victims with permanently weakened immune function, suggests pioneering studies released in the mid-nineties. Dr. Frank Putnam of the National Institute of Mental Health writes: "Abuse seems to be a biology-altering experience. It changes the brain's stress-response system." He followed 170 girls, ages 6–15, half sexually abused, half not, for seven years. He found that the sexually abused girls in his study had abnormally high stress hormones, which can kill neurons in brain areas crucial for thinking and memory. He also found high levels of an antibody that weakens the human immune system, which may explain some of the illnesses that plague women who have been sexually abused. It is important to note that in a follow-up study Dr. Putnam reported that not all sexually abused children have symptoms immediately following the abuse, perhaps "because the abuse was minor, they are more resilient, or they have a coping style that masks their distress." However, both research and clinical evidence show that children who display fewer symptoms initially are more likely to deteriorate over time. I've often heard this in my practice: "I was okay—I didn't have any effects until I had my first child or saw a certain movie or—." When the symptoms or memories resurface or become unbearable, that's an indicator that you are ready to be healed. Perhaps for the first time in your life, you have the courage and ego strength to take your own healing steps.

Strides are being made by the medical community to take seriously the damage to a child who has been sexually abused. Sexual abuse is a public health problem of enormous consequence not only because of the numbers, but because of the long-term effects suffered as a result of the trauma. It's important to let your abuse become part of your medical history so that what was once seen as "unexplained" may become clearer to you and your physician.

I can't stress enough how important it is to take care of our physical selves, and to understand that the abuse often leaves its mark on our bodies as well as on our souls.

When we feel rebellious or perfectionistic, when we "act out" and seek instant gratification, when we are passive-aggressive or don't control our impulsivity, when we want to black out or block out, we're in our Inner Adolescent. But let's not forget, this is also the part of us who loves to be spontaneous, enjoys trying new things, urges us to take a break from too much work or responsibility, loves to act silly with our friends. We don't want to eliminate her, but we may have to tame her as we do our healing work, because she has an unending list of distractions to dazzle us.

Inner Maiden

I can't just write about the Inner Child and the Inner Adolescent without mentioning the Inner Maiden, who is so important to women and to those who love them (a topic we'll get to when we talk about relationships). The Maiden comes into being during the ages of 17–25. She has her roots in our childhood and adolescence, and in our sexual abuse wound. This stage of development is about individuation; it's about the resolution of the identity crisis of our teenage years and the development of our identity in relationships. It's about taking on the world and making a place for ourselves with our peers. Being a Maiden means flirting, feeling our feminine power, and having crushes. As one of my mentors who was sexually abused once shared, "I never got to be a young woman. I never got to experience the 'maiden' part of my life. That's an incredible loss you can never recapture. You can do it over and you can do it differently, but you never get to be 18 again."

This is a complex issue and probably meant for another book, but I do want to touch on the five types of Maiden styles that I have seen in my work with women who are struggling with this developmental stage. Do you identify with one of these types—or is there a sixth one that is a better fit for you?

Romantic Rescue: She is the one who yearns and waits. She has dreams of being rescued by her Prince—she is the romantic. She is the Rapunzel waiting by her window to be discovered and cherished and adored. Her identity will be through Him. She has not yet formed her own sense of self. She will only be complete, whole, or healed by him, with him. Cinderella, Snow White, Rapunzel, a 1950s woman—there are countless examples. She is the one who goes through life with a bag packed for the day when the Shining Knight on a White Charger arrives. Until then, her life doesn't really begin. She is a Half waiting to be a Whole by being chosen and adored.

Dreams of Discovery: She is the one who is waiting to be valued, to be discovered, to be famous, to be on the cover of *People*, to be talked about on TMZ. She no longer wants to be invisible! She says, "I'll finally be appreciated, and people will see my worth. Then they'll be sorry—I'll show them. Resolution will only come when my true value is recognized!" She wants either to *win* the trophy, or to *be* the Trophy to prove her worth and her place in the world. It's still about the Other—waiting to find value from others—and going after what she lost a long time ago.

Sex, Drugs, and Rock and Roll—and Other Addictions and Compulsions: This is the one who is stuck in her adolescence. Her angry Adolescent is in charge of her life today. She keeps her Maiden locked in the tower and doesn't allow her to come into consciousness. As a matter of fact, she doesn't allow much to come into consciousness!! She is about rebelling, fighting authority, partying, dropping out of whatever she dropped into, promiscuity, etc. The Adolescent won't let herself grow up and become a Maiden.

The Child-Woman: This is the one stuck in her child-self. She is helpless, dependent, and needs someone to take care of her and fill her up. She is generally seductive and is not too discriminating in her partners; she uses her sexuality as her currency. She often has an amazing capacity to get people to take care of her, or she will wind up angry and bitter that no one did. Her expectations are high, her sense of self low. As Iyanla Vanzant says in her book *Trust*: "I had to stop being an abused, abandoned, neglected little girl. That was an experience I had, not who I am."

Making It in a Man's World: This is the woman Carl Jung would say is Animus Possessed. She denies and rejects the feminine and identifies with the masculine. She doesn't get the payoffs she wants because she leaves her feminine, receptive side behind rather than integrating it with her masculine side. There is too much vulnerability to her feminine side, so she keeps it under wraps in order to not be hurt. But without her feminine side, she will always be a second-rate man! She's a Joan Crawford kind of gal: "Put on those shoulder pads and grab the world by the balls!" (This is not gender identification; this is gender abandonment: they are two different challenges.)

Belief Systems: The Most Powerful Effects of All

"It ain't what you don't know that gets you into trouble.
It's what you know for sure that just ain't so."
— Mark Twain

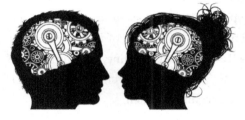

If I had to pick one of the most destructive and lasting effects of sexual abuse, it would definitely be the belief systems that arise from the molest. The power of those belief systems lies in how deeply they are buried, and how intertwined they are with who we think we are. Marilyn Van Derbur, Miss America of 1958 and a strong activist because of her own incest history, explains it like this:

> *What happens to a child's mind when her young body is pried open and violated is that her belief systems are shattered. It's not just the physical invasion of our bodies; it's the trauma that it does to our entire belief system.*

Over time beliefs become reality: the truths we live by, our normal. Rarely do we question them because they are what give us security: "I know how it is, so I know what I have to do, who I have to be, what I have to do to survive." I have played tug of war with survivors who are attached to erroneous beliefs: they have the power of a pit bull to hold onto those beliefs even in the face of clear evidence to the contrary. I have arm-wrestled with them, chased them down, offered them another belief in exchange for the erroneous one—and it's always a tough battle that I often lose!

Identity is often sewn together by these outdated beliefs, so that tugging on one thread threatens to unravel a survivor's sense of self. Beliefs generally arise as the explanation for a situation that's impossible for a child or teen to understand. Our brain, our psychological system, does not like gaps, does not like to be baffled by something it doesn't understand. That void creates too much anxiety, so we find an explanation, we come to a conclusion to explain what happened to us and why. The problem is that the abuse occurred when we were too young to understand, too naïve to figure it out, too scared to come to a correct understanding. So, we spin a story, we create a belief system, and our beliefs become imbedded into our self-definition and our understanding of relationships, the world around us, and our ability (or inability) to cope.

An essential and ongoing aspect of healing is turning up the volume on what is being played inside our minds so we can hear and respond to these long-standing beliefs. We must be vigilant, listening to these internal voices and recognizing the power of the "whisper." I don't believe the healing can happen unless we listen to and question ourselves: Do we accept that belief as true? Do we trash that belief because it's not true? Do we need to alter or update that belief to make it true today? This takes persistent and consistent work, but the results can be life-altering. It's asking the ongoing question: "Is this a feeling or a fact?"

 ## *EXERCISE:* Challenge Your Belief System

I always give sexually abused clients this assignment: fold a piece of paper in half, and on one side of the paper write down the beliefs you hold that stem from your abuse. The list is generally quite long. On the other side of the fold, I ask them to write a "corrected" statement for each belief they find to be erroneous. For example, one woman wrote:

Belief Systems

Erroneous	Corrected
People are scary and they lie to you and manipulate you.	I deserve people who won't turn their back on me.
It's okay to have sex with a married man.	It's okay to have sex with a married man if he's married to me!
I am damaged and unlovable.	I'm okay; my perpetrator was damaged.

Here are the 33 most common beliefs stemming from the abuse wound. Read them, mark the ones that you embrace, and feel free to add your own. Remember, these are common but *false* beliefs that many survivors grow up believing. As you read through them, check the ones that you still believe. By acknowledging the belief and challenging it, the erroneous belief will have less power over you, and you'll begin to change.

❏ I have to do what men want or they will hurt me, or they will not love or want me.

❏ I feel there's something wrong with me.

❏ I'm not as desirable as someone who was not sexually abused.

❏ I'm not lovable.

❏ I deserved what happened to me.

❏ It was my fault—I didn't stop it.

❏ I feel powerless.

❏ No one would stay with me if they really knew me.

❏ I have a hard time taking care of myself. Sometimes I don't think I can.

❏ I'm only good for one thing—sex.

❏ Nobody will protect me.

❏ It's safer to be alone than to be in a relationship.

❏ Every child will be molested—it's just a matter of time.

❏ I'll never be healed.

❏ Being vulnerable is not safe.

❏ I have to do what I'm told.

❏ If men don't want me sexually, I don't feel valued by them.

❏ I don't deserve to be happy.

❏ If I really let myself feel my feelings, I'd go crazy (or die, or be out of control).

❏ It's not safe to be in my body.

❏ My body is ugly and damaged.

❏ Relationships don't work

❏ I don't deserve to be loved.

❏ People can't be trusted.

❏ I can't say no or set limits for myself.

❏ Sex is disgusting.

❏ I need to control everything in my life so I don't get hurt.

❏ I'm ashamed of my sexuality and some sexual behaviors in my history.

❏ I can't express my feelings.

❏ I have to be a good girl to be safe—or I have to be a bad girl to be in control.

❏ I can't ask for what I need.

❏ God doesn't care—if he did, I wouldn't have been abused.

❏ I'll never have enough to feel secure and safe.

How many did you mark? What would you add to the list? Really listen to yourself as you go about your daily life and see how many of these come up and color your perception of yourself.

Depression and Sadness

Depression and sadness go hand in hand with sexual abuse. I have yet to meet a survivor who has not suffered from depression either as a chronic condition or as periods of darkness and despair. Research shows that twice as many sexually abused women suffer from depression than women who were not molested as children. Survivors are twice as likely to report suicide attempts. The wounds go deep, and often the pathway to healing is through the storminess of tears and the ragged edges of loss. There is much to be grieved. The loss of innocence, the betrayal, the violation—all have to be mourned.

Drawing by a young Survivor

Often a survivor's journey begins with feelings of depression and apathy that seem to grab hold of her and won't let go. The feelings of despair can become persistent and overwhelming without a clue as to what caused them. There is often a crisis period when the memories break through or when the pieces come together and create a reality that is hard to accept. As one survivor wrote:

My sorrow is quiet and deep; not a chaos of emotions bombarding me from without, but a solid internal presence filling me with blackness and despair. It is a seemingly bottomless reservoir of bleakness and loss. I cannot name all the sources of my sorrow. There is not always a conscious cause. There is a deep pool of loss of childhood; fear of anger, destroyed innocence, misplaced judgment; monsters who take form with rage, with violence, with irrationality. Because of my sorrow, I am never completely comfortable with being loved, with trusting others, with welcoming joy. I have spent the larger portion of my life carrying this blackness inside. How does one let go? How does one believe? How can hope shine into such a paucity of peace? This is not a slippery slope that I slide down for lack of footholds. This is a thick, amorphous, nearly solid blackness that resides with constant familiarity at my core.

Depression has been experienced by every woman who has gone through the Healing Steps workshops; for some, it has become a chronic state, and for others, brief but dark periods that have become crippling. If you find yourself paralyzed by your depression or are having thoughts of suicide, please seek help. You may be a candidate for anti-depressant medications. However, because medication takes several weeks to reach its full effect, you will need immediate assistance: a combination of psychotherapy and medication evaluation by a psychiatrist can help you through this dark period. Most survivors have thoughts of suicide at one time or another in their lives. Please understand that *this is a passage, not a life sentence.* When you seek help, you are taking a strong step for yourself: you are reaching out and allowing someone to walk beside you.

This is a rough time and has to be faced one day, one hour, at a time. As Laura Davis, co-author of *Courage to Heal*, puts it: when the reality of the abuse breaks through, there is "a watershed moment when nothing is ever the same again." This is a tough and painful period, but the intensity is temporary—and it will lessen with time.

If you persist in your Healing Steps work, you may need to take a temporary break or slow down the process. We talked about "flooding" earlier: you may be drowning in past and present feelings as you progress in your healing work. Consult a counselor who can give you support and can help pace you as you work toward your goals. As I mentioned earlier, the topics presented here were presented in workshops four to five weeks apart, so the content could be processed over several weeks. There is time.

If you are in treatment, this may be a time to increase your therapy sessions to more than one time a week. It is not at all uncommon for there to be intense periods of pain, and prolonged periods of feeling angry and overwhelmed, during your healing process. These periods generally come and go, but there *is* light at the end of the tunnel. Whatever feelings, experiences and memories have been held captive within you are now creating havoc within you. When you open the door and say, "Okay, I'm ready. I will do whatever I can to activate what lies within, so I can deal with it—and then I can move on with my life," all hell can break loose! When we dig into the past, the feelings that accompany our experiences emerge; we may not have had the ego strength to manage those feelings in the past when we were young and unequipped. We now have the opportunity to face them, and to learn some skills so we can manage them. It takes time, it takes tools, and, in many cases, it takes a guide who'll walk beside us. This may be your next step—to reach out and know that there is someone who will listen and give you strength and support to continue on with your journey toward healing. Take yourself seriously, listen to yourself, and if you think you are stuck in the grips of depression, make that phone call today.

What Do You Do?
What do you do with the heartache
when it rushes up with a swell—
crashing into your heart,
a hurricane blowing from hell...
What do you do with the heartache
when it's searing into your brain—
breaking your will with doubts,
can you ever go forward again?

What do you do with the heartache
when it tears a hole in your soul
leaving you empty and aching,
leaving you shattered and old...
What do you do with the heartache
when it becomes a place in your life
filling the spaces around you
with constant reminders of strife...
Where can you go when you're hurting?
Where can go when you break?
Where can you go when the tears won't stop?
Where do you go for relief?
I wish that I knew the answers,
you'd think that by now I could tell;
I've had so many chances to find out—
so many chances to fail.

What do I do with the heartache?
What do I do with the pain?
How do I face each tomorrow
when I'm so worn out from today?
Someday I might have an answer
but for now I just have to wait.
They say that God will not test you
beyond what you can endure;
He must have lots of confidence
in my ability to get through.
Trust is a hard thing to find
when you lay beaten and bruised in the path
but I'm going to try to believe
that this pain is all part of a plan.

Maybe tomorrow I'll understand—
maybe tomorrow I'll see;
for now I'll just hold myself tenderly,
don't decide anything rash.
Try to stop asking these questions,
try to let go of the pain.
What do you do with the heartache?
You live through it—
praying for peace.

— "May," a Healing Step participant, 1991

Anger

 Anger occurs when something we wanted to happen didn't, or something we didn't want to happen, did. When our expectations are unfulfilled, when agreements are broken or boundaries are violated, it is certainly appropriate to feel angry. Anger is meant to alert us to the fact that we have a problem that needs attention.

When a situation is handled appropriately, we can generally let our anger go. It's meant to be fleeting—not a permanent fixture—and unlike wine, it does not improve with age! I once read that being angry for three to four minutes is like eating four to five eggs: anger releases cholesterol that gums up the arteries so that we don't bleed to death (assuming we are in a life-or-death situation). Angry people have three times the number of heart attacks, even when their blood pressure is normal. Being angry with someone for five minutes also disrupts the immune system for four to six hours. Clearly it doesn't serve us to hang onto our anger or to bury it. As Dame Edna commented on an old *Ally McBeal* show, "Just because you bury your feelings in the basement doesn't mean they'll decompose!" Right she is.

It's impossible to have been sexually abused and *not* to be angry—angry at the violation, angry at the betrayal, angry at not being protected, perhaps angry at not being believed, angry at every day that goes by where there is denial by the perpetrator or an eruption of our pain. We're angry that we had to grow up too fast, or struggle in relationships, or figure out our sexuality. We're angry that something unexpected happened that disrupted our lives that we didn't have the skills, the knowledge, or the courage to deal with. We didn't know how to handle that kind of hurt, fear, and disappointment.

Drawing by a Survivor

What do you do when there is nothing you can do? Well, we generally spin around with what we'd like to do, what we wish we had done, what we would do now. Trying to change what cannot be changed, or influence those who do not want to be influenced, will meet with failure and cause further emotional distress. When the source of the anger lies outside of us, we often look outside ourselves for healing, but when we blame someone else for our suffering, then we need something *from the other person* in order to feel better or to go forward with our lives. I'm not talking about accountability here. I'm talking about *blaming someone else for the effects* of the molest. *The effects are ours to repair and heal*: it is not up to the perpetrator, nor the protector who failed us. If we keep handing the responsibility over to the perpetrator, we remain passive and he retains the power to determine the quality of our lives. Numerous times I have heard, "I can't go on until he admits what he has done, until he understands how much damage has been done." It would be wonderful if denial were broken on all fronts; if everyone looked at their part in this travesty and were remorseful; if those involved recognized how they let us down and abandoned us. In a perfect world.

But this isn't a perfect world. And you can stand up for yourself and get the help you need to deal with the anger that remains from your abuse. If you don't own your current anger, or work to release your anger, the person who wronged you in the past remains in power over your present well-being—and now you become angry *and* helpless *and* full of resentment. If you keep repeating your story without working on the accompanying anger, you are simply fanning the flames of that anger. Remember: that original anger is what keeps us tied to the perpetrator. Releasing it is what brings us freedom from the hold he has on us. Releasing the anger does not mean what was done to you was not reprehensible, nor does it mean you are not entitled to be royally pissed off. It simply means you will not be controlled by it. And it's not an easy task—it's more like stump removal than pruning the branches.

If you were abused when you were very little, your anger is probably more primitive and direct. There are things you can do to move that energy in a physical way. Make noise—scream, shout when you are in the shower or in your car. Use words—or not. Making sounds works just as well. We used to beat cushions with pillowed bats called "batakas," but you can pile up some sofa cushions, get on your knees, hold a tennis racquet in two hands over your head, and bring your arms down hard—whack with the face of the tennis racquet. It makes a great whooshing sound. Pair that with a one-word exclamation, such as "no!" or a short sentence, such as "don't touch me"—whack, "don't touch me," whack. Or find a safe and soft mattress where you can lie down and kick your legs and slam down your arms; have a tantrum, you have the right to kick and scream.

We also have to learn how to *recognize* when we are angry, how to *express* our anger, and what to do with the residual anger that haunts us. I think of anger as having five intensities:

- annoyance

- irritation (can be ongoing)

- resentment

- anger

- rage (which generally has primitive roots; we feel it deep inside our bone marrow!)

Anger isn't passive. You can actually feel it in your body. It buzzes and tightens your stomach; it can even blind you, as in a "blind rage." That energy is asking to be acknowledged and released in some way. Remember: emotions are not symptoms of disease; emotions are the symptoms of healing. A beneficial first step is to begin monitoring your anger. When you talk about your molester, or think about your abuse, or focus on the person who didn't protect you, what do you feel in your body? Where do you feel it? Is it annoyance, resentment, rage? How do you know? Get acquainted with your anger—and use it constructively. What is it trying to tell you? Is someone stepping over your boundaries? Is someone's behavior toward you intrusive and/or abusive at the present time? Are people close to you breaking their agreements with you—either spoken or not spoken? Are your expectations being thwarted? And are your expectations realistic?

Begin to see your anger as a messenger calling your attention to something that is not "right" —either within you, within a relationship, or within your world. And remember, whining is simply anger coming through a small opening!! *Don't silence the messenger, but don't give her a megaphone to blast everyone, either. Neither extreme works.*

EXERCISE: Confront Your Anger

Take pen to paper and write a dialogue between you and your anger—a two-person conversation. Ask your anger some investigative questions, such as: "When did you first show up, Anger?" "What would you like to do to _____?" "What would you like to say to _____?" "How can I help you express yourself, Anger?" "What are you trying to tell me about_____?" You can come up with the questions, and let your anger come up with the answers. It's a beginning.

Dr. Fred Luskin, Founder and Director of the Stanford Forgiveness Project, says that if you are more than mildly upset with the actions of others in your life, it is because you are trying to enforce an "unenforceable rule." He believes if you work on challenging your rules when you start feeling upset, then your anger won't last, or won't be as severe. In his book *Forgive for Good: A Proven Prescription for Health and Happiness,* he provides a process that includes asking yourself, "What experiences in my life am I demanding to be different?" and then changing "demanding" to "hoping," which may open you to the possibility that you may not get what you want. In this way, you can begin to deal with the reality of your situation. If you find this idea intriguing, you might want to pick up a copy of his book.

Here are the basics about Anger:

Four Things Not to Do *with Anger*

- Suppress it: consciously dismissing anger from your mind and ignoring it.

- Repress it: forcing it into the unconscious by ignoring it. This creates depression and wreaks havoc in your body.

- Displace it: transferring it to a more acceptable, or safer, object (such as mother, partner, the dog, etc.)

- Sublimate it: re-channeling anger and its energy into something else, such as work, political causes, etc. without working through the original anger. This only postpones anger work.

Four Things to Do *with Anger*

- Express it: in an art form such as drawing, clay, finger painting, journaling. Write it in your journal or in a letter. Or shout it out.

- Act out the energy: through biking, racquetball, or anger exercises such as hitting pillows, throwing darts at a personalized dartboard, using a squirt gun aimed at a target, etc.

- Share it: in a therapy group, in a support group, with trusted others, or with yourself—out loud.

- Meditate and create images of anger: express the color of it, the size of it, the energy that surrounds it—and then let your imagination work with it until you come to a place of stillness, and perhaps resolution. Or just sit quietly and breathe through your nose until you feel a shift in your body. The Baltimore School District has begun to teach mindfulness and meditation techniques to four thousand students, helping them to calm down, redirect their negative energy, and resolve conflicts. Has it worked? The district reports that *all* students have learned an alternative to dealing with their angry impulses, and that school suspensions have been reduced dramatically.

For some survivors, anger is not always at the surface. Anger can be scary—not only someone else's anger, but also our own. So, what happens to anger that is buried or exists below our consciousness? Unfortunately, it doesn't decompose over time; rather, it comes out in hidden ways. Do you procrastinate on assigned tasks, or are you habitually late? Do you frequently "forget" when asked to do something? Are you sarcastic or cynical in conversation? Do you grind your teeth or clench your jaw while sleeping? Do you have a chronically sore neck or shoulder muscles? Are you excessively irritable about "little things"? Are you chronically depressed? If you recognize yourself here, I recommend one of the body therapies, such as the Rosen Method discussed in the next Step, to help you get in touch with what may lie beneath the surface. It's almost impossible to have been sexually abused and not have some degree of anger at what was done to you. Getting in touch with your anger and moving through it is an essential part of healing. A secondary gain for getting in touch with your anger is that it really does help energize you through your healing process.

I loved the story of 79-year-old Barbara, one of the women highlighted in the powerful video documentary *The Healing Years*. At one of her early therapy appointments, she told her therapist that her father had touched her in "funny" ways. As she expanded on her story, her therapist commented that his touching must have made her angry. She was stunned. Angry? At being touched? She had never considered that before. After the session, she got in her car to return home, turned on the radio, and heard Helen Reddy singing "Leave Me Alone." She turned the volume up, joined in, and sang the song full-voice all the way home. She sang—*and then screamed the words* "leave me alone, leave me alone, leave me alone" for days, feeling stronger with every verse. Her therapist's suggestion and the powerful lyrics of the song helped Barbara put words to intense feelings she had long buried. Find the song on iTunes and have a listen; the words may speak to you as well.

I'll conclude with one of my favorite stories about anger. Although it is thought to be a Cherokee parable, the source cannot be confirmed.

Two Wolves

An old Indian grandfather said to his grandson who came to him with anger at a friend who had done him an injustice:

"Let me tell you a story. I, too, at times, have felt a great hate for those that have taken so much, with no sorrow for what they do. But hate wears you down and does not hurt your enemy. It is like taking poison and wishing your enemy would die. I have struggled with these feelings many times."

He continued ...

"It is as if there are two wolves inside me; one is good and does no harm. He lives in harmony with all around him and does not take

offense when no offense was intended. He will only fight when it is right to do so, and in the right way. He saves all his energy for the right fight. But the other wolf, ahhh! He is full of anger. The littlest thing will set him into a fit of temper. He fights everyone, all the time, for no reason. He cannot think because his anger and hate are so great. It is helpless anger, for his anger will change nothing. Sometimes it is hard to live with these two wolves inside me, for both of them try to dominate my spirit."

The boy looked intently into his grandfather's eyes and asked...

"Which one wins, Grandfather?"

The Grandfather smiled and quietly said, *"The one I feed."*

Post-Traumatic Stress Disorder (PTSD)

As we continue to look at the impact of the sexual abuse wound, I'd like to say something about Post Traumatic Stress Disorder. PTSD, a diagnosis found in the *Diagnostic and Statistical Manual of Mental Disorders,* refers to a group of symptoms that some individuals develop after experiencing a traumatic event, such as sexual abuse. There are categories for adults, adolescents, children over the age of six years, and children under six years. These categories describe certain intrusive symptoms associated with sexual abuse—in other words, the aftereffects. It is believed that these symptoms originate from the severe betrayal of trust experienced by the survivor. As Mary Gail Frawley-O'Dea, PhD, executive director of the Trauma Treatment Center in New York City, puts it:

> *It is from this epicenter of betrayed trust that the mind-splitting impact of sexual abuse ripples outward. It is simply too much, and the resulting fracture of the victim's mind and experience often leads to a debilitating post-traumatic stress disorder that affects every domain of the victim's functioning and lasts for years and years after the abuse has stopped.*

Researchers of PTSD have concluded that even a single traumatic event can change the brain's chemistry. When we endure trauma, the body automatically moves into a flight, fight, or freeze response, which causes our heart rate to increase, pupils to dilate, and blood to race to our muscles. After the event, even a minor trigger reminiscent of the trauma can set off "overexcited" reactions, resulting in an unconscious major reaction. The National Institute of Mental Health states that the severity of PTSD is based on the trauma plus certain biological factors. Belleruth Sanparstek, in her comprehensive book *Invisible Heroes*, writes:

> *The new studies and surveys highlight the complex nature of post-traumatic stress. How we get through a terrible event, and the toll that event ultimately exacts, is a convergence of a great many interacting forces: the nature of the traumatic stressor itself; our degree of exposure to it; our age, gender, and ethnicity; our inborn neurological wiring and biochemical predispositions; our psychological history; our social support networks; and our coping behavior before, during and after the event.*

Another universal finding she cites is that children are more vulnerable to PTSD than adults, and women/girls are more vulnerable that men/boys. Even with young children, the male to female difference holds up, "compounding vulnerability for young girls and leaving two strikes against them: once for being a child and once again for being female."

Some common symptoms experienced by abused women are flashbacks (intrusive recollections or nightmares) which are beyond conscious control, dissociation (an adaptive response to escaping trauma that is more dramatic than what most of us have experienced when we "zone out"), exaggerated negative beliefs or expectations about oneself, and, of course, hypervigilance. Dissociation is the single strongest major predictor of the eventual development of PTSD, and it is the most common way for survivors to "not be present" during their abuse. As one survivor explained to me, "Dissociation served me much of the time. I had developed a remarkable ability to demarcate the sections of my emotional life. I walled off sections that were the most intolerable and locked them away. It was the only way I could survive."

Dissociation devastates a child's emotional and cognitive development, causing dysfunction and distress later in life. It's experienced as *numbing out* or leaving your body, which ultimately creates a memory barrier—a primitive, yet effective, method of protecting ourselves.

The hypervigilance experienced by an abuse survivor is an exquisite sensitivity to any stimuli that is reminiscent of the abuse, along with a heightened state of awareness and reaction to a disruption in the environment. Someone suffering from PTSD can be triggered by a seemingly neutral occurrence into an earlier state of arousal. For example, a Vietnam veteran I was seeing immediately hit the floor when he heard a car backfiring outside my office—an overreaction by someone needing to protect himself from a perceived life-threatening event.

I have observed many men and women in my office regress as they worked on their abuse—their physical postures changed, their voices changed, their childhood selves became evident as they remembered and experienced early pain. The reactions, defenses, and crippling pain are embedded into our psyches and need to be brought to the surface and examined so we can move forward in healthier, more productive ways.

If you do seek therapy to support and guide you through the healing process, you may be diagnosed with PTSD. That does not mean you are crazy or mentally unstable. What it does mean is that the psychiatric or psychological community is acknowledging the seriousness of your childhood trauma and giving it the same respect and importance as those who have experienced combat, or who have been held hostage, or been kidnapped, or been in a serious automobile accident. There are extraordinary life events that leave their mark on us and need to be understood, treated, and respected. This is one of them.

We have looked at some of the elements that add to the creation of our individual abuse wounds. We have looked at the importance of when the abuse occurred. We have come to recognize that when we experience stress in our current lives, we may regress to that unfinished developmental stage when the abuse occurred. We have examined our belief systems, and we have become aware of the negative self-limiting and self-effacing messages we send ourselves. We have touched on PTSD (and you can certainly Google it to see if you recognize symptoms in yourself). We have briefly looked at physical issues (and we will further examine body and sexual issues in the next Step). The abuse is over, but the effects may not be.

> *The past exists only in memory, consequences, effects.*
> *It has power over me only as I continue to give it my power.*
> *I can let go, release it, move freely.*
> *I am not my past.*
> *The future is not yet.*
> *I can fear it, flee it, face it, embrace it,*
> *And be free to live now.*
> — Author Unknown

Characteristics and Aftereffects We May Share as Adult Survivors

Now it's time to look at the aftereffects we may have in common as adult survivors of sexual abuse. This is a working list for you; so please cross out what doesn't fit for you and add what does. As was previously discussed, our wounds are like thumbprints: no two are exactly alike.

- Frequent periods of depression or a chronic depression that seems to color your life. Sense of apathy, not caring. A feeling of emptiness.

- Hypervigilance: always waiting for the other shoe to drop, a state of watchfulness not directly related to a current situation. May include an extreme startle response.

- Difficulty with trust: not trusting yourself, not trusting relationships, not trusting "life" to treat you fairly; difficulty discriminating whom to trust.

- An inaccurate, and generally negative, perception of yourself.

- Poor self-esteem: not only feeling "less than," but also not having a sense of self at all.

- Addictions, which attempt to reduce anxiety, and take you away from uncomfortable and painful thoughts or feelings. These include, but are not restricted to food, alcohol, sex, intense relationships, drugs, television, work, the Internet, shopping, electronic devices.

- Eating disorders, always associated with *not enough* or *too much*. Four times as many sexually abused women suffer from anorexia, bulimia or overeating.

- Internalized shame: sexual abuse survivors tend to carry shame for themselves as well as shame and pain for the family system as a whole.

- Isolation: deep feelings of loneliness, and often a lifelong search for nurturing and belonging.

- A strong need to be understood.

- Confusion regarding sexuality: difficulty with sexual arousal, promiscuity, avoidance of sexuality, struggling with letting go or having an orgasm, hypersexuality, confusion between affection and sexuality.

- A desire for intimacy, together with a fear of being close to another person—often resulting in dysfunctional relationships.

- Pseudo-maturity or immaturity, inappropriate dress, manner or behavior.

- Dissociation: detachment from self, emotions, and what is happening in the environment; sometimes, inability to control when dissociating.

- Somatic complaints: stomach aches, back problems, gynecological issues, etc.

- Difficulty setting limits and boundaries; difficulties claiming personal space; difficulty saying "no." A learned helplessness, resulting in excessive passivity or compliance, producing depression and erosion of self-esteem.

- Difficulty with nurturing and caring for yourself. Often nurturing capabilities are either absent or turned outward toward others.

- Struggles with anger: not feeling it, expressing it inappropriately or aggressively, or suppressing it.

- Pervasive guilt: always apologizing for what you did, what you said, or who you are; overly responsible.

- Stuck in the blame game: always looking to see who the perpetrator is. "Who did that to me?" "Who caused me to feel this way?" Someone else caused it, someone else has to fix it!

- Destructive patterns in relationships: inability to create relationships, withdrawal from established relationships. Often recreating *triangular* relationships.

- Reckless and risk-taking behaviors: having sex with strangers, driving at high speeds, playing at the edge of illegal activities, cutting/defacing one's body, etc.

- Excessive secrecy, lying, exaggerating, covering up as a pattern, not as a necessity.

- Feeling powerless, victimized in life, resulting in passivity or being rigidly controlling of others and events.

- A fear of not being *normal* because of the abuse.

- Suicidal thoughts or attempts.

- Profound grief over the loss of a broken childhood.

Drawing of the loss of childhood by a survivor

A Healing Step woman wrote this meaningful passage about her wounded self—and the disconnect she feels. In her writing, she encompasses so many of the struggles discussed in this Step:

Where are you—where do you long to show up? I don't know why you scare me—probably because you are where I stuffed all of my pain and heartache. You are where I feel abandoned and weak. You are the one nobody saw or cared for. You are the one who had to figure it out the best you could all by yourself—and I seem to have done the same thing to you. I realized that you could take care of yourself, so you became invisible to me, although I've always known you were there—because I have never felt whole—always like some huge chunk of me is missing—bitten out. You are weary of me with good reason; I have not been available to you. I put everyone else first. Was that you trying to get my attention when I started to get sick? When I got into that depression? Are you the weight that I can't shake? Have I so ignored you that you are just trying anything and everything to make me see you?...You are the little girl and the warrior. I see where those parts peek out in my life, little glimpses, but I know there are more parts—the feminine, the courtesan is in there, too. You have so much, so many sides, so many gifts, and they are struggling to take flight. The external search is futile, everything that I need and want is right here on the inside—I just need to get to know it and bring it up inside of me and it will flourish and grow. That is where I need to be—in the amazing complexity of my being!

This insightful and powerful passage was written by a woman who, as an innocent little girl, should have been treated like a princess; instead she was repeatedly taken to a motel called The Glass Slipper, where she was violated by her stepfather. Her journey has been tough. Like so many survivors, she carried the physical assault as well as the assault on her self-esteem—none of which was her burden to carry. And like so many survivors, she was reluctant to open her wounds and allow herself to be comforted.

If you do the healing work and have patience, your symptoms *will* decrease, and the pain *will* end. As Marilyn Van Derbur emphatically states at the end of her powerful video *The Healing Years*, "It doesn't have to hurt for a lifetime."

 ## EXERCISES: **Then and Now**

 To make this Step real and meaningful for you, it's important to take on at least one of the following tasks, based on the effects of your abuse. It is preferable that you complete all three. This is a difficult assignment if you just want the abuse to end. But the power *now lies in the aftermath*. It's important to look at where you are at the present time, and what challenges need to be addressed so you can continue to heal. So, take a deep breath, and begin with the exercise that speaks to you right now.

Make a Collage of Your Inner Child/ Adolescent/Maiden

The first exercise is a creative assignment, so you will need:

- A large sheet of paper

- Scissors

- Glue/paste

- A stack of old magazines and/or catalogs. If you don't have any magazines, print pictures from online images, or ask your friends and neighbors for old magazines and/or catalogs; everyone has an excess and will be happy to donate.

Make a collage for your Inner Child, your Inner Adolescent, your Inner Maiden. First, decide which part of yourself you want to work on. Then look for pictures, words, and images that relate to the one you have chosen. Let your intuition and imagination do the choosing. Cut out the images, place them on your paper, and move them around until they look right to you. Then glue them into place.

In terms of the Maiden, you may not fit into any of the five examples I gave you—so create your own. Consider questions such as: How did I leave home? What did I envision for myself after high school? Who were my female role models? Did I want to be in a partnership? What characteristics did I look for in a partner—or did I want a partner? Did I want a career? Children? What were my early dreams?

What did you learn about yourself in doing this exercise? Did anything surprise you? Are you willing to make a collage for all three parts—your Inner Child, Your Inner Adolescent, and your Inner Maiden?

Color Your Anger

One of the best exercises you can do to get in touch with your anger is to *color* how your anger *feels*. Just get out a large pad and let go with colored marking pens, pastels, paints—whatever you have. Red finger paint is great for this exercise. It's messy and sticky, like our anger! Before you stop, ask yourself, "Is there anymore?" If there is, keep going until you know that's it for now. It doesn't matter how old you are, or how many times you do this exercise, it will be both a release and a guide for you.

Write in Your Journal

Allow yourself some private time, give yourself the gift of truth-telling, and address each of the "aftereffects" listed on pages 136-138.

- Did they pertain to you "then"?

- Do they pertain to you "now"? Examples?

- Which ones are your greatest struggles today?

It's helpful to share your writing with your therapist, a support group, or a friend. Discovery is only part of the process. The next step is about taking a healing step to move you closer to your goal. What would that step be?

Self-Care

If you have not had a physical or a gynecological exam, this is the time to make an appointment. Two-thirds of women survivors feel their doctors should ask them about their abuse history because of its importance to their health today. Don't wait to be asked—tell him or her! Most survivors also want providers who will tell them what's going to be done to their bodies, when, and why. Know that you have the right to set limits with your doctor: you can stop the exam if it gets to be too much, and you can have someone come with you into the examination room. Be sure to talk to your doctor about mammograms, too. Having your breasts checked is not abuse; it's just good preventive care.

Good healthcare also includes seeing your dentist every six months for a standard cleaning. I mention this because there are survivors who are triggered by the feelings of intrusion or "powerlessness" they experience when they go to the dentist. If this is true for you, talk to your dentist or hygienist about your concerns. Take a friend with you for support and know that you are in charge: you can end the appointment whenever you are feeling uncomfortable.

Don't wait; be your own advocate. Start the process of taking care of your precious body through a regular regimen of preventive healthcare.

Therapies That May Be Helpful

 Cognitive Behavioral Therapy (CBT) is recommended if you are struggling with belief systems that are holding your hostage. CBT is a form of talk therapy that helps you recognize the thinking that is keeping you "stuck." When you are interviewing therapists, ask them if they have had training in CBT and if they use it when working with sexual abuse survivors.

Mindfulness techniques have also proven to be helpful in quieting the mind and allowing you to be in the present. Mindfulness has been practiced for over 2,500 years. The techniques can be learned from a trained therapist, and simple exercises are available online should you want to begin. Mindfulness is simply the act of being intensely aware of what you're sensing or feeling at the moment without judgment or without interpretation. Mindfulness exercises can help direct your attention away from the negative belief systems of the past, helping you to better engage in the here-and-now. This is an excellent technique for both reconnecting with and nurturing yourself.

Eye movement desensitization and reprocessing (EMDR) is a therapeutic technique combining exposure therapy (facing what you find stressful or frightening) with a series of guided eye movements. This technique helps you process traumatic memories and changes how you react to these memories. EMDR has been shown to be helpful with the symptoms of PTSD. If you are interested in this technique, ask your therapist if s/he is trained in EMDR; if not, ask for a referral to someone who has received the training.

Medications such as anti-depressants or an appropriate anti-anxiety prescription may be helpful. For some, temporary treatment is effective; for others, treatment may be ongoing. If you or your therapist feel medication may be warranted, I strongly recommend you see a psychiatrist for a full evaluation. They are the experts in psychopharmacology; and with the increased number of medications now available, you need an expert not only to prescribe for you, but also to follow up with you. Getting the right dosage with the fewest possible side effects is a very delicate process. The right medication can have a significant impact—and so can the wrong prescription, so do your due diligence.

 ## Suggested Reading

The Creative Journal: The Art of Finding Yourself and *The Well-Being Journal: Drawing on Your Inner Power to Heal Yourself*, both by Lucia Capaccione

Quiet: The Power of Introverts in a World That Can't Stop Talking, by Susan Cain

Freedom: My Book of Firsts, by Jaycee Dugard

Revolution from Within: A Book of Self-Esteem, by Gloria Steinem

Invisible Heroes: Survivors of Trauma and How They Heal, by Belleruth Naparstek

The Highly Sensitive Person: How to Thrive When the World Overwhelms You, by Elaine N. Aron

I urge you to buy a copy of *The Healing Years*, a documentary focusing on three women and their individual stories of abuse and recovery. One of the women is former Miss America Marilyn Van Derbur, who has dedicated herself to healing from the devastating effects of sexual abuse. (Check out her website.) She also has a powerful, new video in which she describes the unexpected results that ensued when she decided to tell her own story. Janice Mirikitani who contributed two verses of her powerful poetry to *Healing Steps is also featured*. A video such as this is especially valuable if you are unable to participate in a group, where so much of the value lies in hearing another woman's story.

*"The truth about our childhood is stored up in our body,
and although we can repress it, we can never alter it.
Our intellect can be deceived, our feelings manipulated,
our perceptions confused and our body tricked with
medication. But someday the body will present its bill, for
it is as incorruptible as a child who, still whole in spirit,
will accept no compromises or excuses, and it will not stop
tormenting us until we stop evading the truth."*

— Alice Miller
Thou Shalt Not Be Aware: Society's Betrayal of the Child

Step Five
Sex and Your Body

"Mr. Dufy lived a short distance from his body."
— James Joyce

 Margaret Mathews, a pen name for a survivor, writes in *The Healing Woman*, "I used to live in my head. I really did. It's no wonder—since my head was the only safe place to be, as my body endured years of physical and sexual abuse in childhood. When I did make occasional visits to the body below my neck, I was assailed with fear, pain and grief. Of course, I got the hell out of there as soon as I could because no head in its right mind would stay long in regions of such severe discomfort."

According to my Healing Steps women, this was one of the most difficult workshops to attend—or even contemplate attending—because the women had to revisit their bodies and perhaps spend some time there. The whole subject of sex and your body would evoke groans and "do we have to" from the workshop women. It's very confrontational because most of us avoid talking honestly about these issues with one another, and we don't work well with them privately as we usually hit a few walls of confusion before we slip into a pool of self-doubt. Sound familiar?

Whenever I hear women discussing their bodies, the tone is always negative—whether the discussion is in a support group, an individual session, or in my personal life. It's about what isn't right—there's "not enough" (breasts, height, hair, lips) or "too much" (thighs, stomach, nose, waist). Should we happen to forget, print ads and other media remind us and offer to solve our problem of being who we naturally are. The cosmetic industry is booming; cosmetic surgery has become a regular beauty routine along with injections of strange materials under our skin. Late night infomercials tell us how to lose, gain, and change. It's interesting that men generally think of their bodies as instruments of action, in which function is more important than form; what their bodies *can do* is what's important. Women are socialized to look at their bodies *as objects* to be examined, faulted, or praised.

We all know that it's difficult for women—not just those with an abuse history—to feel confident and comfortable in our bodies. Our body image is affected by our families, our peers (especially during adolescence), social pressure, life experiences, and—by far the most influential—the media. Researchers frequently point to the negative impact the media have on a woman's perception of herself. The media define cultural standards of beauty as well as preferred body size. By adolescence, young people are receiving 5,260 "attractiveness" messages a year from network television commercials alone!! *It stands to reason that a primary variable in how you feel about yourself is the number of hours of television you watched growing up.*

Research also tells us that between 80 and 91 percent of all American women are unhappy with their bodies, which in turn affects their self-esteem. As a result, many women resort to dieting to achieve their *perceived* ideal body shape. We're not talking about changing eating habits to become healthy; we're talking about dieting to achieve an *ideal*. A Harvard University study looked at 12-year-old girls who were classified as underweight and found that two thirds of them identified themselves as "fat." By age 17, only 3 out of 10 girls have *not* been on a diet and 8 out of 10 adolescents are unhappy with what they see in the mirror. Carolyn Coker Ross, MD, a pioneer in the treatment of eating disorders, found that 43 percent of first through third graders want to lose weight and 81 percent of 10-year-olds fear being fat.

This obsession with thinness has produced a $20–$60 billion industry. In 1975, most models weighed 8 percent less than the average healthy woman; now it's 23 percent less—and fully half of the United States is on a perpetual diet. Ten million women are suffering from eating disorders resulting in constant dieting, bingeing, and purging. And the ideal look for adult women is often presented by 14- and 15-year-old models. It has gotten so bad that young men are sometimes chosen to model women's fashions. The ideal body type for couture fashion is 5' 11" tall with no hips or chest—a figure that most women, even top models, do not have. God forbid we have a bump or a clump, right?

Studies show that not only are 8 out of 10 women dissatisfied with how they look, but more than half see a distorted image of themselves. Over 72 percent of women who are in a relationship undress in the bathroom before having sex because they are uncomfortable with their bodies. Cindy Crawford once remarked that even she doesn't look like herself in ads because of all the retouching done to perfect her image.

It seems we live in a world of exaggerated extremes—flat buttocks or inflated buttocks, no breasts or huge breasts; we either plump it up or try to get it off, accentuate it or hide it. What about embracing all the sizes and shapes we are? Clearly accepting ourselves and our bodies is a universal issue for women, but there are even more significant struggles that survivors have to wrestle with.

Sexually abused women often feel powerless, worthless, and objectified because their body has been used by another in an abusive way. They may hate their bodies for betraying them. In an effort to cope, many women become obsessed with controlling their bodies, often in an unhealthy way. They retain tight control of what goes in and what comes out (anorexia, bulimia, overuse of laxatives), or they exercise excessively. Others carry body-shaming thoughts, often abusing their own bodies by cutting, hair-pulling, burning, or neglect.

Overeating is another common "solution" to survivors' depression, anxiety, and fear—and it is certainly destructive. As has been pointed out to me by more than one survivor, being overweight is a defense, a protection, a guard, against getting attention and having to handle any advances (even if not predatory). "Being overweight is like wearing a sign that says, 'Don't look at me. I have a wall around me so I don't feel so vulnerable and at risk,'" said one eloquent survivor. "It's my 'meat suit.' My body got me into trouble so now I'm going to hide it in order to be safe."

Body image is a major issue for most women, but it's especially toxic when rooted in trauma. For women who have been sexually abused, this is often layered on a foundation of painful inadequacy, damage, and shame. Body hate raises your risk for illness and disease, for depression, for experiencing more stress and anxiety, for relationship problems, etc. It becomes a barrier to living a fulfilling and satisfying life, which is why this Healing Step is so important.

The goal of this Step is quite simply to communicate openly and honestly about body image, our bodies, and our sexuality. It's crucial to know and accept where you are with both your body and your sexuality, and to reclaim both. Why is that so uncomfortable? Does it have to do with your sexual abuse, or are there other factors? Why would accepting and taking care of your body be such a challenge?

Common Body Challenges of Survivors

Knowing how you sabotage yourself in your relationship with your body is crucial. Here's a list of common ways in which we deny or dishonor our bodies. Read them over and mark the ones that you relate to. (You will notice that some are repeated from the challenges listed in Step Three.)

- **Dissociating:** An unconscious defense stemming from PTSD. Leaving your body behind, like the Joyce quote: "I lived a short distance from my body." Too often, survivors live outside their bodies, watching themselves.

- **Detaching:** Not owning your body, not claiming responsibility for it. With the touch that comes from sexual abuse, there is a deep separation from "self" and from one's own body.

- **Desensitizing:** Numbing your body, developing a high tolerance for pain or discomfort. "Whatever comes along, I can handle. It doesn't touch me."

- **Disliking your body:** Obviously, this attitude is shared by many women, but survivors tend to place negative feelings about their abuse onto their bodies. Treating your body like your abuser did and abusing it in some way—addiction, cutting, or other self-injurious behaviors—is common.

- **Distorting reality:** Perceiving your body as being too damaged, too thin, too fat, etc. This often leads to anorexia, bulimia, compulsive over-eating.

- **Depriving yourself of touch:** People suffering from extreme body-image disturbance often report lack of holding, being held, hugged.

- **Adopting a "little girl" or "adolescent" persona:** How you dress or present your body denies the reality that you are a woman.

- **Overidentifying with your sexual desirability:** Your worth is measured solely by how attractive you are to men. Rejection means you're not okay.

- **Wearing baggy clothing:** Your clothes do a good job of concealing your body.

- **Ignoring or overemphasizing physical problems:** Both extremes put you out of touch with the reality of your body.

- **Developing gynecological problems**.

- **Blaming your body for getting you into trouble or for responding to touch while being abused:** As one woman observed: "Rejecting my body makes total sense to the hurt little girl inside me. It was my body that got me into trouble."

- **Not taking care of your body**: You don't get pap smears or mammograms, you don't go to the dentist.

- **Feeling powerless, worthless and objectified:** Your body was used by another, so now it—and you—feel like damaged goods.

So, the question for all of us is: how do we move from disregard or dislike to accepting our bodies? It's amazing how most of us take care of what's important to us—our cars, our gardens, our children. We read the latest books, listen to the experts, exchange ideas on our favorite blogs; and yet, as sexually abused women, we tend to ignore the care and feeding of our bodies.

I was guilty of this. I always held the belief that the purpose of my body was to carry around my head. My husband, understanding this, designated himself my body monitor: "Have you had lunch?" "Did you make that doctor's appointment?" "What are you doing for that headache?" When my body crashed in 1988, it was a real wake-up call. Much as a car needs to be serviced, my body needed to be tended to and honored if I expected it to continue to serve me. Don't wait until your body stalls at the worst possible time. For me, it was when I was scheduled to be the keynote speaker at a major sexual abuse conference in San Francisco. I had to say "no" to a wonderful opportunity, and "yes" to finally acknowledging the importance of putting my body first.

The initial step to change is always heightened awareness and ownership of a particular feeling, belief, or guiding principle in your life. As Dr. Phil often says, "You can't change what you don't acknowledge." Now that the abuse is over, it's safe to "come home" to our bodies. Often our body issues are not evident until we reach a point in our lives where we feel safe enough to slow down, return to our bodies, and develop body awareness. That time is now.

A final word about dissociation: remember that dissociation is a separation that happens at the moment of overwhelming harm or threat—or perceived harm or threat—when there is no other place to go. This separation often shows up as a split between the body and the *self* and can be very stressful. There is a need to "pull yourself together"—literally. Here are a few simple things you can do when you are struggling with dissociation and feel yourself leaving your body.

• Engage in a physical activity, such as walking or other simple movement—anything to move the energy down to the lower half of your body.

• Start a mundane physical task, such as washing dishes or gardening, especially without shoes and socks so you feel closer to the earth.

• Do a grounding exercise: plant your feet on the floor, close your eyes, and imagine each foot connected to a solid root going through the floor—all the way to the center of the earth. Imagine opening the bottom of each foot and permitting energy to flow up your legs, through your spine, to the top of your head. Feel the connection between you and the earth—strong, solid, and present, in the here and now. Take several deep breaths and then gently open your eyes.

• Take slow, deep breaths while focusing on an object directly in front of you.

• Take a yoga class, and become more familiar with being in your body.

 EXERCISE: **Examine Your Body Closely**

 This first exercise is a very powerful one. It may lead to some anxiety and a tendency to avoid. If so, it is absolutely essential that you push through whatever resistance you have. Use your feelings of resistance as part of the exercise. Write about what you are feeling or thinking when you contemplate doing the exercise. What excuses are you using for not doing it? What do you fear? What don't you want to see or feel?

Now let's do it. Give yourself plenty of time and privacy; don't try to squeeze it between other scheduled events, and don't do it when you are likely to be interrupted. Your body will thank you.

- Stand in front of a full-length mirror, naked, and look at yourself. Take time to really be with your body. Notice how you feel as you look at yourself: notice your thoughts, your inner dialogue, your self-criticism or self-appreciation. Give yourself at least five minutes. Now, look at the *being* within your body: look into her eyes. Notice your feelings and your thoughts as you connect with her.

- Now draw the body you saw in the mirror. Capture what is important to you as you remember your image.

- Mark the place or places that were hurt, abused, or violated during your abuse. You may want to use different colors to marks different body parts. Notice: did you include these body parts in your original drawing—or leave them out?

- Write the answers to these questions *on your drawing: How do I feel about the parts of my body that I marked? What are my thoughts about these parts? How well have I been taking care of these parts of my body?*

- Did this raise your awareness in any way? If so, what did you learn about yourself and your body? What does your body need and what can you commit to do to care for it? Are there words of acceptance and compassion that you can give to those parts of your body that had to endure the abuse?

 ## EXERCISE: Writing to Increase Body Awareness

 Refer back to the list of ways you deny, ignore, or abuse your body. In your journal, give examples of each behavior or attitude you've observed in yourself. Are these behaviors or attitudes still part of your life today? Do you want to change or modify them in some way? What would it take from you to make a change? What would be the first step? How might you sabotage yourself?

Now write:

The three things I like least about my body are _____.

The three things I like most about my body are _____.

I think my abuse has affected my body image in that I _____.

EXERCISE: Visualization

Prepare a recording of the following visualization. You can record it yourself, or you can have someone record it for you. Be sure to pause in the appropriate places so that, as you listen, you have time to bring forth the images requested in the visualization. The point is to be able to just sit quietly, listen to the recording, and follow along with the visualizations.

When you do this exercise, allow your body to settle into a comfortable position. Do not cross your legs or arms; rather, allow your body to rest comfortably with a sense of openness and receptivity. Let your thoughts drift away. If they begin to intrude on this exercise, just bring your mind back to the sound of the voice on the recording.

Option: If you are one who simply can't visualize, I encourage you to copy into your journal the passage in paragraph 6 of the following visualization (beginning with "I am so sorry you were violated...") and repeat it out loud to yourself until the words feel natural to you.

Concentrate solely on your breath for a few moments. Feel its coolness as it enters your nostrils. Feel your breath move down into your body, and notice the place where it stops and begins its upward movement. Just keep following your breath for a few more moments, breathing in peace and relaxation, breathing out tension and tightness. Breathing in, breathing out. Just letting go. No place to go, nothing to do but allow yourself to be within your body right now.

Now become aware of how you're experiencing your body. Feel where your body is making contact with the floor, sofa, or whatever you're lying or sitting on. Feel the contact that is being made against your back, your buttocks, the backs of your legs, your feet. Feel where your arms and hands are. See if you can make your hands feel warm—good—a little warmer. Now feel a tingling in your fingers.

Now focus your attention on a place in your body where there is a feeling of tension or tightness. Just let your awareness float there naturally. It will know exactly where to go. Focus on this place. How big is it? Are the edges of it jagged or smooth? What color is it? How thick or dense is it? Just notice it. Now, see if you can change the color of it. If it changes, fine; if not, that's okay, too. Now see if you can change the size of it—see if you can make it smaller. See if you can make it dissolve completely into the pool of your relaxation.

Now bring your attention to your whole body once again. What emotion is your body expressing right now? Where do you feel that emotion in your body? See if it has a color or size as well. Just notice it. Just let it be there and just notice it.

Now bring your attention to a time when you were being molested. Just let it come naturally. Let the sensations come into your body—know that it's safe right now to feel the sensations in your body. Where in your body do you feel the sexual abuse? Just let yourself feel it for a moment, noting where the sensations are. Just let the sensations be there. Just notice them.

Now focus on one particular part of your body where there is a sensation. Let that part of your body speak to you. What message does it have for you? Listen to it. Respond to the message. Now say to this part of your body, "I am so sorry you were violated. I am so sorry you have had to carry so much for so long. I will do all that I can to honor you and to heal you—starting now. I will begin by not hurting you—by protecting you—by not allowing others to hurt you—and by caring for you. Right now, I will make that commitment to you. I will bathe you in a healing light that is just the perfect color for your needs in this moment." Take a moment and let the light surround this place on your body—bringing it comfort and healing. Let the light penetrate the wounded place, and feel the contact and the healing as it occurs. Let that area warm under the gaze of your compassionate Spirit. Feel it all melt into the pool of relaxation. Good.

Now tell your body that you realize this is only a beginning— but it is the first step in reclaiming your body as your own responsibility. You will care for it, love it, honor it, and protect it.

Say these words to yourself—or out loud: **This is my body. It belongs to me. The abuse stops with me.** *(Repeat)*

Focus once again on your breathing and feel the power of these words as you repeat them: **This is my body. It belongs to me.**

Now bring your focus back to your entire body and feel your body returning to a state of well-being. Breathe deeply and slowly, and once again become aware of your body in contact with the floor, or the sofa or chair. Be aware of the sounds around you, the temperature in the room and the placement of your arms and hands. When you are ready, drift slowly back to your usual state of consciousness. Allow yourself to stretch that wonderful *body of yours and gently open your eyes.*

How We Make Changes

Let's face reality: if taking care of our bodies were a priority for us, we wouldn't be struggling with this chapter. When something does not come naturally to us, we need to create a plan outside of ourselves. What do you need to change in order to take better care of your body? And how do you make the changes you need to reach those goals?

Here are three tips to help you keep the agreements with yourself:

- Create a well-defined structure for yourself: One of my clients, who was impeccable about keeping her business appointments, decided to make appointments with herself—written in her organizer, with alerts on her phone—for physical exercise: one hour, two days a week at a gym; and a one-hour walk on the weekend. Another client booked pedicures for herself twice a month from April through October. Another client did not allow herself to eat anything after 7:00 pm, as she was a "snack with TV kinda gal." What kind of structure would support your goals to better care for yourself?

- Don't undervalue convenience: When something is a chore for us, when we resist doing it, convenience becomes extremely important. So, barter with someone who'll come to your home to teach you yoga. Or harness a friend to hit the ball with you at the neighborhood tennis court. In our neighborhood, we send out emails inviting others to join us on neighborhood walks. Make things easy for yourself. There are TV channels that offer exercise and yoga programs or stretch-alongs every morning. You don't even have to get out of your jammies.

- **Be accountable to someone**: This is one of the secrets to following through. Have a friend or find a partner whom you can report to—or make an agreement with your therapist to help coach you into a healthier lifestyle. I happen to work well for rewards, so I reward myself after making those doctor appointments, ordering my supplements, or taking a walk. A reward could be the gift of uninterrupted reading time or meeting a friend for lunch after the doctor's appointment. What would be a reward for you?

 ## *EXERCISE:* Write a Prescription for Healing and Change

Your body is your own. It belongs to no one other than yourself. Get acquainted with it—it is your lifetime companion; it deserves to be served as well as it serves you. This is a reciprocal arrangement; it breathes for you, keeps you alive, warms you, moves you from one place to another, allows you to hug another, helps you write, bathe, feed yourself—so it's important to take care of it and yourself.

The great Dr. Albert Schweitzer once said, "You have an inner doctor who knows just what your body needs." So please, be your own doctor, and fill in the prescription below. What do you need to take better care of yourself?

R℞

PATIENT NAME _____

ADDRESS _____

_____

_____

Prescription:

SIGNATURE _____

DATE _____

A survivor in Healing Steps named Cheryl writes of her personal journey with her body:

Over the years of healing from the pain of my sexual abuse, I gradually regained awareness of my body's intuition, wisdom and impulses. Earlier in my life, my survival had depended upon suppressing my awareness of the information my body was sending me in order to keep the "peace"—or at least to survive until I was independent enough to seek help and healing. If I had been conscious of my body's impulses and information, my legs and feet would have run away from home! I would have spoken about my pain, my fear, and my anxiety, instead of holding it in my stomach, intestines, genitals, and heart. My family could not tolerate my expression of emotions, so instead I experienced ulcers, pre-cancerous cell growth, incapacitating cramps, severe back pain and sleeplessness.

After working in jobs that I didn't like for years, I had an opportunity to choose a new job path. I felt guided from within to take massage therapy classes. When I took my first class, I became aware that I could not bear to be touched by my classmates or teachers. I was very surprised by my reaction but have come to realize that "touching" for me had only been through sex, and I could dissociate during sex. While learning to receive and give massage, I could not dissociate. This began my journey of reclaiming my body.

Gradually, as I consciously reconnected and accepted each part of my body, I gained more flexibility in my body and my mind. I was not as rigid. Many of the painful disorders resolved or were no longer as painful. My body is a kind of barometer now, giving me information before my conscious mind perceives that information. I've learned to trust myself through my body's wisdom; following that wisdom has brought me a fulfilling life.

Now I am grateful for every felt sense of joy, delight, and love; as well as the feelings of sadness, anger and even fear. I know that my entire body-mind is always working toward equilibrium. Instead of thinking, as I did in the past, that my nervous system was weak or overly sensitive, I now try to honor how hard my nervous system has worked to bring me this far.

The safety and emotional support I felt in Healing Steps was a very big part of my nervous system recovering from the unconscious "freeze" state I had been in for so many years. Step by step I came to trust the women in my group and eventually to trust myself. When I was stuck in the "freeze" while in Healing Steps, Sharyn would suggest how I might use our current Step as a way to move through it. Through Healing Steps I was more often able to discern when I was in the fight/flight/freeze state, and to ask myself, "Do I need this freeze survival mechanism now? Am I really threatened now? What is true for me right now— even though my jaw is tightening, my fists are clenching, my breathing is shallow?" Asking myself these questions reminded me that I was in a community of people, my Healing Steps group, who had all survived similar experiences of abuse and now we were supporting each other in our healing. The sense of community and support and the examples I saw in others are what allowed me to think that I might be able to move into a place of "rest" instead of constant vigilance and defensiveness in my life. It is in this place of rest that I now experience feeling love and being loved. Being in my body is a good place to be.

What is so poignant about Cheryl's willingness to thaw and to experience all her feelings is that she is a woman who was impregnated by her father, and given an abortion by her grandmother. Her body was not a safe vehicle for her. In order to withstand so many assaults, she remained intact by *not* consciously experiencing what was happening in her body. She dissociated—until she found the inner strength to trust in herself. Now she can deal with whatever happened in the past *and* embrace the love she has found in the present.

I share with you a simple meditation which has always spoken to me:

> *My Body is a temple*
> *Caring for my body gives me a place to worship*
> *Listening to my body brings me wisdom*
> *Challenging my body fulfills my potential.*
> — *Hummingbird Words: Affirmations for Your Spirit to Soar* and
>   *Notes to Nurture By*, by Marvel Harrison and Terry Kellogg

Body Therapies That Can Be Helpful for Healing

 • **Massage:** Massage is not only relaxing and healing, but it can be very therapeutic for someone who has been sexually abused. I'm not speaking of intense sports massage, but rather of gentle massage with kneading strokes that promote both circulation and a sense of well-being. Massage can also be helpful for headaches, depression, and relieving stress. It stimulates the release of endorphins, the brain's natural painkillers. Some massage therapists have been trained in Trauma Touch Therapy, in which special consideration is given to individuals who have been sexually abused. There are many lessons to be learned through receiving nurturing touch—lessons in self-acceptance, surrender, and accepting care and pleasure in a safe environment. As a good friend who is a massage therapist reminded me, "One of the benefits of massage for survivors is the empowerment that comes when the survivor realizes what safe touch is for her, when she learns to ask for what she needs or wants, and when she practices setting boundaries for herself."

• **Rosen Method:** This practice holds that experiences and memories are stored in the body in the form of tension, which can cause pain and chronic muscular tension. By making contact with the tension in the body with gentle hand pressure, monitoring the breath of the client, and asking questions, the Rosen practitioner facilitates the release of stress and pain, both physical and emotional. Rosen Method Bodywork is sometimes called "listening touch" because the practitioner is trained to listen to what the client's body has to say through gentle, non-invasive touch.

• **Myofacial Release:** Myofacial release is designed to release deep knots in the connective tissues in the face and jaw, often caused by clenching teeth and tightening jaw muscles. This can be a painful therapy while it is taking place, but it offers a release for long-held pain.

• **Reflexology:** Reflexology is based on the premise that pressure points on the feet correspond to the glands and organs of the body. Finger pressure to the reflex areas on the hands and feet can be helpful for releasing tension in blocked areas of the body.

- **Shiatsu:** In this Japanese style massage, precise finger pressure is applied to body meridians through which "chi" (energy) flows, causing emotional as well as physical release.

- **Reiki:** The Reiki Master lightly places hands on areas of the body being treated in order to balance physical and emotional energy, as well as to release blockages. This is a very healing therapy and is often paired with massage.

- **Yoga:** Hatha yoga was developed by the ancient masters to open the body so that "prana" (life force energy) can flow freely, supporting transformation at all levels. There are many different kinds of yoga, so do some research and see what's available in your area.

- **Kegels:** These are exercises developed by Arnold Kegel, MD, to strengthen the PC (pubococcygeus) muscle, a hammock-like muscle stretching from the pubic bone to the tail bone, in order to help women with urinary leakage problems. The exercises turned out to have a pleasant side effect—increased sexual awareness. They actually help you become more aware of feelings in your genital area and increase sexual arousal. You can find instructions on the Internet.

- **Fitness for Survivors:** This fitness package for survivors includes exercises designed to replace dissociation with physical awareness. It includes information on how to do Kegel exercises, and ends with a soothing relaxation to aid in stress reduction and healing. For more information, contact Shereen Motarjemi at Fit Healing Productions.

- **Model Mugging class:** This is not actually a body therapy; rather, it is a very effective way to discover your own strength. In a Model Mugging class, you learn how to protect yourself from attack and become empowered through practice and knowledge.

- **And the most convenient and inexpensive of all:** Stretch, walk, and move your body on a regular basis. Put on your favorite music and dance. Give or receive a hand or foot massage. Enjoy a bubble bath with your favorite scent, some music, and a lighted candle. Walk barefoot in the sand or on the grass. Step into a bakery and take a deep sniff. And tonight, go outside and look up at the moon and stars. It won't cost you a cent.

Sexuality

"As I get older, I just prefer to knit."
— Tracy Ullman

"I often felt that my perpetrators were reaching for my soul,
trying to take something from me that was long lost in themselves."
— Staci Haines, in her wonderful book *The Survivor's Guide to Sex*

Historically, women have not openly discussed their sexuality, nor has it been acceptable to do so. If they did, many were not honest. Women have long felt competitive with other women, comparing themselves as a way of judging their worthiness and value. Traditionally there has been good reason for this: we have long been in competition for the men of the tribe, the boys in the schoolroom, and the executives in the workplace. It was our relationship with a man that defined not only our social status, but also the quality of our life and the lives of our children, and certainly our access to money and goods. As women have become more educated, more independent and self-sufficient, we see this changing—*changing*, but not disappearing.

Women have also felt inadequate as their image was defined, idealized, and erotized by men in the popular media. Most of us can't relate to the women on the adult channels, or the sexual responses reported about the women in Penthouse magazine or on the Internet. For the first half of the twentieth century, any knowledge of women's sexuality was based on Freud's theory of the superior and inferior orgasm, or the findings in the 1939 Kinsey report. It wasn't until

1966 when Masters and Johnson began to develop a more accurate picture of a woman's sexuality that long-held myths were finally dispelled. When the birth control pill (Enovid) came along in the 1960s, there was a radical change in how a woman perceived her sexuality. This was the first time a woman could separate sexual pleasure from sexual reproduction. Reliable birth control—controlled by a woman herself *without* either the agreement or knowledge of her sexual partner—was a major step in a long, slow process of sexual empowerment for women. Within five years, six million women were on the pill! For the first time in human history, women had choices.

During the 1970–1980s, many long-held views of female sexuality came to be challenged and reassessed. It became important for all women to have access to sexual healthcare and education, and the freedom to make their own choices regarding birth control and family planning. Women marched, wore t-shirts that said "Uppity Women Unite," and made their presence known. And the 1973 Roe v. Wade landmark decision by the United States Supreme Court gave women the right to choose a legal abortion. Whether or not you agree on the issue of abortion, what this means for all women is that the right to make this important decision is a woman's choice—not the government's. The Women's March on January 21, 2017, was evidence that women are still ready to stand up for their right to make their own choices about their bodies and their reproductive rights.

In the 1970s Lonnie Barbach also threw the doors wide open with her book *For Yourself: A Woman's Guide To Female Sexuality*, which encouraged women to know their own bodies. She taught women the importance of learning about their sexual responses through exploration and masturbation. This was a critical step for all women: to own their sexual pleasure and to not rely on their partner's experience—or lack thereof. By the way, Dr. Barbach's book is still available and was revised in 2000.

There are also very clear instructions on self-pleasuring in Staci Haines' *The Survivor's Guide to Sex,* which I heartily recommend. Haines openly discusses her own sexual abuse and is a strong advocate for adults molested as children. She has written a book that will tell you everything you need to know about your sexuality—and more.

In April 2016, a front-page article in the *San Jose Mercury News* heralded "No Prescription Needed for Birth Control," meaning that women could finally secure birth control without the expensive process of going through a doctor. The 2013 California law (SB 493) went into effect after state health officials finalized the regulations, and women in California were given significant new alternatives. The process continues. Movement is slow, but we have to remember that "we've come a long way, baby."

As women and sexual beings, we've had a complicated history. A woman's sexuality encompasses a wide range of determinants including her upbringing; her sexual identity; her private and public sexual behaviors; and the social, political and spiritual influences that weave throughout her life. Now let's add in a history of sexual abuse to further complicate self-image and security (or insecurity) about our sexual selves! If we didn't feel like a sexually "normal" woman in our culture, the sexual abuse secured our fears. Remember that our first intimate relationship was fraught with betrayal, exploitation, grief and rage—so it is a tangle of mixed feelings and confusion. Best we don't talk about that part of our sexual history; most of us have a pat story about our first sexual experience that we pull out when needed. How could we say, "Oh, do you mean the first experience *outside* the family or with someone my *own* age?"

That is what Step Five is about. It's about not only examining our connection to our own body, but also about reclaiming our sexuality. *If our sexuality is being defined and controlled by our sexual abuse experience, then our sexuality is still in the hands of the perpetrator.* As a 15-year-old molest victim told me, "It's so easy to have sex. It feels normal just to do it without thinking about it. I'm used to just going along with it." Or as a woman struggling with her sexuality said:

> *I was sexually overstimulated as a child, which caused me to relate to the world in an overly sexual manner. I get myself into sticky*

situations by behaving in inappropriate ways. In the past I had trouble distinguishing a rational way of being sexual; I sometimes still have that problem, but it's much more manageable now. My sexuality became like a drug. I became addicted to the power it had over people—especially men. I felt I was no longer a powerless abused child, but rather, a powerful sexual goddess.

Shari was an artist who did much of her healing through the powerful and haunting images she created. She reflected the feelings of many survivors when she told her Healing Steps group:

There is very little about my sexuality that the abuse did not affect. Basically, I got stuck and never grew up with regard to sex. I turned off. Sex wasn't fun; my body wasn't good, it was dirty. I was always taken, as opposed to being a giver. I avoided sex. I hid behind baggy clothing, a fat body, busyness, whatever. I tried to disappear. Being touched was being violated. I was not comfortable being touched by either sex. Sex became a tool to keep something, or to get something. It was a performance rather than an act of affection. To totally let go and just enjoy? Good grief—no!!

To clarify, I am not saying you have to be sexual. Part of freeing yourself from both the Inner Perpetrator and the Outer Perpetrator that we discussed in the third Healing Step is understanding that you do not have to be sexual unless you want to be. Granted, that may present issues if you are in a relationship, but this needs to be honestly discussed with your partner instead of dealt with in ways that are probably frustrating for both of you. It is difficult for most couples to talk to each other about sex, but it is particularly difficult for survivors.

Embarrassment is a major barrier for many survivors; it can be embarrassing to discuss your history, your preferences, your struggles. It can also be embarrassing to listen to your partner and know how to respond without being defensive or judgmental. Some couples feel that frank talk takes away the spontaneity of lovemaking, making it "too clinical." What is true is that discussing sexual likes and dislikes will enhance your sex life; and if you say nothing, you'll probably continue to lead a less-than-satisfying intimate life.

There will be a discussion about the importance of straight talk in Step Six, which focuses on the key elements of good relationships. Honest communication is essential in every relationship, but it is even more important when one of you has been sexually abused and is embarking upon a healing journey. What is important here is the issue of timing and focus. As a survivor, you need to respect your own pace. Deciding to work on sexuality is your decision alone—and when and how you do it is also your decision.

The focus in Step Five is on sexual awareness, sexual healing, sexual safety, and regaining ownership of your body and your sexuality. I define sexual safety as emotional safety (trusting your partner), psychological safety (trusting yourself to make good decisions on your own behalf), and biomedical safety (preventing unwanted pregnancy or transmission of disease). All are important in order to reclaim your sexuality and to feel comfortable with any kind of sexual encounter. When you're ashamed of your sexuality, you're ashamed of your very identity.

Becoming a Woman

"One is not born a woman, one becomes one."
— Simone de Beauvoir

At this juncture in recovery, it's essential that we see ourselves as women before we can develop our sexuality as women. In previous Steps we have discussed our Inner Child and our Inner Adolescent—and hopefully they have become more alive for you as you've continued through the Steps. If we do not move into our Woman at this point, our sexuality takes on the "flavors" of our other developmental stages. For example, our Inner Child brings her fear, her disgust, her inability to care for herself appropriately into our sexual lives—she doesn't feel like there is a choice about being sexual, and she can't be discriminating. She freezes rather than saying "no," or she dissociates. We have to heal our child's wounds and take full responsibility for her "woundedness." We cannot use what happened to her as an excuse for acting in a childish manner. We need to be aware of her needs and learn how best to take care of them. We need to correct some of her childlike belief systems, so she can learn the reality and truth that may have been withheld from her. We do need to incorporate her playfulness and spontaneity into our sexual lives, but *we cannot let her take charge of our sexuality.*

If we remain in our Inner Adolescent, we may act out, be promiscuous, use sex as a weapon or "power tool." Our Inner Adolescent is so headstrong: she would love to run the show. As a matter of fact, she usually feels entitled to do so! She takes unnecessary risks with the arrogance of a teenager: "Nothing will happen to me, right?" She doesn't use protection, drinks too much, and cares more about being "chosen" than "choosing." We know that sexually abused adolescents are less likely to practice safe sex, putting them at greater risk for STDs and unwanted teen pregnancy. Trying to navigate their way through a hookup culture is difficult for any teen, but put an unhealed Inner Adolescent in charge, and she is bound to find trouble. Do remember, however, that this is also the part of our psyches that can be innovative and think outside the box. She is the one who delights in developing an individual identity and a sense of style that is unique. She is also the one who creates friendships and finds chums—and so she can help you create a support team. So, appreciate her—just don't let her be your guiding force when it comes to your sexuality!!

If you grew up in a dysfunctional family, evolving into becoming a woman also means giving up being the daughter you wanted to be. It is particularly difficult for some women who have been sexually abused to grow up because they have not had the chance to fully live out being taken care of and protected as "a cherished daughter." They often unconsciously refuse to move into womanhood and are frozen waiting for and wanting what they can never get. It's a very painful place to be. Teresa, one of the Healing Steps survivors, was so devastated by her mother's lack of attention and abandonment that finding a mother figure became the central focus of her life. Her mother's apparent lack of concern allowed her molestation to continue for years. Her focus was healing the emptiness and longing that permeated every aspect of her life. Feeling intense grief over her abandonment, she would fill herself with food as she waited for the perfect mother to come along, one who would make up for what she didn't get—and certainly deserved. It was only when she came to the realization that her mother did the best she could and that her own lack of care was about her mother's limitations—and not hers—that she was able to move forward.

The pain associated with knowing that you will never have that unconditional love you crave is devastating—and the loss must be grieved. If this is the case for you, I hope you will share your pain and disappointment with a professional who can support and guide you through this difficult passage. Many of these issues were discussed in Step Two: Where Was the Protector? Reviewing that chapter may be helpful to you.

As the inner Maiden, we may hold an unrealistic, overly-romanticized view of sexuality. We may believe our partner will "make the earth move," fill the hole in our yearning to be adored, and take care of us forever. The Maiden is trained into dependency and expectation: "When I fall in love...," "When I meet my soulmate...," "When I get married...." Like the women stuck in waiting to be a cherished daughter, this woman is waiting for rescue so that her own life adventures can begin. Or the Maiden may get caught in the web of unrequited love, or the never-ending passions of a Danielle Steele heroine where the drama becomes more important than the relationship. Romance is important, but don't live in a castle of dreams. A relationship based solely on romantic notions will only end in disillusionment; there is no place else for it to go. But stay tuned, Maidens: in Healing Step Six, we will discuss what it takes to develop a relationship that honors *you*, because as most women know (and men often don't understand), a relationship that doesn't include the healthy Maiden is a rocky one filled with resentment. It is not enough to bring the Maiden into a relationship; we must also bring in the maturity of a woman to temper the fragile and innocent heart of the Maiden.

A Woman is designated not by age, but rather by the continuing movement of her growth. She moves through each stage of development with awareness and healing so that all parts of herself become woven into the wonderful complexity that defines her as she is today.

So, what designates the passage into becoming a woman? A coming of age rite like a Bat Mitzvah? Our first menses? Turning 18 or 21? Graduating from college? If you have been a victim of abuse, I believe the process is ongoing. To become a woman is to heal, to develop the parts of yourself that were damaged and hurt, and to bring those parts into right alignment with one another. This is an ongoing and empowering process. With each Step your woman will emerge stronger, less burdened, and ready to open the door to her life. She may look like this:

- A Woman takes responsibility for her "parts"—both physical and psychological. She does not project them out, hand them over, or get lost in them. Her choices in life are not based in unresolved issues or in her abuse. She does not see nor react to relationships based on the Victim/Perpetrator/Rescuer triad we discussed in Step Three.

- A Woman sets her own goals and direction in life, all the while retaining the ability to be flexible when need be. She takes responsibility for staying on track and does not blame others for her setbacks. She feels empowered and free to make choices to move her life in the direction *she* wants to go.

- A Woman keeps her agreements and does not play the "blame game."

- A Woman has moved from being a needy or entitled daughter to being an adult. She is self-sufficient and able to care for herself. She doesn't expect others to support her financially (unless it's by conscious agreement in a partnership) or to "bail her out." She takes on life's mundane responsibilities: she is neither a dependent daughter nor a witless wife who doesn't bother her pretty little head with things like finances, expenses, and other "grown-up" concerns. She exudes a sense of self-confidence.

- A Woman takes care of her body, her needs, and her sexuality by being aware of all three, making decisions about all three, and knowing how to care for all three.

- A Woman sets limits and boundaries to take care of herself and any child she is responsible for.

- A Woman contributes to the community, bringing her ability to nurture, her deep sense of relationship, and her spirit to others. Her life has meaning and spiritual purpose.

These are my definitions of being a Woman. They may not be yours, but what is important here is that you do form a vision of what being a Woman means to you. You can't expect to be a woman comfortable with your sexuality until you know you are a woman who can at least take care of herself and set boundaries to protect yourself from what you don't need or want.

Your mother, or your mother surrogate (grandmother, aunt, etc.), was a primary role model for you, so you need to examine what you learned from her growing up. At the end of this Step, I have included a questionnaire which will be helpful in furthering your understanding of yourself as the woman you are today. Take the time to write your answers and thoughts in your journal; they will help you become aware of how you define yourself as a woman.

Now Let's Talk About Sex

Openness about sexuality among women has changed in the last decades, but I'm not sure the honesty factor has changed. As women, we "act" open, we laugh at Amy Schumer, we talk about our vaginas, we openly appreciate attractive bodies, we expose more of our own bodies, and we feel free to love whom we love—but are we ahead of where we were a decade ago? I'm not so sure. Sexuality is still a very difficult issue to discuss when you've been sexually abused. Leona Tockey—a former colleague, survivor, and mentor of mine—stated that "our sexuality is so interwoven with our identity, with our sense of who we are, that when sexuality is damaged, so is identity. The reverse is also true." Clearly the development and expression of sexuality is a very significant aspect of who we are and can substantially be altered by sexual trauma.

When we discuss sexuality, we are really talking about several issues. We are talking about our sexual self-concept, meaning how we see ourselves as sexual beings. Do we see ourselves as sexual beings at all? And, if we do, what are our feelings, thoughts, appreciations and criticisms about ourselves? What about our sexual attitudes? And what about our sexual behaviors? Our sexual histories? Our choices? Our current behaviors? *Which are symptoms and which are simply choices?* If we are celibate, is that a healthy choice—or a neurotic decision? And orgasms—do you have them, want them, worry about having them? Do you think your sexuality was affected by your molestation? How about your beliefs about men and sex—were they influenced by your abuse? There are so many questions to contemplate when we open the door and decide to meet our sexual selves.

Generally, symptoms of troublesome sexuality are *any feelings, thoughts, or sensations that echo your past abuse or inhibit healthy sexuality as defined by* you. Often, whatever developed as a defensive pattern during the molest becomes a survivor's sexual response. For example, the emotional response of panic, or disgust or shame, or suspicion, or regression in the moment becomes the present-day emotional response to sexual activity. You may feel numb or anxious and want to avoid the whole thing, or you may dissociate, as Diane Keaton did in the movie *Annie Hall* when she floated out of her body and busily made a grocery list while having sex with Woody Allen. A priceless scene!

There may be a physical "imprinting" that makes inappropriate sex feel so pleasurable and exciting that you may compulsively seek out risky sex. Or the opposite could be true: the physical aftermath of sex may be painful or nauseating. You may confuse your partner with the offender: 60 percent of survivors have flashbacks during sex. Or you may feel childlike or "dead" inside, as many women have shared.

It isn't true that women who have been sexually abused are necessarily more promiscuous than other women, but it is true that women who have been sexually abused are more anxious about sex, experience more sexual guilt, and are thus less sexually satisfied than other women. The two most significant factors that affect sexual adjustment for survivors? Self-blame for the abuse (82 percent of women blame themselves when no "physical force" was used); and the conditioned responses—the feelings, thoughts and sensations—that remain within the survivor due to the past abuse.

Most often, however, when we talk about the actual effects of sexual abuse on our sexuality, we are talking about the top ten symptoms as listed by Wendy Maltz in *The Sexual Healing Journey*, one of the definitive books on healing sexuality after abuse. I recommend picking up a copy of this book, as it is a comprehensive manual for you on your journey. In Chapter Three of her book, Maltz presents a complete inventory of sexual aftereffects. Take a look, and see what may resonate with you. This helpful inventory will assist you in forming a sense of who you are sexually at the present time.

Below I have listed the challenges mentioned most frequently by the Healing Steps women. Do you identify with any of these struggles?

- Difficulty with trust

- Fear of sex

- Withdrawal from touch

- Dissociation—difficulty with being present and staying present

- Lack of interest in sex, or even of being physically close; difficulty being aroused

- Difficulty letting go and "surrendering"

- Flashbacks and/or "dark" thoughts during sex

- Need for power and control during sex

- Difficulty in saying "no" and in setting limits, which often lead to avoidance of relationships or sexual situations

- Sex without intimacy

- Assuming a passive role in sex, with underlying resentment; seeing sex as an "obligation"

- Pre-orgasmic

- Provocative behavior often followed by attitude of naïveté which tends to validate generalized belief that "men are only interested in my body and/or sex"

- Seeking love and intimacy *only* through sex

- Sexual addiction/compulsion often leading to inappropriate relationships

I'm guessing that like the rest of us, you are already aware of what your particular struggles are in this area. You may not talk about them, but I'm sure you think about them. Sometimes survivors avoid sexual experiences entirely, sometimes there is a numbing of physical sensations, sometimes there is a passivity of just "going along" and faking enjoyment. (The passive-victim role always breeds resentment in relationships.) Often, sex occurs without intimacy. Sometimes instead of passivity, a survivor will exhibit an aggressive and controlling attitude so as not feel powerless. Obviously, the issue of *surrender* can be a major stumbling block for survivors, and this often leads to difficulty with orgasm. It's not uncommon for survivors of sexual abuse to have dominance fantasies, even fantasies about rape, which can lead to feelings of shame and guilt. Sometimes there is a compulsivity about sexuality, which leads either to compulsive masturbation or promiscuous sex.

Often there is a tendency toward illicit sex, secret affairs, and sex that sets up a triangular relationship with men or women who are unavailable. Breaking taboos with someone who is married, someone who is dating your best friend, or someone who is unattainable or unavailable in some way is common among survivors, because it's *familiar*—and it can be more comfortable than caring, truly intimate, non-secretive sexual behavior. As one woman expressed it, "Dirty sex is familiar sex."

If you do have a sexual history that feels "cloudy," take the time right now to answer the following questions. Writing down your answers would be even more healing. By the way, I open my Sexuality workshop by asking each woman to write her sexual secrets on a piece of paper. I then collect them and place them in a basket in the middle of the room where they sit until the end of the workshop. The tension and fear of disclosure is palpable. In the afternoon, without disclosing the secrets to other group members, each woman works on what, if anything, is disturbing to her about her "secrets." The following is the home version of the same exercise:

EXERCISE: Exploring Your Sexual Secrets

1. Write down your sexual secrets, including any misgivings, embarrassments, or feelings of guilt and/or shame you may have about your secrets. Were your secrets about sexual behaviors, or thoughts or fantasies you may have had? Read them over. Are there any more you need to put down? Think carefully: review your sexual life.

2. Do you remember what you were feeling in each of the cases of actual behaviors you wrote about above? Do you remember what you based your decisions on? Did you make a decision, or did you just react or respond in a sexual situation? Do you think any of these could be related to the abuse in your past?

3. Are you still blaming yourself for what occurred in each incident? Were you at fault? What would help the "you" in each of the incidents mentioned in #1 to forgive yourself and move on? Is there any action required here?

4. How would you feel if others knew about your sexual secrets? From whom are you withholding your secrets? What do you fear if they discovered your secrets?

This is an important area to examine when we are wanting to reclaim our sexuality. The past weighs us down. Our secrets wrap us in guilt and shame. We don't have to share our sexual past with anyone else (except for the sexual abuse itself), but we do have to be honest with ourselves. We all have a past. We've all made decisions and choices that we may regret with the passage of time and the increase in self-awareness. So, let's include our sexual history in the mosaic of our complex sexuality—it is but one piece of who we are, and we would not be complete without it. As the silent film star Mary Pickford once said, "If you have made mistakes—there is always another chance for you. You may have a fresh start any moment you choose, for this thing we call 'failure' is not the falling down, but the staying down."

We all wonder: are we "undersexed" or "oversexed," and does it even matter. And who decides that anyway—some obscure researcher, or is this a personal matter that we can decide for ourselves? And what is *normal* anyway? Of course, there is also avoidance of sexuality—or as one member of Healing Steps said, "The truth is, I wish I didn't have to have sex. And I wish I didn't even have to talk about it." So, do we have to talk about it? Yes, we do have to talk about it. Talking about sexuality is essential for healing and ending the shame, the guilt, and the errone-ous beliefs we may still have about ourselves. However, the most important issue is taking back our sexuality and integrating it into who we are today.

In this particular Healing Step, we focus on reclaiming our sexuality—making it our own, and not letting someone outside ourselves determine what is right, what is *normal* for us. The only boundary I would set for you (and I do feel strongly about this, because I don't want you to remain stuck in the past) is that you not hurt yourself or someone else *either physically or emotionally* with your sexuality. You have been abused by someone not showing restraint and respect. You have been injured by someone who did not rein in his impulsivity. You have been hurt by someone who was self-indulgent and concerned only about his own needs.

Don't "offend" with your sexuality. If you have in the past, then this is the time to begin to unravel that behavior, acknowledge it, and, if appropriate, make amends so that you can move on to a healthier lifestyle. The Alcohol Anony-mous Twelve Step program recommends creating a list of all the people one has harmed and making amends with these people (being accountable for your behavior and apologizing for the hurt you have caused), except when doing so would injure them or others. This may be a healthy and freeing exercise for you.

Guidelines for Reclaiming Your Sexuality

What does *reclaiming your sexuality* mean to you? Remember, everybody's abuse is individual so the impact on their sexuality is individual as well. Does it mean enjoying sex more? Does it mean changing a negative association you have? Generally, reclaiming your sexuality means making a change in either your thought patterns, your behavior, or your experiences. It involves a great deal of unlearning, as well as learning. Our physiological sexual response is inherent, as is our orientation, but our sexuality is learned—the kind of person we are attracted to, what is stimulating for us, what is okay to do, how to do it, etc. The good news is we can re-learn, we can practice, we can go at our own pace, we can be in charge of the process. We have time.

I'm very aware that healing your sexuality is a major challenge and takes time. This book is only a starting point in your journey. I hope you will not stop here, but rather you will find satisfaction in however you define yourself sexually. Reclaiming your sexuality always begins with having a relationship with your Inner Child, so she can trust you to take care of her, to protect her, to not ask her to take on a role that is inappropriate for her. If you have not done the Inner Child work in Step One, please go back and finish that work. Otherwise, the foundation is not present for you to do this work. It's important that you connect with her so that she can be excused from your sexual life; *this is not the place for her.* You can bring in some of her qualities, such as playfulness, imagination, and wonder, but when you bring an unhealed part of yourself into your adult sexual life, you bring in baggage that is not needed. She needs to be reassured that what is going on is safe, and that you are not going to pull her into an abusive, powerless situation and hang her out to dry. She needs to trust you to make good decisions.

 Once you have an alliance with your Inner Child, you can learn to feel safe in your body again. The abuse is over. It is safe to come home. As we've discussed, many survivors abandon their bodies as a way to survive. Some temporarily flee during their abuse as children, and some disappear even during consenting sex as adults. It's important to know you now have control over your body. You are not a child, you are not physically weak or helpless, you can say "no." Or can you? This is one of the toughest parts of reclaiming your sexuality. So often sex can feel like an obligation or something to put up with, something your partner has a right to rather than something

that is yours and that you choose to share with someone. It is crucial to learn to develop limits and boundaries. You have an invisible bubble around yourself—it is a physical boundary that marks your territory. What is inside that bubble is yours. It's yours to protect, to keep to yourself, or to share. You have a right to privacy (your thoughts and feelings) and you have a right not to be touched or hugged without your invitation. This right is yours to give—*not* someone's to take.

If need be, look in the mirror to remind yourself that you have aged since the abuse. You are no longer a helpless little girl: you are a woman. You have decided not to mistreat your body like you were mistreated. You have decided to take care of yourself. Stand tall, feel the strength of knowing the choices are yours and no one else's. From this day forward, your sexuality is yours to do with as you please. If you have a difficult time even imagining what it would be like to own your own body, find a role model—someone who feels comfortable with herself sexually; someone who enjoys a healthy sex life; and someone who is also self-protective, assertive, and able to handle awkward situations—maybe, a character in a novel or someone on TV. Then watch and learn.

As I sit (in 2016) writing about our bodies and our sexuality, I'm watching a breaking news story scroll across my computer. It is about a Stanford swimmer found guilty of sexually assaulting an unconscious, intoxicated woman outside an on-campus fraternity. In this case, two grad students spotted the Stanford student attacking the woman, and they physically held him to the ground while calling authorities. Had they not intervened, this would have been just another campus incident, a crime of opportunity that takes place far too often on college campuses. My point is this: please, Government, stay out of making choices regarding women's bodies; and please, men and boys, stay out of women's bodies when not invited. And women: stop getting trashed and abandoning your body!! If you want to reclaim your body and your sexuality, begin by *protecting* it. And ladies, be a friend to each other. When you see another woman in need of help, or drunk, or out of control, take care of her, remove her from a potentially dangerous situation, and get her to safety. And to our government and to the men out there, step in and protect women when they need you. Take a stand against those who perpetrate *against* women.

Be a hero—and thank you to Peter Jonsson and Carl-Fredrik Arndt for stopping to assist the woman on the Stanford campus and making sure the perpetrator was brought to justice. You are true heroes. The Stanford student who assaulted the woman was sentenced to six months, banished from Stanford, and now must register as a sex offender. He was released from jail after three months. This sentence, which outraged women and men around the world because they felt it was too lenient, led to California Assembly Bill 2888, which makes sexual assault of an unconscious person a crime with a mandatory prison sentence. Perhaps it is stories like this that will bring attention to the epidemic of rape on college campuses.

Other stories have heroes, too. I recently listened to a Ted Talk by Jessica Ladd, who has developed a reporting system for sexual assault—one that allows victims the privacy they desire while addressing multiple rapes committed by the same students on campus. I hope this becomes a basic service on every campus across our country.

And finally, here in Silicon Valley we host an annual *Walk a Mile in Her Shoes* event, during which approximately 250 men strap on high heels and walk a mile to raise awareness about sexual assault. Their efforts also raise money for the 1,100 women seeking support at the YWCA Rape Crisis Center each year.

In late 2016, California state lawmakers approved a bill to eliminate the statute of limitations on filing certain rape and child molestation charges. Previously, California had limited pressing charges in such cases to 10 years post-crime, after which you could not press charges in such cases. But the Senate and House have cleared a "no limitation" statute and California's governor has approved the legislation to revoke that limitation. As one supporter noted, "there is no limit on the emotional scars"; therefore, there should be no limit on the opportunity to press charges when you have been violated. Senate Bill 813 states that rape (now defined as "all forms of nonconsensual sexual assault") will no longer be subject to a statute of limitations. According to the California Women's Law Center, 17 states have abolished statutes of limitations on rape; hopefully, others will follow suit. Enough is enough.

Exercises for Reclaiming Your Sexuality

Sexuality is a difficult topic. So when you take on the following exercises, make sure that you feel safe and that you have time to focus on them without interruption. Turn off the electronics, put a "do not disturb" sign on the door. If you feel anxious, take a few deep breaths to re-center yourself. Know that you are not alone: this topic is generally met with anxiety and avoidance. Manage the anxiety, and don't give in to the avoidance. By the way, there are two kinds of avoidance: nurturing avoidance and crippling avoidance. Nurturing avoidance is not doing something that is harmful to ourselves. For examples: choosing not to spend time with toxic people; deciding to stay home rather than doing drugs with a particular group of friends every payday, etc. Crippling avoidance is when avoiding something is harmful to us. For example: avoiding the dentist; avoiding a work assignment; avoiding doing a certain Healing Step!

 ## *EXERCISE:* **Visualization**

 I feel very strongly that this is a necessary exercise to do before any of the others. Once again, I ask you either record this visualization for yourself or have someone else record it for you. You may need to do this exercise more than once before you feel you have completed it. Make sure that you have your journal and a pen nearby to write any thoughts or feelings you may have. Remember, all these exercises are designed for you to learn about you. Put on some relaxing music, get comfortable, and begin.

When you are comfortable in a sitting position, take four or five deep cleansing breaths. Make sure that your arms and legs are not crossed and that your body is in an open and receptive position.

Imagine your Adult Self standing outside the place where your molestation took place. See your Inner Child at whatever the age she was when the abuse took place. Have your adult make contact with the Child, and tell your Child that the Perpetrator is holding some-

thing very valuable that belongs to her. Explain to her that you are going to confront the Perpetrator. You will tell him: "You thought you owned my body and my sexuality and could do whatever you wanted with them. Well, I'm now taking them back ... this is my body ... I own my body and my sexuality ... they no longer belong to you."

Tell your Inner Child to stay outside where she is safe. Perhaps your "Nurturing Self" stays with her, or perhaps someone you trust cares for her. And perhaps you need someone to accompany you as you go inside to take care of business.

Now let your imagination create the perfect scenario for you. Go inside with the strength of your conviction that this is the right time to reclaim what is rightfully yours. Go inside—strengthened by the energy of all the other women who have courageously gone before you to take back what was taken from them so many years ago.

Imagine standing tall and confronting your Perpetrator. Picture the Perpetrator in a way that makes you dominate—perhaps he is only four inches tall, or perhaps he is confined behind bars, whatever makes sense to you. Say what you need to say to him—this part is yours. (Silence on the tape for at least two minutes). Is there anything else you need to say? See if there is anyone else that may lay claim to your sexuality or your body. If so, let your Adult confront that person, too, and take back your sexuality until there is no one else to lay claim to your sexuality. You may be surprised at the people from your past who show up. Just let the experience unfold until you feel complete with this part. Do whatever you have to do to reclaim your body and your sexuality.

When you feel you have reclaimed all the pieces of your sexuality, and your body is back where it belongs (around you), then leave that place feeling strong and capable. Just let the image of that place fade from view. Celebrate or honor being the owner of your sexuality: it's all yours to get to know, to have a relationship with, and to make choices about. Now promise yourself that you will take loving care of your body and that you will protect your sexuality. If you

do not know how, tell yourself that you will learn—and perhaps get
some guidance from someone you trust. Find your Inner Child. Give
her a hug, take another four or five deep breaths, and when you're
ready, open your eyes.

EXERCISE: Reflecting on the Visualization

This can be done as an art project or a journaling exercise.

Some women imagine taking from the Perpetrator a box that houses their long-forsaken bodies and/or sexuality. Imagine yourself with this box. How big is it? What does it look like? How is it secured—tape, padlock, dusty straps? Is the top easy or difficult to remove? If you are drawing, this is the time to draw the box with as much detail as you can. If you are writing, use your words to describe the box.

Once you've envisioned the box, open it and see what's inside. Let it be whatever it is—and draw or describe whatever you see. Are you surprised by the content? Does it make sense to you? What are you going to do with it? This is a big decision.

After completing this exercise, some women have found an object similar to the one they envisioned in the box; others have created an object that symbolizes their new-found bodies and/or sexuality. The object is then placed in a position of honor in their home, and it comes to signify ownership and responsibility for being the sole caretaker of this very precious part of themselves. Would this be meaningful for you?

EXERCISE: Developing the Feminine

Reflect on these questions in your journal:

- How did you feel about yourself as a female child?

- What was your relationship with your mother?

- How did your mother, or female caretaker, feel about being a woman?

- Did you admire your mother?

- What were her values as a woman? What did she teach you?

- What did she teach you about your sexuality?

- What parts of yourself were allowed expression when you were a girl?

- What were your activities, ambitions, and dreams when you were 10?

- What decisions did you make about yourself as a girl?

- How were you influenced by female characters in the media or literature? Who were your favorite female characters?

- Did you have mentors or models who inspired you with the way they lived their lives? In what ways?

 ## *EXERCISE:* **Becoming a Sexual Woman**

Reflect on these questions in your journal:

- What do I enjoy sensuously?

- What do I enjoy sexually?

- What don't I enjoy sensually or sexually?

- What would I like to do or try sexually?

- What was my most memorable sexual experience? Why?

- What was my worst sexual experience? Why?

- A healthy sexual encounter for me includes: _____ _____ .

- My fears about being sexual are:_____ _____ .

- When it comes to setting limits and boundaries around sex, I _____ and _____ .

- My darkest secret about my sexuality is: _____ _____ .

✔ *EXERCISE:* **Mask Art Project**

Needed: One plain mask, which can be purchased at a craft store such as Michaels; marking pens, paints, glitter, feathers, whatever your heart desires for embellishments.

Take the plain mask and use the embellishments to create your Woman. The possibilities are as unlimited as your imagination. Paint, glue, decorate, feather; she is yours to create and discover. Now put on the mask—*be* her. She may be an inspiration, a discovery, or a familiar "you." Honor her, talk to her, get to know her; most of all, integrate her into who you are becoming.

Suggested Reading

The Survivor's Guide to Sex, by Staci Haines

The New Our Bodies, Our Selves, by The Boston Women's Health Book Collective

Heal Your Body, by Louise L. Hay

Love the Body You Were Born With: a 10-Step Workbook for Women, by Monica Dixon

Women's Bodies, Women's Wisdom: Creating Physical and Emotional Health and Healing, by Christine Northrup

Binge Eating & Compulsive Eating Workbook, by Carolyn Coker Ross, MD,

Incest and Sexuality, by Wendy Maltz, MSW, and Beverly Holman

The Sexual Healing Journey: A Guide for Survivors of Sexual Abuse, by Wendy Maltz, MSW

Healing Your Sexual Self, by Janet Woititz

Thou Shalt Not Be Aware: Society's Betrayal of the Child, by Alice Miller

For Yourself: The Fulfillment of Female Sexuality, by Lonnie Barbach, PhD, [a classic book on orgasm]

"Teach Girls Bravery, Not Perfection," a Ted Talk by Reshma Saujani

Collage

Scraps of memories – bits of fantasy
A colorful dream – a fairytale scene
And not much reality.

Each contains a part of me
And each contains a vision of you
Glued together – they fuse together
And make a collage of us.

It's what I wanted it to be
What I made it to be
What I hated it to be.
            — a survivor

Step Six

Relationships:
How Not to Bring the
Past into the Present

"Spiritual partnership is a union between equals for the purpose of spiritual growth. If you know that, you understand that everything that comes up in the relationship is all about growing both of you to a new place."
— **Gary Zukav**

"To increase the odds of meeting your soul partner, just travel further and further into the life your heart longs to inhabit."
— **Unknown**

We have spent the last five Steps looking within us at the effects of our sexual abuse. We have looked back with disappointment, anger, and pain at what happened to us in our childhood, including what was done *to* us and what was not done *for* us. We have looked at ourselves in the mirror as we faced our bodies and examined our feelings about sexuality. Now it's time to look around and see who we are surrounding ourselves with in our lives today. This is our life drama, and we have cast each of the supporting players for a reason. Who is in your world? Take a moment, close your eyes, and picture the people that you choose to spend your life with. Do they know about your abuse? I'm not suggesting that you tell them; I'm just wondering. If you are in a relationship, does your partner know your history? What is the most important relationship in your life at this time?

It's often difficult for us to discuss our relationship challenges with others. "Wait, that's not true," you say. You talk about your relationships—or lack of— with your girlfriends, your co-workers, with anyone who will listen, right? I'm guessing that when you discuss relationships, you talk about your satisfaction or dissatisfaction with the focus being on what your partner does or doesn't do *right*. Rarely do we talk about our own part in the relationship—where we struggle, how we handled an argument, what we could have done to make the day go more smoothly, our partner's unmet needs, etc. It's very difficult to take a hard look at how we show up in a relationship: we usually minimize our part, get defensive, or turn a blind eye. It's almost impossible to see ourselves as others see us; and that is what this Step is all about. As sexual abuse survivors, our tendency is either to minimize our power and impact in a relationship, or to overemphasize our needs. We struggle with appropriate boundaries and how to set them. Intimacy is a challenge because it is always based on trust and vulnerability (need I say more?), and most survivors avoid intimacy while deeply craving it. And, of course, if there is incest in your background, you grew up in a family of secrets, alliances, coalitions and dishonesty—none of which will be helpful in establishing the kind of relationship you want today. As I was writing this book, I reviewed numerous evaluations filled out by the participants in the Healing Steps workshops. When I asked, "What topic would you like to see expanded by having additional workshops?" over 95 percent of the women said relationship or partnership issues. Clearly, this topic is significant to all survivors.

There are five things I know to be *always* true about relationships:

- **Relationships are paramount to our well-being.** In order to feel peace, in order to be whole, we need to be in healthy relationship with ourselves and with the people around us. The relationship we have with ourselves is the most important one because it determines how successful our other relationships will be. We all know that the healthier we are, the healthier our relationships will be. Looking for love before developing a strong sense of self is like trying to find the mate to a shoe you've never seen before!

We also have to have a relationship with our community, with the world in which we live, and with our spiritual selves. Relationship brings about a sense of calm, a sense of identity, and a sense of connection—all of which allows us to have the ultimate possibility of growing into ourselves. You may remember Maslow's hierarchy of needs—with the need for belonging being necessary to fully actualize our potential as a human being. We all have an innate desire to be part of a tribe or a clan, to identify with our ancestors, and to know our personal history. We have only to look at the popularity of websites such as Ancestry.com and television shows such as *Who Do You Think You Are?* to recognize the universal longing to identify our roots. No one wants to be ostracized from their clan, nor do we want to have a family circle close ranks, leaving us on the outside. And yet, that is what often happens when a victim of sexual abuse tells someone outside the family about a molestation that has occurred within the family. Too often I have witnessed a woman's pain of rejection by her family after making the decision to tell an outsider of her abuse. And regardless of the dysfunction of the family, the abuse victim still longs to be included and embraced by her family of origin. The fear of being abandoned by or ostracized from one's family provides powerful motivation to keep the abuse secret.

It is also difficult to be in a primary relationship when you are going through the initial stages of the healing process. Flashbacks are common; and raw feelings can overwhelm a relationship. Abandonment fears often cause survivors to shut down before the healing process is completed. At the end of this chapter, we'll discuss some ideas to help you and your partner alleviate some of the stress you may experience as you move through these difficult and painful times.

- **We need to remain "conscious" in our relationships.** In her powerful book *Guilt is the Teacher, Love is the Lesson,* Joan Borysenko reminds us that "rather than thinking in terms of good and bad, it is more helpful to think in terms of conscious and unconscious, aware and unaware."

Relationships ask something from us each day. They are not like air plants that demand little to survive: you have to tend to them. It is said that the concept of regularly tending to a relationship is different for men and women. Women see relationships like rose bushes—a lot of time, research, and discussion goes into selecting a rose bush. And roses require regular maintenance—watering, fertilizing, pruning, dead-heading, etc. Women selecting and caring for a rose bush will read about roses, talk to experts, and compare their roses to their neighbors'. They know how important it is to choose the right rose bush, and they don't expect to plant and then just ignore their rose bush.

Men, on the other hand, see relationships more like evergreen trees. A great deal of time is spent looking and comparing different species of trees; and after one is selected, an inordinate amount of time is spent in determining correct placement, stabilizing it with heavy twine and stakes, and hand-watering it for the first few weeks. After a few months, the twine and stakes are removed and the tree is left to fend for itself in the corner of the yard. There is little or no maintenance until the tree shows clear signs of distress. Notice of a dying tree is usually met with a throwing up of hands, and an exclamation: "What do you want me to do? I did everything I was supposed to do. There's clearly something wrong with this tree!"

I've seen this dynamic played out over and over in my office—men and women do have different points of view about the care and feeding of a relationship. Men tend to be problem solvers, and they often avoid problems when the solutions are difficult to fathom. Intimate relationships with women often fall into this category, and as a result, men wind up confused and overwhelmed. A wonderful guide into the mind of a man (which is different from ours) is Michael Gurian's *What Could He Be Thinking?* I enthusiastically recommend reading it if you truly want to be in a conscious relationship with a man.

- **Relationships go through stages.** The first three stages—attraction, courtship, and falling in love—are relatively easy to manage, since excitement and anticipation propel us into showing up as our best and most attentive selves. We have to manage our anxiety, of course, but that's a small price to pay for experiencing all those intense bonding hormones. We are in a state of euphoria. We are obsessed, possessed, and unstressed! The world has taken on a special meaning. During this stage, we often unconsciously pick a mate who we hope will allow us to heal our childhood wounds and to grow beyond our limited view of our self, and our hormones produce the "perfection" we see in our partner during this stage. Not quite as romantic a notion as finding our Prince Charming, but certainly a powerful motivating force in determining whom we choose as our mate.

However, we soon move into the stage I call "the slipping of the masks" and difficulties begin. We become aware of our differences. Power struggles emerge, and disappointment and disillusionments present themselves. This is the stage when we start to tell the truth—and to see the truth. As our selective perceptions and wishful thinking diminish, we start to resent our partner for not being who we want him or her to be. We feel let down and sometimes duped, and we are faced with an important challenge: Do we let go of the relationship? Do we try to beat our partner into submission? Or do we surrender and accept this person as a wonderful, yet flawed human being (much like ourselves) who may not always meet our expectations, but whom we want to build a life with? It is at this point that the real work of a relationship begins.

• **Relationships are about transformation.** In the beginning, a new relationship indeed brings out the best of us. When we fall in love, we see our best selves mirrored back to us. We put our best foot forward—we are generous, understanding, patient, flattering, accommodating, and cooperative. We may even fall a little bit in love with ourselves; we're so witty, so charming, so radiant, so sexy. Hormones are being released, our partners are wonderful, and we are certainly different from other couples we know.

But relationships are like old 45-rpm records. We bought them for Side A, but we also get stuck with Side B! In his provocative book *Journey of the Heart,* John Welwood, PhD, suggests that relationships are all about transforming Side B. We can choose to see transformation as the purpose of relationship, or we can get locked into always being "right" in the right-wrong dance so common in a relationship. Relationships are meant to dredge up the parts of ourselves that need work, so that we can grow and become even more than who we are right now. Where else do we allow those hidden aspects to show? And where else can we learn so much about ourselves?

Our primary relationship asks a great deal of us. Through daily exposure and commitment, it provides a stage for all of our individual parts to reveal themselves and do their individual dance. It is here that we work out our unresolved issues and traumas from childhood; it is here that our shadows come out and do their ugly and destructive dance; it is here that our fears, our insecurities, and our critical nature come to the surface. It is here that we can work on issues that otherwise remain underground when we are not in an intimate relationship. A close relationship is a powerful light source, and like any strong light, it casts a long shadow. When you stand in the light of your closest relationship, you must learn to deal with your shadow. At the same time, your partner stands in the same light, casting his or her own shadow. No partner will ever match the fantasy we hold in our mind; no partner will so completely meet our needs that we have no emptiness or longing left inside. As I have said many times, relationships are not for the faint of heart, but they are ideal for growing into who we envision ourselves to be.

- **We need to own our part in the relationship.** It's difficult to acknowledge what we do that creates hardship for our partner, what we do to instigate arguments, what we do to sabotage communication, and how we make matters worse by the manner in which we express our anger or hurt. It's hard to see our part, to own our part, to be accountable, and to make the necessary changes in order to maintain and strengthen our intimacy. This always begins with awareness of who we are in relationship: how we show up, what scares us, what skills we may lack or have never learned. We need the confidence to know that saying "I'm wrong" or "I should have been kinder" or "I'm sorry" will not annihilate us or give our partner ammunition to shoot us down. And if our partner does take a pot shot at us, then we have to know how to manage that as well. In order to have a healthy relationship, we must make the necessary changes in ourselves; understanding and awareness are crucial but are not enough. In order to be open to the transformative opportunities in our relationships, we must focus on our own changes, not on how to change our partner.

I had been very cynical about forming lasting relationships. I put all men in one category—domineering, distant, controlling and non-supportive. I was very angry, very punishing, and extremely egocentric when it came to establishing communications during disagreements. I was also overly needy and expected men to take care of me. I wanted too much sympathy and expected a great amount of validation from men. I had a number of one-time affairs during relationships that were understood to be exclusive. With coworkers and friends, I would be seductive, yet elusive. Friendly, yet distant. I could not form friendships with men without evoking sexual elements. I had also taken little responsibility for my behaviors and would often transfer my feelings onto the man I was seeing. Post-therapy, I am involved with a man who allows me to acknowledge my weaknesses, to work on breaking old patterns, and to accept my past and go on with the future. I believe in myself and I believe that I can make a relationship work.

— a survivor

 In this Healing Step, we will look at how to increase your awareness of how you show up in relationships. Obviously, one of the key elements affecting your relationship is the sexual abuse in your history. As Dr. Phil McGraw stated in one of his television shows, "If you have an open wound from sexual abuse, it will contaminate your relationship until it is healed." Even if your partner does not know you were molested, he or she will still feel the effects of your unhealed abuse, *as will you.*

The Arc of Relationship

Before I talk about the common challenges I've seen in survivors' relationships, I'd like you to assess the variables that have influenced you in your relationships—or have impacted your decision *not* to have intimate relationships.

Take a look at the Arc of Relationship diagram (page 198), which I used frequently in my workshops. It provides a useful tool to help reveal the impact our families, our sexual abuse, and our previous relationships have had on us. As you look it over, think about your own experiences, decisions, and belief systems.

Here are some examples of what women in my workshops have learned from it:

- In the section about the relationship with her mom, one woman observed that her mother would leave a relationship as soon as there was discord or stress. She learned that when things get rocky, you just leave. As she put it, "I was a runaway as a teen and an expert at dissociating when things got tough. I guess I believe that exiting is how you handle a relationship that's not working."

- When talking about the section on how sexual abuse affected her, a group member wrote that she would go numb and shut down whenever she was abused. "Now I freeze whenever anyone tries to get close to me. I feel nothing. I can't even tell you how I feel about my partner. How do I feel about anyone in my life? I don't know."

- And in the section about siblings, a soft-spoken woman talked about her relationship with her brothers, who were quite dominant and extroverted. She felt like she "never had a chance. I was the quiet one, so I just gave up. And I tend to do that now. I have no idea how to take a stand for myself, so I don't. And then I feel resentful."

EXERCISE: Examining Where You Learned About Relationships

Each segment in the Arc of Relationship highlights an area of your life where you learned about relationships and your place within them. Write the answers to the follow-up questions, taking your time so you can be as complete as possible in your answers. This may take you several sittings, but don't rush the assignment as it is designed for you to learn about the influences on your relationships today.

ARC OF RELATIONSHIP

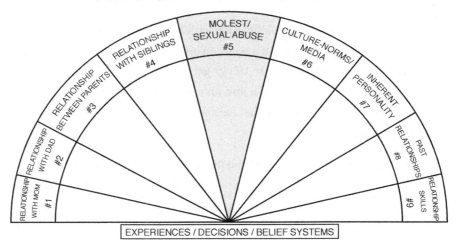

EXPERIENCES / DECISIONS / BELIEF SYSTEMS

HOW WE SHOW UP IN RELATIONSHIPS

Wedge #1: Relationship with Mother or Mother Surrogate

1. What is your first memory of your mother?

2. Was your mother absent physically, emotionally? If so, how did that affect you?

3. Write a paragraph of what you remember about your mother and her relationship with her parents, family, partner, friends, coworkers.

4. How did your mother handle differences with your father?

5. What advice did your mother give you about relationships?

6. How did your mother show her love for you? Or did she? How did she show her anger toward you?

Wedge #2: Relationship with Father or Father Surrogate:

1. How would you describe your relationship with your father?

2. Describe how you witnessed him interacting with your mother.

3. How did you know when your father was angry? How did you handle it?

4. What characteristics did you like or admire about your father? What didn't you like?

5. Do you find any similarity in your choice of partner to your mother's choice of your father?

6. Was your father critical of you? In what ways?

Wedge #3: Relationship Between Your Parents or Your Family

1. How was affection expressed in your home? Or was it?

2. Who was in charge? How did you know?

3. How was anger or a difference of opinion handled?

4. How did each parent "manage" the other?

5. What was your role in their relationship?

Wedge #4: Relationship with Siblings

1. Did you have siblings? Steps? Half-siblings? Or were you an "only"?

2. Where were you in the birth order? Do you think that made a difference?

3. What was happening in your family when you were born?

4. How did you get along with your siblings?

5. How did you settle differences or arguments with your sibs? Who settled them—you, your sibling, or your parents?

Wedge #5: The Molestation or Sexual Abuse Wound

1. How did you explain the abuse to yourself as a child?

2. How do you explain it to yourself now?

3. How did you cope with the abuse as a child?

4. Do you find yourself behaving in a Victim, Perpetrator, or Rescuer role? In which aspects of your life?

5. Do you believe your abuse affects your relationships today?

Wedge #6: Culture/Norms/Media

1. What were the expectations for women when you were growing up?

2. Who were your role models? In the media? Why those particular people?

3. Who were the celebrity couples in your world of TV, movies, music? What did they demonstrate to you?

4. What expectations did your family, teachers, and friends have of you? For your future? Did you share those expectations?

5. Have changes in the culture affected you? If so, in what ways?

Wedge #7: Inherent Personality

1. How would you characterize yourself?

2. What have friends and family always said about you?

3. Have you ever taken any personality inventories, such as the Myers-Briggs, or studied typology, such as the Enneagram? If so, what have you learned about yourself? If not, you may want to check out these two typologies online as they both can provide valuable information about who you are.

4. Which of your personal sensitivities tend to show up in relationships?

5. If you tend to be outgoing in relationships, how do you think your abuse affected you? If you tend to be less relational and more inner-directed, how do you think your abuse has affected you?

Wedge #8: Past Relationships

1. Have you had many past relationships? Would you characterize them as successful; or did they have a short shelf life, or end too soon?

2. Is there a pattern to the partners you've selected? Did your previous partners have the capability to tend to your needs? The willingness?

3. What was your part in ending these relationships?

4. How did you handle the differences that came up in these relationships?

5. What did you learn from your past relationships? List for each one.

Wedge #9: Relationship Skills

1. What is the best thing you bring to a relationship?

2. What is the biggest challenge to you in a relationship?

3. Think about the most significant relationship you have had to date. What have you learned from your partner?

4. How do you manage anger and frustration in your relationships? Is there room for improvement?

5. What communication skills would be the most helpful for you to learn?

After you have answered the questions above, put your answers aside for a day or two and let your responses settle. Once the ideas have "percolated" within you, take out your journal and write about what you've learned from the Arc of Relationship. I recommend you dedicate at least one to two pages to each section. Feel free to create additional questions for each wedge. For example, you might consider these questions:

- What did you learn from the first crush you had? How about the first time you had sex?

- What did you conclude about relationships from watching your mother in her relationships?

- Did your relationship with your father influence you in how you see yourself as a relationship partner? Did he value you? Did your parents value each other?

- What does social media tell you about relationships?

- Do you believe it's possible to have a successful relationship? What would that look like? Do you have anyone in your life who has what you would consider to be a successful relationship? What are the elements of their partnership that you admire?

- If you have been in a relationship that didn't work, are you aware of your part in the breakup? How are you *not* a good partner? Has there been a pattern to the partners you have chosen?

This exercise is not about change: it is about awareness, because we can't change what we don't know about ourselves, right? So, use this writing exercise to heighten what you know about yourself and the relationships in your life. This is also a good topic to discuss with your support group or your friends. Also, check out the "Relationship Assessment: State of Your Unions" exercise at the end of this chapter.

Focusing on Molestation

"History is not destiny."
— Unknown

"I have woven a parachute out of everything broken."
—William Stafford

There are many commonalities shared by women who have been sexually abused when it comes to relationships. I'm going to list some of the major challenges that repeatedly come up in the Healing Steps workshops, as well as some suggestions on how to manage them. As you read, see if any apply to your relationships, past or current.

Top Ten Relationship Challenges For Sexual Abuse Survivors

1. Projection

It is very common for you, as a survivor, to experience your partner as the perpetrator—and thus your enemy. It's important to learn to discriminate between your partner and your perpetrator—especially during this very intense time of recovery from your past abuse. It is normal during this process to slide easily between the past and the present; "then" and "now" become very slippery. Early experiences can feel like present realities. Sensitivities are heightened, pain deepens, anger is just below the surface, emotions come up when you least expect them—and to a degree, that may surprise you. Your vulnerability is almost palpable, and no one in your world quite knows what to do with it. You don't want these feelings: you want to shake them off like a pup shakes off water, but unfortunately the drops of acidity often get splattered on the people about whom you care the most.

If you find this confusion happening, if your partner begins to morph into someone untrustworthy or threatening, make eye contact with your partner, take several deep breaths, and remind yourself who he or she is: "This is the man (woman) who loves me. This is Billie, not___." Call your partner by name as a way of reinforcing his/her identity and holding yourself in present time. Don't allow the memory of your perpetrator into the relationship or into the bedroom. Often the confusion occurs while being intimate, as it's very difficult to respond in a natural way while you are in the heart of your healing. When that occurs, it is important to create a timeout, so you can center yourself. It is tempting to project your feelings of anxiety and fear onto your partner, to and make him "the bad guy" just to give yourself relief; remember the Bounty Hunter in Step 3? As the Dalai Lama said, "Once you've been bitten by a snake, you are very cautious—even of a coiled rope." Don't turn your partner into the abuser to reduce your anxiety or to reenact the Victim-Perpetrator relationship we discussed earlier.

This is an exercise I often assign to survivors to bring clarity to the issue of who the Perpetrator really is when they are feeling hurt or angry in a relationship. I have them construct a Hurt Museum made up of all the times they have been hurt, betrayed, or violated in a relationship, by anyone, from the time they were small. Of course, there is the abuse which deserve a large monument in the museum. But there also may have been a time when someone bullied them or made fun of them. There may have been a boyfriend who stood them up—or broke up with them just before a big dance or betrayed them with their best friend. The idea here is to actually draw a layout of exhibits of all the hurtful events in your past, much like exhibits you would see in a museum.

Example of a Hurt Museum

Actually putting these events on paper will help you figure out if your strong reaction is due to what is occurring in the present, or if it's connected to one of the exhibits in your personal Hurt Museum.

2. Trust

Trust, which includes being able to trust as well as being trustworthy, is the foundation of any relationship. Without it, anxiety and resentment permeate every interaction. When we are in recovery, we are still healing from misplacing our trust and being deeply hurt. We are unsure about whom to trust, and we struggle with our feelings of exposure and vulnerability. There is no greater venue to highlight our own personal challenges with trust than in our relationships. Partners are human beings, and they will let us down—but does that mean they are untrustworthy? In my experience, survivors have either a high tolerance for inappropriate—and perhaps primitive—behavior on the part of their partners, *or* they overreact to a minor slight in the relationship with a major reaction. Those in the former group often miss or disregard the early signs of deceptive or shoddy behavior on the part of their mate; they either aren't aware of, or disregard, the warning signs. And those in the latter group can be so vigilant, so protective, and so out of touch regarding whom to trust that they see an outlaw where there is only a potential hero.

Discrimination is a struggle, so what to do? Be as honest and vulnerable as you can with your partner after you have determined that he is trustworthy. I admit this is tricky. How do you know if you can trust someone—are there guarantees? So often women who have been sexually abused believe it is dangerous to get close to anyone because they believe they will be betrayed, exploited, or hurt. Do you believe that? It's important to remember that trust is built over time and is based on the actions and reactions of your partner. Keep your eyes and ears open. See if your partner keeps agreements with you, whether they be about exclusivity, intentions, promises to do something for you, being on time for dates or events. Anyone who has ever been in one of my groups knows my mantra: "Life doesn't work if you don't keep your agreements." How does your partner handle agreements? In a slip-shod manner? Or is he or she reliable? Do you know you can trust your partner to say what he means and mean what he says? And about that question of guarantees, there aren't any guarantees about behavior; there is only your ability to handle it. You are tough, you are resilient, and you know where to go for help and support should you need it, right?

When you've been sexually abused, it's hard to know whom to trust and it's hard to trust yourself to make good decisions about relationships. Survivors often come to the conclusion that intimate relationships are not safe. Your ability to discriminate, and to make good choices for yourself, is important in order to create safe havens in your life. In an interview on Oprah's *Super Soul Sunday* television show, Iyanla Vanzant said, "Trusting yourself means trusting yourself to make right choices, trusting yourself to hear that inner voice and follow it,

trusting yourself that when people betray you or abandon you, you *will* be okay."
It's important to remember: *how much you trust others is dependent on how much you trust yourself to be able to handle whatever comes your way.*

[Untitled]

I leave my door
unlocked at night
accept rides
from so-called strangers.
lollipops too.
I give my thighs away,
throw money
off of bridges
and pet
growling dogs.
I trust mechanics,
television ministers
and my own judgment.
— Deon Gates
Reprinted from *Healing Woman Newsletter*

Time is the most valuable tool in inviting someone into your life on a permanent basis. Give the relationship time to develop, time to really get to know your potential mate in a variety of settings, and time to have normal life experiences. This "getting to know you" period is a wonderful phase of a relationship; don't rush it—linger and savor it, you can never recapture the wonder of it. Have the patience to let a relationship unfold naturally; give it time to evolve into whatever it is meant to be. Be friends first, and ask yourself: *do I like this person and admire their character—not just love or lust for them?* I heard it said once that there are people who take the heart out of you, and people who put it back. Take the time to find out which one your partner is.

3. Expectations

Your partner doesn't owe you anything because you were molested as a child. Whaaat? Of course, we can *hope* your partner offers compassion and understanding and whatever protection might be needed if the abuser is still in your life, but you can't expect special allowances because you were molested. This is a tricky one. What I've observed from so many women in my workshops is that they expect their mates to make up for what they didn't get because of the abuse. It goes something like this: "How could he _____when he knows I was molested?" Or as my good friend Susan, who was molested from the age of three until she was an adolescent, says, "My mantra in my marriage used to be 'I deserve, therefore you owe me.' " A woman in one of my groups was tearfully emphatic when she said, "He should understand I can't help it: I was sexually abused and I don't want anyone to raise their voice, or ask for sex when I'm feeling vulnerable, or ask me to do *that,* or wear a yellow shirt like my abuser used to wear or _____." You fill in the blanks. What are your expectations of your partner? What should he or she automatically "know" about you that stems from your abuse?

During your recovery, there will likely be a period where a long-forgotten part of yourself surfaces and (as the director of the New York Trauma Center once wrote) shows up as "greedy, grandiose, and insatiably entitled." This can obviously wreak havoc in your relationships and with those around you as your expectations tend to increase along with your awareness of what you didn't get as a child. There does come a time when the realization of what was taken from you seeks resolution within you—and that's when grief and mourning really begin. Your inner work is to feel the sadness for yourself because you didn't get what you deserved, it wasn't fair, and you'll never be able to go back and create a different reality for yourself. There is a much-deserved mourning period for the childhood that never was, for the idealized parent who never existed, and for the fantasy family that you will never experience. The pain is deep and has to be worked through, not acted out with your partner—because he didn't cause it and he can't fix it. This passage is dark and painful and is certainly a time to use the tools that have been presented in previous chapters.

In the meantime, don't expect your partner or your friends and family to know what your triggers are unless you not only tell them but also teach them *what you prefer and what doesn't work for you* as you go about your daily life—especially when you are in the throes of your recovery. Remember that such behaviors are only a *preference* for you; they are not about the "right" way to be in a relationship. And don't expect your partner to automatically know how to support you because he or she loves you, as in: "If he really loved me, he would know what to say, what to do, what I like on my birthday, etc." The truth is, if your partner does know, it probably has more to do with luck than love!!

 Often a survivor will unconsciously use the wounded part of herself to test her partner, hoping to receive what she has longed for—whether it be understanding, compassion, attention, or validation. And she often feels let down when she doesn't receive the expected result. It is very easy as an incest survivor to feel like a victim, to feel wronged or betrayed when your expectations are not met. Asking for *what you need* is so important. You know what that is, so you can teach your partner how to respond. Most people are well-intentioned, but ignorant about sexual abuse, and their inability to care for you is often based on *not knowing* rather than *not caring*. When you feel like a victim (you *were* a victim when you were abused), you may become demanding or petulant or angry—and then your mate becomes victimized by your abuse history. It's important to know that the greatest number of arguments in a relationship center on a Victim-Victim scenario: it's a fight to the finish regarding who was the victim of the other's behavior. This scenario is a common occurrence in the recovery process.

4. Commitment and Capability

Be clear about these two "C" words. What are you committed to when you think about your partner? Are you committed to just being in any ol' relationship? Do you get anxious when you think of commitment? Does commitment mean being trapped in yet another family situation where abuse might take place? As an abused child, you may have learned that people who care about you may also hurt you and that "families" can be unsafe. Often, survivors adopt the mantra "leave before you care," or "if someone cares, it's only a matter of time before they hurt you or abandon you." This pattern often results in inviting people into our lives who do exactly that which reinforces our belief system. There is such comfort and power in being "right"!! And if you are in a relationship, what are you committed to? Are you committed to your partner's growth and well-being? Is your partner as important in the relationship as you are? Are you committed to looking at those aspects of yourself that rear their ugly heads more than you would like them to? Or are you committed to being right at all costs, to being the victor instead of the victim? Are you committed to "peace at any price"?

The second "C" word is *capability*. Is your partner capable of being in an intimate relationship? Are you capable of meeting all the demands involved in a continuing relationship? Do you both have the skills and experience? So often we confuse *intention* with *capability*; and what's true is that we may have good intentions but lack the capability to be honest, or manage anger, or listen to our partner while holding onto our own intense feelings. Oftentimes, survivors in the midst of recovery are not *capable* of being in a stable relationship because they *are not stable* at the moment. Emotions can run the gamut from neediness and clinging behaviors to white-hot rage and other distancing behaviors. Dependency can turn to paranoia in a split second, creating havoc. Patience is a virtue, as we know, and a great deal of patience is required of both parties during healing. Generally, the extreme emotions ebb and flow, and over time the storm passes. Everyone in a family needs to weather this period, which is why I strongly recommend counseling for each member of the family so each can understand what is happening and what they can do to care for themselves.

The most successful relationships are based on whether the individuals have both the *ability* and *willingness* to resolve differences. *Capability* is different from *ability*. We can develop the *ability* to negotiate our differences, but we may not be *capable* of doing so in the context of a relationship. And without *willingness*, all the *ability* or *capability* goes out the window. Willingness to be vulnerable, willingness to admit to your part of the dynamic, willingness to be wrong, willingness to see the issue worked through to the end, willingness to know when enough is enough—all these are important in yourself and in your partner. It's important to ask yourself: Are you *capable* at this time in your life of being in an intimate relationship? Do you have the *ability* to resolve the challenges that come up in relationship? Are you *willing* to do what it takes to make the relationship work? Finally, are your limitations due to an unusually stressful period in your life (such as recovery), or are you just not ready for the demands of an intimate relationship?

5. Boundaries

 Boundaries are essential in relationships. It's important to learn what your boundaries are and how to protect them, as well as to understand what boundaries your partner may have. *A boundary is a line of protection that establishes your personal territory.* We have to learn where that line is and what we need to do to protect it. I don't believe it's possible to have been sexually abused and not experience boundary issues in subsequent relationships. Sexual abuse is the ultimate boundary violation, and since 90 percent of molestations occur with someone known to the victim, the abuse becomes a boundary violation of the worst kind. Often you won't know what your boundaries are until you feel violated in a relationship, and then you are confronted with the difficulty of what to do and how to react in an appropriate way. To further complicate this issue, there are a wide variety of boundary issues in any relationship; and in a relationship where a partner has been sexually abused, landmines are just waiting to be detonated. Rarely do couples discuss their boundaries until a landmine gets stepped on—and then reactions are generally heated, not discussed.

Most abuse victims have an exquisite sensitivity to certain behaviors. They might be sensitive to a partner walking in on them unexpectedly when they are naked ("knock, please"), or to a partner telling someone else about the survivor's abuse ("it's solely my story to tell if I choose to"). It is of the utmost importance that in order to have your boundaries honored and respected, you have to communicate them to your partner. However, it is also important that you take a look at what you have asked for so your requests are not too vague, such as "don't ever do anything unpredictable," or "don't do anything that reminds me of Uncle Dan." These are too global, too general. It takes practice to be more specific, but then so do most things in a successful relationship.

To conclude, if your boundaries are too rigid, you will feel isolated, abandoned, and alone. If there are too many obstacles to navigate in order to be close to you, you will scare people off. Is that what you want? On the other hand, if your boundaries are too permeable, you will wind up feeling invaded, used, and confused and will often lack a sense of self. Rigid boundaries lead to separation, and blurred boundaries lead to enmeshment. It's important to develop a healthy rhythm of closeness/separateness that works for you. Will there be some anxiety when you begin setting boundaries for yourself? Absolutely, but the price is definitely worth the payoff.

Here are some common signs of unhealthy boundaries in relationship:

- Acting on your first sexual impulse.

- Being sexual for your partner and not for yourself.

- Going against your personal values to please others.

- Allowing others to touch you in ways that are uncomfortable for you.

- Telling all.

- Not noticing when someone else displays inappropriate boundaries.

- Not noticing when someone invades your boundaries.

- Accepting food, gifts, touch or sex that you don't want.

- Taking as much as you can for the sake of "getting."

- Giving as much as you can for the sake of "giving."

- Letting others direct your life.

- Letting others define your reality.

- Believing others can anticipate your needs.

- Falling apart so others will take care of you.

- Any kind of self-abuse whether it be sexual, physical, food-related, financial, or chemical.

6. Power and control

Power and control can cause tension in any relationship, but this dynamic is particularly significant for a survivor. When you are being molested or abused, you have no control; you have no power. The perpetrator depends on this fact, and the grooming process is calculated with that in mind. On a deep level, most survivors swear they will never allow themselves to assume the position of victim again, but as we know, many do find themselves dominated in relationships—until they have the courage and the tools to free themselves. That's how we learn—by repeating the same patterns over and over until we find the courage and wisdom to break free.

There are survivors who stay away from intimate relationships in order to avoid the whole power-control dynamic. The majority of survivors, however, want to be in a primary relationship and must confront this dynamic in order to learn. In my practice, *power and control show up not only externally—in terms of one partner exerting power over the other—but also internally when our unhealed wounds exert power over our behavior.* When survivors fall in love, I've noticed two distinct patterns of behavior: one group will be represented by "Cindy" and the other by "Martie"—both fictitious women.

Cindy feels off balance in her relationship with Charlie, not trusting "this love thing." She does well in superficial relationships, but as intimacy and commitment grow, panic begins. When I tell her, "It's good to question this 'love thing,'" she looks relieved. "This state," I explain, "is very real, very powerful, but short lived—it lasts maybe a year or so at best, so don't trust that you two can maintain this intensity into eternity. Do enjoy it, and if what remains after the year is good and solid and right for you, then choose it."

The lack of trust for Cindy, however, extends to her partner's behavior. She questions every action and reaction: "What does he really want?" "Does he mean what he says?" "What does he really mean?" "Does he still care for the last woman he dated but just doesn't want to tell me?" Cindy is hesitant, cautious, wary, and very suspicious of any behavior resembling manipulation. She can be accusatory where there is no ill intention. She sees trouble before it has a chance to appear. She protects herself by being vigilant, hyper-alert, and suspicious. She becomes an expert on male behavior by reading every book she can find about men and relationships. She over-interprets her partner's words, repeating what was said, figuring out what was meant; and she feels she'd better be ready to move on as abandonment is probably just around the corner. She's always waiting for the other shoe to drop.

Cindy is being controlled, not by her partner or her relationship, but by her previous abuse, by her belief systems about men and relationships, and by her vulnerable position in the relationship. Her lack of esteem and self-worth causes great pain and doubt for her. Her relationships don't stand a chance of surviving because she wears her partner down with her self-doubts, her need for reassurance, and her eternal questioning. And, of course, her relationships do end and her beliefs become self-fulfilling prophecy.

Then there is Martie who goes in full bore, taking charge, blinders on, no boundaries, ready to move in after the first date. She is like many survivors who move too fast in order to decrease anxiety. She knows what he's thinking and feeling. She's got the whole relationship playing out in her head; she just needs a body to fill the space. She grabs the power, script in hand, and is devastated when it doesn't play out like she expected.

When she brings her partner into a therapy session with her, she explains his behavior to me—including his motivations—and she tells me what he's thinking and predicts what he's going to do. Her safety is in "'knowing,'" and she has no tolerance for listening or taking in new information.

Martie is being controlled by her inner processes in a dramatic attempt to avoid being controlled in the relationship. She only feels safe when she is in control of a relationship, so she is quick to grab control. When a survivor needs to be in control, anger and rage are always an ongoing issue. There is little to no flexibility: it's "my way or the highway."

There are many different styles of power and control. I've highlighted just two. How do you exert power in your relationship? Overtly or covertly? The goal, of course, is to enjoy a sense of personal empowerment, one that stems from the ability to be assertive when need be, the ability to set limits and boundaries as necessary, the willingness to share your feelings, and of course the willingness and ability to compromise and accommodate.

"Where did you learn that love's supposed to be easy?
It's only easy if one person is in charge and the other just follows the rules."
—Kate Brennan, *In His Sights*

7. Feeling Unworthy or Damaged

It is easy to feel "bad" when you've been abused—bad because you believe you contributed to the abuse, bad because you were abused and now you feel like damaged goods, bad because you didn't tell, bad because you did. And in a close relationship, nothing can create as much havoc as feeling unworthy or damaged. Once we hand ourselves over to another person, a mere glance can bring up all of our self-doubts. Do you believe you are inferior to other people because you did not have "normal" experiences when you were young? Do you believe that anyone who knows what happened to you sexually will not want anything to do with you? I hope not. How you feel about yourself affects the quality of your relationships and the quality of the partner you choose. Do you believe that only worthless individuals would be interested in you? Do you believe that no man could care for you apart from a sexual relationship? Are your needs as important as those of your partner? Are you afraid he will leave you if he knows what happened to you as a child? Are you carrying the shame that rightfully belongs to the perpetrator? Please don't rip off the Perpetrator by carrying his shame: allow him to carry it so it becomes his burden, not yours! Are you repeating the abuse dynamic (remember the V-P-R triangle in Step Three?) in an attempt to resolve a dysfunctional relationship? One way to get clear on this is to think about the relationships you've been in: Is there a pattern? Do you play the same role in every relationship? Do you allow the "Needy Child," the "Angry Adolescent," or the "Moody Maiden" to run the relationship?

Another classic role where survivors get stuck is that of Rescuer in the V-P-R triangle. The Rescuer relates to others by taking care of them. Her primary value is to be of service. She has a high tolerance for bad behavior—and she tolerates way too much. She assumes responsibility for her partner's behavior and feelings, and she often makes compromises at great personal expense. She stays too long in a bad relationship and feels she's the one who can change her partner's behavior. Is this you? She is often unconsciously invested in having an emotionally crippled partner, so she can maintain a role that is comfortable and safe for her. This role is less dramatic and painful than that of Victim or Perpetrator, but it still leaves her stuck. Often, a co-dependent relationship develops—a basic agreement between two people to stay locked in unconscious patterns that limit each other's potential: "I won't call you on your stuff, and you don't call me on mine"; "You don't call me on my spending, and I won't call you on your alcohol use"; or as one of the Healing Step women commented, "I don't complain about my husband's gambling, and he doesn't get on me about my Internet shopping. We justify our own indulgences by not mentioning the growing resentment about each other's addictions." She went on to say that she always picked partners who allowed her to get away with her destructive behaviors; if they confronted her, she showed them the door. In the past, she would rather have ended a relationship than face up to her own bad behavior because negative behavior meant she was indeed as damaged as she always believed she was.

A survivor's lack of self-esteem can also lead to an enmeshed relationship. Here a survivor picks a partner to merge with. She needs another self upon which to feed; it's as if there is not enough of her to form a "whole." A good image here is the traditional three-legged race, where two people run a race, arms around one another, each with a leg in the same gunny sack. They are completely dependent upon each other and have to move at a slower pace because of their mutual dependence. In this kind of relationship, there is an unspoken agreement not to support each other's individuation, but rather to remain in a self-defeating and self-destructive pattern that has no room for individual growth. It's amusing in a gunny sack race, but not so amusing in life.

Sometimes it's hard to see ourselves in relationship, and this is where a therapist or trusted friend can help. Don't feel guilty about inviting a less than worthy partner into your life. Just know that the part of you bringing the same SOB into your relationship is also giving you the opportunity to stand up and say, "No, thank you. I'm finished with this dance and I'm ready to move on."

8. Inappropriate Relationships

Inappropriate relationships are not uncommon for survivors. Most survivors are relieved to hear that they are not alone in picking the wrong partner—one who is abusive, emotionally unavailable, addicted, married, committed to someone else, etc. Affairs, which occur frequently, often recreate for the survivor the original triangle present during abuse: the relationship is "forbidden," an alliance of secrecy forms between two people to the exclusion of a third, and a false sense of power takes over, one that translates to "look what he is willing to do for me—I am *that* alluring and desirable." Sexologists agree that our sexual response is not learned, but what we respond to *is* learned. Since sexual feelings were often awakened in a forbidden relationship, survivors often find the forbidden situation exciting or sexually stimulating. If this sounds like you, here is another opportunity to take a hard look at what you might be doing and to walk away from someone who is using you in this way (or to walk away from someone *you* are using).

When the abuse wound is not healed, we are unconsciously attracted to our "unfinished business": we recreate unhealthy dynamics, and we attract people who exploit our vulnerabilities. It is said that as adults we create relationships with others that mimic the relationship we had with the parent with whom our unfinished business resides. Is that true for you in your choices? You may be someone who moves in and out of relationships quickly; or you may push away close, intimate relationships even though you want them. You may notice a pattern of becoming sexual early in a relationship and then losing interest. If you have dysfunctional patterns in your relationships, please help yourself by seeking a qualified therapist to help you sort out what is contributing to your choices. You deserve better—and the only one who can stop the craziness is you.

9. Distorted Belief Systems

Distorted belief systems are not uncommon when you have been violated; and in my estimation, such belief systems are one of the most significant contributors to bad relationship choices. Distorted beliefs cannot be seen: they reside just below our awareness. And they often develop when we are young, naïve and inexperienced, as we attempt to protect ourselves from being violated.

Often, we hold tight to these distorted beliefs—which over time have crystallized into "truths." If we give up on them, we will no longer be safe. Here are some common examples of erroneous beliefs:

- "I'm only good for one thing."
- "You can't trust anyone. Sooner or later, they will betray you."
- "Give them an inch and they'll take a mile."
- "Men only want one thing."
- "I can't say no. It's just the way I am."
- "I'll never have children. They'll just get molested."
- "No one would want to be with me because I'm used goods."

Erroneous beliefs weave through every aspect of the abuse wound and act as a barrier to our moving forward. Some are easily available, and some reside deep inside us and have to be pried out with persistence and tenacity. It's worth the time and trouble to do so, because if we don't become aware of the conclusions we came to as a result of our molest, we will be sabotaged at every turn. And what makes it all the more confusing is that we often unconsciously pick companions who will validate our erroneous belief systems. Remember, we are attracted to our unfinished business. Joan Borysenko, in her book *Fire in The Soul,* suggests that when a difficult situation arises, always ask yourself, "What is this situation asking of me?" In my experience, the psychological and spiritual growth for all of us lies in this question. It's also how you can uncover your own erroneous belief systems.

"The greatest discovery of any generation is that
human beings can alter their lives by altering their attitudes of mind."
—Albert Schweitzer

10. The Shadowy Parts

The shadowy parts of ourselves are revealed in intimate relationship. That's the good news and the bad news. It is good news because only when the negative aspects surface and begin to play havoc with our lives do we tend to them. The bad news is that we are often in a position of not knowing how to deal with these forces, and we tend to displace or project the darkness onto our partners. In intimate relationships, we often expect to arm-wrestle with our partner's dark side—but we are surprised to find that the greatest battle is often with our own shadow.

"Welcome the dark parts of love and deep unknown layers.
Let them speak, too. Swim in the swirl of love. Love with all your
faucets turned on. We are gifted in love even if we don't know how yet.
I'll see you in the caves of discovery."
— Sark, in *The Bodacious Book of Succulence*

If you are reading this book, chances are you are from a dysfunctional family. If you were sexually abused, you were violated in the context of a relationship, perhaps in your family. Chances are, you didn't tell or receive counseling at the time of the abuse, so you had to make sense out of what happened to you on your own. And how did you do that? What kind of tools did you possess to put the pieces together and to come out with an accurate conclusion about the event and your own part in it? What kind of relationship skills did you gain in your childhood and from your parents to handle what had happened to you under their watch? What kind of training did you receive to handle the anger, the pain, and the betrayal you felt?

So now you are in a relationship where you can be vulnerable and let down your guard. And at the same time, your relationship activates all that dormant material in your life, bringing it to the surface. It may seep out slowly, or it may explode to the surface when you least expect it—and since your partner is the only one around, surely all these intense feelings are his fault, right? Suddenly your beloved morphs into an enemy intent on destroying you. You can do one of two things: you can be the Victim, or you can be the Perpetrator. (Remember Step Three?) This dynamic always raises its ugly head in conflict. And conflict can be addictive.

Conflict addiction is like any other addiction; it involves one of the most powerful drugs known to science—adrenaline! The conflict addict spends her time and energy either preparing for, engaging in, or recovering from arguments and conflicts. The dance involves that push-pull between being the victim and being the perpetrator of the emotional violence. Recent research shows that conflict addicts, like drama queens, become dependent on self-administered shots of adrenaline—and they don't feel good unless they get their fix. The solution, of course, is to develop an increased tolerance for periods of serenity, but in the meantime the cycle continues.

Or can you actually do something different? Is that possible? Absolutely, but it takes work to move from being reactive to being consciously active. And that brings us full-circle back to what we discussed in the beginning of this chapter: being a *conscious relationship partner*.

Before we discuss being a conscious relationship partner, let's take a look at the unconscious patterns that may be part of your relationship.

EXERCISE: **Review the Top Ten Relationship Challenges**

Review the relationship challenges. Write any insights, examples, or "ah-ha's" you may have. See what you really believe about boundaries, power and control, expectations, etc. Do any of these challenges appear in your relationships today?

Being a Conscious Relationship Partner

Here is my *idealistic* definition of a conscious relationship partner:

When you are empowered, you are knowledgeable about the inherent challenges in relationships, and you are willing to seek advice and counsel when needed. You know yourself—your "bright side" and your "dark side." You have accepted what happened in your past, and you understand how your past affects your present. You recognize the importance of smart communication skills, and you are able to access them effectively when needed. You are able to listen, learn, and accept your partner's point of view, and you treat it with as much importance as you do your own. You communicate your needs and feelings in a spirit of reciprocity and compromise.

You are entitled to respect and thoughtfulness from your partner, and you know this is reciprocal in any successful relationship. That means you give what you hope to get. You feel centered and are able to ground yourself when necessary through time alone, meditation, or another practice that you have found to be effective. Anger is part of every relationship, but you have learned to manage yours and have committed to resolving issues as they come up. You know to take a time out if things get too heated and to set another time to sit down when the fire is not so hot. You work out signals with your partner when either of you needs a timeout, and you respect your partner's need just as you expect him to accept yours. Words are sharp and can pierce your partner's heart, so you are cautious about what comes out of your mouth in the heat of anger. You won't sacrifice your relationship in order to be "right"; you demonstrate self-control.

A sure indicator of my intent to be "right" at all costs is when the man who loves me morphs into my enemy right before my eyes!! I feel constriction in my solar plexus, and I'm ready to annihilate at all costs: it's do it to him before he can do it to me. I'm lost in my self-righteousness, there's fire in my eyes, and there is nothing I won't sacrifice to be right in that moment. But I have learned. When I feel those clues in my body, I know I have to create space away from him. Then I take some deep breaths and ask myself two questions: "Is this how I want our relationship to feel right now?" and "What do I need to do to help put the two of us back on track?"

This second question is always difficult, and the answer is always the same. I have to be accountable for my part in the interaction. When the fire is gone from my eyes, I go to him and apologize for my part in our scuffle. I recognize it, acknowledge it, and apologize for it; that's the remedy and the only remedy I know that's helpful. If that's too difficult, I leave him a voice message or send an email—words are words. What I know is that when he gives me that gift of recognition, acknowledgement, and apology for *his* part, I feel so relieved and grateful. My heart becomes available again, and I am ready to go forward with him by my side.

As a conscious partner, you will have talked about anger with your partner, discussing what is acceptable and what is not. Because you both know what your histories have been in previous relationships, you will know where the hot spots are. You will also know what the high-risk words and phrases are—"you always," "you never," "you're just like your mother/father," "you don't listen," etc.—and you'll catch yourself when they slip, or explode, out of your mouth.

You will have worked through the effects of your past abuse, your addictions, your losses, and the issues surrounding your family of origin. You recognize that challenges come up, and you are willing to grapple with them when they do. And most of all, you are willing to accommodate change and growth in yourself, in your partner, and in the relationship. You know that a relationship is a living, breathing entity that changes and evolves over time.

As a conscious partner, you know how to speak up for yourself, to ask, even to demand when appropriate, and to invite your partner into your world. There is a place in the relationship for your Inner Child, who is a master of spontaneity and playfulness, but you will not lead with the Child, nor will you expect your partner to be the Child's caretaker. As a conscious partner, you will introduce your partner to your Maiden, so her romantic expectations and desires can be communicated. You will not silently monitor your partner like an internal sniper ready to shoot down any perceived wrong choices. You will not blame your partner for your past or expect him to create a future for you. You feel equal to your partner and have no need to "deflate" or "inflate" yourself in order to be in relationship and earn love. You know who you are, where you've been and where you are going; and you have the courage to invite someone to make the journey with you.

A conscious partner also does not stay in a relationship that is dysfunctional or abusive; you know that survivors often stay way too long out of false loyalty or fear, and now that you are an adult you know you have the power to leave.

I began my definition by saying this is an "idealized" view. This is the kind of partner I would like to be, and the only way I can keep working on my skills is to know what I'm aiming for. Do I get angry and show up in a primitive way when a nerve is touched? Sometimes. Do I go around and around with my partner on the same frustrating issues? Yep. But the difference is I know it—he knows it—and we talk about it, sometimes relentlessly. And then we try harder. We are imperfect, but we are committed.

This is clearly not a task to be mastered, but rather it is a life-long adventure and challenge. And it is not a journey for the faint of heart. We all have to soul-search and decide the kind of relationship we want—if we want a relationship—and then do the best we can to select a partner who shares our vision.

 What is your vision? What is your definition of a conscious partner? Do you know of anyone who matches your criteria or has the same values as you when it comes to relationship?

In one of my New Year's Healing Steps groups, we focused on becoming more conscious partners—and we made some Relationship Resolutions. You may want to write your own.

Here are ours:

Relationship Resolutions

- Keep my agreements. Doing so creates trust; not doing so creates resentments.

- Nurture my relationships so that they may strengthen and grow. Nothing grows without sustenance—not my friendships, my primary relationship, my work, or myself.

- Show respect by demonstrating my intent in words and action.

- Develop the willingness to resolve differences over the desire to be "right"; listen, communicate, and be cooperative.

- Expect the best from myself—and not settle for anything else.

EXERCISE: Relationship Assessment: State of Your Unions

Write your answers the following questions in your journal or binder:

About Members of My Family:

- What is the state of my relationship with each member of my family?

- Do I want any of these relationships to change?

- What would it take from me?

- Am I willing?

About My Friends:

- What is the state of my relationship with each of my friends?

- Do they reflect who I am? [Every great spiritual master from Jesus to the Dalai Lama to Dr. Phil has emphasized that the "company we keep" will either elevate us or bring us down.]

- Do I want any of these relationships to change? What would it take from me?

- Am I willing to make the changes necessary to enhance or strengthen my friendships? Do I need to widen my circle of friends—or perhaps let go of certain relationships that are no longer in my best interests?

About My Significant Other:

- What is the state of my relationship with my partner at the present time?

- What do I need to do to strengthen this relationship right now?

- Am I willing to do that?

About My Work Associates:

- What is the state of my relationships with the people I work with?

- Do I want to change any of the relationships?

- What would it take from me? Am I willing?

About My Children:

- What is the state of my relationship with my children?

- Do I want to change these relationships?

- If so, what do I need to do to change the dynamics I now have with my children?

- Am I willing to do so?

About Scarcity of Relationships:

- Do I want more relationships, friendships, or perhaps a significant other in the coming year?

- If so, what am I willing to do to make that happen?

- List at least five concrete steps that will bring you closer to your goal.

One of my favorite poems about relationships is "Comes the Dawn." The authorship has been claimed by several writers and even the title is controversial. I read it at the end of each of my relationship workshops, and I'm delighted to share it with you here:

Comes the Dawn

After a while you learn the subtle difference
Between holding a hand and chaining a soul.
And you learn that love doesn't mean leaning,
And company isn't security.

You learn that kisses aren't contracts
And presents aren't promises.
And you begin to accept your defeats
With your head up and your eyes open,
With the grace of a woman, not the grief of a child,
And you learn to build all your roads
On today because tomorrow's ground
Is too uncertain. And futures have
A way of falling down in mid-flight.
After a while you learn that even sunshine
Burns if you get too much.
So you plant your own garden and decorate
Your own soul, instead of waiting
For someone to bring you flowers.
And you learn that you really can endure,
That you really are strong,
And you really do have worth,
And you learn and learn,
With every goodbye, you learn.

— Author Unknown

For the Partners of Survivors

The longer you have been in your relationship and the more committed you are, the better equipped you are to deal with the stresses that occur when a survivor is moving through her issues. Also important are your partner's coping mechanisms, her support systems (hopefully it's not just you), and her willingness to accept responsibility for her "stuff." If you view the relationship as a place to challenge yourself and grow, you will find more success. Knowledge and boundaries are your two best friends during this time. I heartily recommend educating yourself about the healing process, so you can understand how rational some of your partner's "irrational" responses might be.

Many survivors come to a time when they are breaking through all the barriers they have built around their molestation, and they find themselves haunted by memories and overwhelmed with raw feelings, which are often directed at you. For some survivors, this experience comes about as a slow leak: your partner may exhibit increased sensitivity to her feelings or her moods, or she may become quick to anger. She may start having nightmares. Seeking the expertise of a qualified therapist is highly recommended for the two of you so you will understand what she is going through and how best to support her. You need support as well because this is a journey that can get rough in spots. You also need to know that this will not go on forever; it usually has a beginning, a middle, and end during which she integrates her experience into who you knew her to be. She is taking a courageous step, one she would not be embarking on unless she had the ego strength to work through whatever is presented to her.

I want to stress that this is not just about her; this is also about your relationship, and it is certainly about you. Whether you knew what happened to her or not, your relationship was affected by her abuse wounds, and your relationship will be stronger if you can weather the storm. It's a complicated process, different for each couple, and with a great many unknowns—which is why I recommend relying on a therapist to help guide you through the passages. You may not need to participate in therapy on a regular basis, but just having someone who understands the ups and downs of this journey and can help you make sense of what you can expect, is extremely helpful.

How do survivors see their partners' participation in therapy sessions? Here are what survivors have said:

> I think it would have helped a great deal for my husband to be in therapy—at least once in a while. He had no comprehension of what had happened to me. Perhaps group sessions would have been the best, so he could have heard other spouses' feelings, as well as other survivors'. It would have taken the "strangeness" out of my story, and I wouldn't have looked so extreme. I wanted him to be angry,

willing to defend me; somehow that would have translated into support for me. He was and is still very patient and tolerant when I go "weird" sometimes. — S.S.

Yes to couples therapy! If communication is blocked, your therapist can be used as a clarifier, a buffer, a mediator. And if the relationship is stifled as a result of the abused woman's experience (for example, if her experience and her memories become disruptive and both parties cannot resolve the situation alone), go together to a counselor for help in moving through the impasse. In an ideal situation, I would like my partner to be an active listener, to accept the information given, and not to push for more than I am willing to give. I would want him to understand that the molest was not my fault; and to support my decision to seek therapy, confront the molester (or not), and allow me to pursue whatever I feel is right for me to resolve my history. — R.C.

No on therapy together. There are some things that I don't want to be part of our relationship. I don't want him to ask questions or want details about what happened so many years ago. If he goes alone, fine, but not with me. — S.H.

Being the partner of a survivor can be challenging. This is an opportunity for you to hone your relationship skills. And remember, you have boundaries and rights in this relationship, too. You can say, "I want to hear what you have to say, but I can only listen for 20 minutes and then I need to go work out." Or if the material is difficult to listen to and fuels you with anger or disgust, you can certainly tell her. Dr. Mary Gail Frawley-O'Dea, former executive director of the Trauma Treatment Center in New York City, emphasizes, "While those in relationship with survivors can model setting limits on what they will tolerate in relationship with another, an empathic understanding of the source of the survivor's sometimes outrageous behavior is essential to hold in mind."

Paul, the husband of a survivor and a Healing Step participant, wrote:

When we met, the childhood abuse suffered by my future wife was not in her consciousness. The memories came up slowly during sex in the first year of our marriage. The first difficulty in this unplanned journey was hearing the stories about the abuse of the person I love. Seeing my partner in so much pain and anger was hard; and with each new memory the pain was relived.

The second was much more difficult and unexpected. All my partner's anger toward the perpetrators was then focused on me. I believe that happened because I was a safe recipient. At first that was okay with me, but I slowly got worn down. Nothing I did was right; for example, I was either not attentive enough or too attentive.

Our relationship seemed to be on a knife edge. Would we stay together? Things could go either way. Phase three for me was working on developing my own interests. I had to be both independent from the relationship and also part of it so as not to destroy it. I had one foot in two very different worlds—one where I was not criticized and in control, and one where I was out of control and had to accept constant anger that I did not feel I had earned. Time moved very slowly. This phase took years. I developed interests outside the relationship that were nonnegotiable. I started writing, painting, spending more time by myself and with my friends. I think the most valuable decision I made was getting a dog. My dog loved me unconditionally—she was always glad to see me, always wanted to do what I wanted.

Phase four was slowly merging back into a relationship where we could trust each other and not attack one another with anger. A great source of pain was realizing that the process would take years, not months. Our sex life has never recovered, but I feel that my wife is the person I want to be with.

I believe that we are drawn to a person subconsciously in order to work out our own psychological issues with our partners. I also believe that if we bail on a relationship, the same issues will come up in the next relationship. So, is this the relationship I want to put effort into? Also, working out my issues from my childhood (having a suicidal and mentally ill mother) along with my wife's issues was very expensive. We have spent many thousands of dollars on counseling. We had to skip vacations, keep older cars, not get new furniture, etc.

Is it worth it? Every penny. If I had to do it over again, I would do the exact same thing. My wife and I became better partners and better people. Because of all our personal work and counseling, we are in a position where we can help others in the family. Thankfully, we also have very good boundaries, which helps in all areas of our life.

As you can see from Paul's statement, it's difficult to be invited into this world, and when you are so close to the victim, it brings up myriad feelings. Of course, it's especially difficult if the abuser was someone in your partner's family or someone currently in her life. Your urge to lash out and confront the perpetrator can be just as intense as what she's going through. Most partners feel helpless when they see someone they care about going through such raw emotion. They feel frustrated at not knowing what to say or do. Are they doing too much or too little?

You may feel helpless when your partner goes through extended periods of depression or seems to snap your head off when you question how long she's been dealing with her abuse. Mates who want to solve problems and bring closure and relief to their partners experience a great deal of frustration because of the limitations on what can be done. The journey of recovery is one that has to be walked by the survivor; you can accompany her, you can support her, but she has to wrestle with the demons herself. Don't neglect yourself. Become better informed about PTSD and recovery from childhood sexual abuse. Read books for partners of victims and get some sound advice on what you can do to take care of yourself as well as the relationship during this time. Two helpful books for partners are *Outgrowing the Pain Together: A Book for Spouses and Partners of Adults Abused as Children*, by Eliana Gil,

PhD, and *Survivors & Partners: Healing the Relationships of Sexual Abuse Survivors,* by Paul A. Hansen, PhD.

My best advice is: don't go on this trip without a compass and a guide. Both are as close as the Internet or your neighborhood bookstore.

EXERCISE: Letter Writing for You and Your Partner:

Part I: Write a letter to each other using the following format.

"Dear _____,"

"What I appreciate about you as a relationship partner/friend is _____."

For abused person: "What I want you to know about my abuse experience is _____."

For partner: "This is what I want you to know about how it is for me to be in a relationship with a partner who has been abused: _____ _____."

For abused person: "You can help and support me in my healing by _____ _____."

For partner: "You can help me in my growth by _____."

For both: "For me, sexual abuse has entered our relationship in the following areas [for example: Our affection and touch? Our playing together? Our problem solving? Our intimacy? Our communication?] _____ _____."

For both: "I think the following would really help our relationship: _____ _____."

For both: "In order to strengthen our relationship, I would be willing to _____ _____."

Signed by both: "With love and respect, _____"

Part II: Read the letters to each other, listening but not responding to any of the content.

When you have both finished, discuss: What was it like to write your letters? What was it like to share your letters? What was it like to hear what your partner had to say? Was this new information? Is there anything you learned about each other that you can bring into the relationship to make it stronger?

The following is a handout that was a particular favorite of the Healing Steps women and summarizes the relationship goals just discussed in this chapter.

Relationship Goals: a Baker's Dozen

1. Build trust: It's the foundation of the relationship. Trust means the ability to trust + being trustworthy.

2. Set realistic expectations: Answer the question: what is a partnership to you, and what do you expect of your partner?

3. Be friends first: Like and respect the other person, not just love them or feel the intensity of the chemistry. Give your partner support, listen to one another, enjoy the companionship and appreciate how great it is not to have to do life alone.

4. **Believe that it's important for both partners to get their needs met:** This assumes that you know your needs, and the needs of your partner. It also assumes you can verbalize your needs—and you don't expect your mate to be a mind reader! However, remember that communicating your needs does not necessarily mean that your mate can, will, or should meet them.

5. **Communicate your needs in a spirit of reciprocity and compromise:** Express your feelings—especially your resentments and anger—in appropriate ways. Be verbally generous with your appreciation and love for your partner, too.

6. **Consciously understand who you are:** Accept your wounds, your sensitivities, your strengths, and most importantly, your defenses.

7. **Keep your agreements.**

8. **Maintain your integrity:** Say and do the honest thing. Know when to share and not to.

9. **Be a good listener:** "Intimate listening" is putting your own feelings and beliefs on hold, stepping into your partner's world, and seeing issues from his or her point of view. Your intention is to understand your partner's internal logic. This takes practice and dedication.

10. **Know your boundaries and the boundaries of your partner:** Communicate your boundaries, and respect the boundaries of your mate.

11. **Know how to connect with your partner:** Express appreciation, resolve a disagreement, be accountable for your words and behavior, and show affection.

12. **Box up the games:** Tit-for-Tat, Finger-Pointing, I'll Define You, Pushing the Boundaries, Who's the Perpetrator, I'm the Victim—put them all away.

13. And most important of all: **be willing and able to resolve your differences.**

 Suggested Reading

Why We Love: The Nature and Chemistry of Romantic Love, by anthropologist Helen Fisher

What Could He Be Thinking? by Michael Gurian

Conscious Loving, by Gay Hendricks, PhD, and Kathryn Hendricks, PhD

Journey of the Heart, by John Welwood, PhD

Getting the Love You Want, by Harville Hendricks

Struggle for Intimacy, by Janet Geringer Woititz, EdD

The Hard Questions, by Susan Piver

Recommended books for partners:

Survivors and Partners, by Paul A. Hansen, PhD

Partners in Healing, by Eliana Gil, PhD

What About Me? A Guide for Men Helping Female Partners Deal with Childhood Sexual Abuse, by Grant Cameron

Allies in Healing, by Laura Davis

The Unbroken

There is a brokenness
    out of which comes the unbroken, a shatteredness out of
which
blooms the unshatterable.
There is a sorrow
    beyond all grief which leads to joy,
and a fragility
    out of whose depths emerges strength.
There is a hollow space
    too vast for words
through which we pass each loss,
out of whose darkness we are sanctioned into being.
    There is a cry deeper than all sound
whose serrated edges cut the heart
    as we break open
to the place inside which is unbreakable
        and whole,
    while learning to sing.

— Rashani *

*This beautiful poem was graciously shared by Rashani Réa, who wrote it in 1991 following the death of the fifth member of her family. She shows us that there is deep grief in loss, but also that below the pain and the sorrow, there is that place within us that remains strong and whole.

Step Seven

Recovery:
Moving Toward Wholeness

⤜⧓⤛

"We are healed by what we turn toward, not what we turn from."
— **Unknown**

"Nothing ever goes away until it has taught us what we need to know."
— **Pema Chodron**

*"Before Healing Steps, I didn't even realize I lost, or just didn't
have, fundamental aspects of my development that I needed to be a
whole person. Now I can go back and take what is rightfully
mine and not feel anything but good about it!"*
— **Eileen, a survivor**

Wholeness—a worthy goal, but what does it mean? How does
the concept of being "whole" tie into the journey we have
embarked on when we began the exercises in this book? It
has become clear as we've traveled through the previous six
Steps that being wounded or "stuck" has a great deal to do
with parts of ourselves left behind, parts of ourselves denied,
and parts of ourselves ignored or distorted. We've also seen

the importance of being aware of those parts of ourselves that are in charge of our behavior and thought patterns. Hopefully, we are clear on the appropriateness—or inappropriateness—of who we designate as our "CEO," the one making all the executive decisions. We certainly hope that our designated leader has our best interests in mind. John Sanford—Jungian analyst, Episcopalian priest, and author of many of my favorite books—writes, "In Christian language, only by the grace of God can we become whole. Yet, at the same time, a person who would be whole must undergo a great pilgrimage and journey—he must search, often painfully, for the ground and fulfillment of his being." William Paul Young, author of the best-selling book *The Shack*, puts it this way: "The movement toward wholeness is when the way of our being matches the truth of our being." In an intimate discussion about his own journey on Oprah's *Super Soul Sunday*, he observed that "the process of transformation is not about becoming something that we aren't; it's about unveiling what we are the whole time." This is indeed a great pilgrimage and a journey of discovery.

But how do we know if we have in fact "recovered" from our sexual abuse, or have integrated otherwise neglected parts of ourselves on our way to wholeness? The question asked of me in every workshop is this: "Do I have to forgive my perpetrator in order to move on with my life?" A very important question which will be addressed later in this chapter.

History is not destiny. We all have the freewill to overcome the obstacles created by our abuse, to grow into ourselves, and to reinvent ourselves according to who we aspire to be. Given all the work we've done to heal, what are the most crucial steps we need to take to create a satisfying future for ourselves? We all want a future in which we feel empowered, we experience less pain, we feel we are living in a world that we have created for ourselves, rather than one where we passively accept whatever comes our way. As Maya Angelou once said, "The question is not how to survive, but how to thrive with passion, compassion, humor and style." Wholeness is clearly more than the absence of pain and haunting memories: it is the experience of being fully alive.

Seven Basic Challenges

So how do we get there? Here are the seven basic challenges to recovery, all of which you have encountered in previous Healing Steps—and all of which will show up in different areas of your life at different times. These are your life's challenges:

Have the willingness and courage to heal from your sexual, emotional, and physical abuse.

This challenge includes the most important concept of all: accepting that the abuse occurred. You cannot change what has already happened. The subsequent aftereffects are yours and yours alone to heal. You cannot hand off your pain, you cannot ignore your pain, you cannot project your pain; your only choice is to lovingly embrace your pain and to heal it. The healing process is not over just because you have gone through this book or completed your therapy. It's a lifetime commitment. Sark, author of *The Bodacious Book of Succulence,* so wisely said, "Healing doesn't care about the years. It is ageless and timeless. It waits for our souls to shift into acceptance."

Healing includes having knowledge of and understanding your Inner Child, Adolescent, Maiden, Inner Perpetrator, and all the different parts of yourself that we have discussed throughout Healing Steps. It's crucial for you to be in right relationship with them, to care for them, and not to ignore them. If you do, they will go underground and create havoc in your life. Guaranteed. Nor can you hand them over to others to be managed, as you will be chronically disappointed. We really need to create a healthy and functional "inner family," all working together to support and guide us toward a life that is creative and fulfilling.

We have to be aware of our "willingness selectivity," meaning: "Yes, I'm willing to work on my _____ but not my _____." When we are feeling stuck, or when we face a loaded situation, we must remember the question: "What is this situation asking of me right now?" When the answer evokes a reaction such as "oh, no—I don't want to do that," we must be willing (and courageous enough) to do whatever will lead us to an expanded sense of who we are, and what we are capable of. Each crisis is an opportunity for growth, an opportunity to heal, an opportunity to discover a new strength within. Are you brave enough to risk failure? Brave enough to make a tough decision? Courageous enough to take a risk and tolerate discomfort?

Take a moment to reflect on the previous Healing Steps. Which ones did you skim? Were there any that you passed over entirely?

Irene Claremont de Castillejo writes in *Knowing Woman*: "I believe one has to return to one's past, not once but many times in order to pick up all the threads one has let fall through carelessness or inobservance. I believe, above all, one has to return again and again to weep the tears which are still unshed. We cannot feel all the grief of our many losses at the time we suffer them. That would be too crippling. But if we would really gather our lives into a single whole, no emotion that belongs to us should be left unfelt."

Affirmations:
"I will not give up on myself."
"I will honor each part of myself as a valuable piece of my Wholeness."
"I have the willingness and courage to take the next Step in my healing."
"I am a child of the universe born to shimmer and shine."

What are your affirmations?

Honor your core self.

The ability to esteem (honor) your*self*—and not to be dependent on others for validation—is a critically important skill. It includes the ability to love, value, and appreciate yourself appropriately without inflation, deflation or distortion. It also includes the willingness to be in contact with your inner *self* even during times of difficulty and stress, to *be there* for yourself. Self-nurture requires that you do not neglect or abandon yourself. When you were abused, you were treated as though your needs were clearly not important. Don't repeat that painful pattern with yourself. You are worth so much more.

Have you ever been in a situation where you were not true to yourself? Have you ever made a decision knowing deep inside that your choice was not in alignment with your core self, not in your best interest? That choice may have wreaked havoc with your heart, your finances, your career—and yet you may have stubbornly stuck with it. In such cases, you may have pummeled yourself with recriminations: "What was I thinking?" "Why didn't I listen to my gut?" "I knew he was trouble," "Why can't I learn?"

The difficulty in not listening to ourselves, in not honoring our inner voice, is that we come down so hard on ourselves and we lose self-esteem. When you receive such messages from yourself, write them down in your journal. The value of doing so is twofold. First, you respect your inner voice by saying, "Hey, I'm listening. What you have to say is important," which reinforces your relationship with yourself. And second, you can come back to what you've written and evaluate it. "Hmm—interesting. I wonder why my Inner Self is saying slow down with Alex. Is there something I'm missing here?" Perhaps, the balance between your impulsive side and your thoughtful side could use some strengthening. Resolution between these two sides of yourself helps to create a more solid core self—one that allows you to make better decisions and thus feel better about how you handle your life. Gloria Steinem ends her book *Revolution from Within* with the words, "There is *always* one true inner voice. Trust it."

Affirmations:
"I accept myself as perfectly imperfect."
"I will talk to myself in a loving, encouraging way."
"I will take the time I need to be self-directed."

Your affirmations?

Set appropriate limits and boundaries, and allow them to become the foundation for trusting yourself.

Set boundries with others to protect yourself. Do not expect others to protect you or become enraged when they do not. Don't be a victim of someone else's negligence, and even more importantly, don't be a victim of your own negligence. Set limits on the incoming perceptions or information from other people, and don't automatically accept their point of view as reality. Listen to their words, take them in, examine them, and actively decide if they fit for you. Discrimination is a tool to be honed over time. Act assertively—not aggressively or defensively—to enforce your limits and boundaries. In other words, don't be a Perpetrator in order to protect yourself. Make sure your boundaries are neither too rigid, nor too easily penetrated. Be patient with yourself—this takes practice.

Affirmations:

"Today I will not say yes when I want to say no."
"I will not allow my feelings, thoughts, or actions to be dictated by others."
"I am committed to protecting myself emotionally and physically."
"Today I will be fearless."

Your affirmations?

Be in relationship with yourself and others in appropriate ways.

The ability to be intimate takes skill and evolves over time—for everyone. When you've been abused in any way, the challenge is even more daunting, but hopefully after doing the exercises in Step Six, you will feel better equipped and not be so hard on yourself. Intimacy requires trust, honesty, openness, and a willingness to be vulnerable. It asks that we be fearless, that we be willing to listen, that we be willing to make mistakes and be accountable for our mistakes. It requires time, skill, and patience. And it's not for everyone. Not everyone values relationship, nor wants to be intimate. That's why it's so important to know what your needs and wants are—and what you desire in a partner. Knowing yourself will help you make an appropriate choice and help you avoid being "blindsided" after the magic disappears.

As you know, communicating discriminately is an important factor in relationships. Often, we think being open and honest means having no filters. But "telling it like it is" has created more destruction in relationships than not speaking up at all! As Pia Mellody so brilliantly said, "Own your own reality, and share it *politically* with others." Words are forever. Words create wounds. You can learn some wonderful techniques from the relationship books I recommend, techniques that will help you communicate effectively, without damaging your relationship.

 I bring this up because your new-found willingness to speak up, to tell your truth, and to share your feelings can bring with it a great deal of passion and energy, but little expertise in discriminating communications. You need both. So, go slow and learn—and the results will lead you in the direction of closer and more intimate relationships with the people in your life.

Affirmations:
"I can be close to another person without losing myself."
"I share my needs with those close to me."
"I take advantage of the growth opportunities available to me in safe relationships."
"A roadmap is guiding me to rewarding relationships through the complexity of my own history."
"My time and energy are as valuable as your needs."

Your affirmations?

Take full responsibility for your dependency needs.

It's so important that we own our own *needing* and *wanting,* and not show up in relationship like an empty soul waiting to be filled. (Remember my friend Susan's mantra: "I deserve, therefore you owe me"?) We do, however, need to be able to ask others for help when appropriate without any guilt or shame—and not be anti-dependent! An anti-dependent is the survivor whose mantra is: "I can handle it myself. I don't need anyone or anything because that only leads to disappointment." So often anti-dependents fear being told "no," perceiving that response as rejection rather than as limit-setting behavior by the other person. Remember, survivors are often not well-attuned to setting limits. Facing others' limit-setting behavior can rekindle feelings of not having your needs met, or of no one being there for you.

There is a dance that many survivors do between being too dependent, too anti-dependent, and, of course, being co-dependent. Where are you in this tricky triangle? The challenge here is to maintain a balance between giving, receiving, and asking; it is a healthy balance between vulnerability and strength. Only you are responsible for knowing and meeting your needs. So, if you have been looking for love in all the wrong places, or if you've been looking for someone to take care of your Inner Child—*stop*. Realize that caring for yourself is your responsibility, and no one can do it better. *Stop* waiting. *Stop* turning your Child over to others and winding up disappointed and disillusioned. *Start* caring for yourself. Do this, and you'll find the strength and inner power that may have been elusive up to now.

Affirmations:
"I am fully responsible for myself,
and I let others take responsibility for themselves."
"I lovingly accept the space between us.
I am whole and complete by myself."
"I will face my own emptiness—you need not fill me up."
"I take care of myself and accept what I need from others."

Your affirmations?

Create moderation in both your internal and external life.

 Being sexually abused is an intense and powerful experience, both when it is happening and in the aftermath. Moderation and balance are not paths walked easily by most survivors.

To present extremes in this kind of behavior, consider the Boomers and Peepers. Boomers tend to exaggerate, overdramatize, overdo, and seek intensity in their lives. They are the high-stimulation folks who need a few degrees of intensity in their lives to feel normal. If the intensity's not there, they will create it. Boomers take up a great deal of space in a relationship. The Boomer's challenge is to stay centered, and not to rely on crisis or drama to feel alive. Events don't have to be bigger than life, nor does every situation need to be faced with great intensity in order to convey importance.

Peepers are the opposite. They play Hide and Seek: "I'll hide, you seek." Peepers hide themselves behind excuses; they shut down, blank out, make themselves unavailable, so they have to be sought out, pursued. This behavior is often a passive power play used to prove that a partner "really cares enough to find me and to see what's going on with me."

 Being either a Boomer or a Peeper is offensive to others. Both styles keep you from being present in your interactions with others. I'm not talking about traits like introversion and extroversion here. I'm talking about *defensive styles* developed with the unconscious intent of taking care of ourselves in some way. They are a learned way of being in the world that may have solved a problem at one time. But what solved a problem then can *become* a problem in our relationships today.

Moderation and balance also means looking at the addictions and the compulsions in our lives. We need to take a hard look at the overuse of *anything,* no matter how benign it may appear. If a behavior takes you away from your life or distorts your reality, it is a barrier to fulfillment. Too much time at the gym, too much compulsive cleaning, being tied to your electronics, being absorbed in work to the exclusion of a personal life, adopting a partying lifestyle—these are all maladaptive behaviors. What's on your list?

Affirmations:
"*I maintain balance in my relationships,*
trusting their constant ebb and flow."
"*I am able to stay centered in the midst of internal or external chaos.*"
"*Everything in moderation.*"

Your affirmations?

Connect with the spiritual dimension within yourself.

The spiritual aspect of your life provides the strength, the knowledge, and the encouragement you need to continue your journey toward wholeness. Spirituality gives life meaning and helps us transcend ourselves. It has been said that we are not human beings having a spiritual experience, but rather *we are spiritual beings having a human experience.* As humans, then, we need to access our inner spirit. Elizabeth Kübler-Ross, MD, puts it this way:

> *People are like stained-glass windows*
> *they sparkle and shine when the sun is out,*
> *but when the darkness sets in,*
> *their true beauty is revealed*
> *only if there is a light from within.*

I believe spirituality is also about intention. Our spirit is the deepest part of ourselves, and I believe it is untouched and preserved even in the most violent of abuse situations. Whether you call this part of yourself your Higher Power, your Inner Knowing Self, your Inner Therapist, God, the Wise Old Woman (or a similar archetype), *it's important to know there is always one true inner voice.* Listen for it, amplify it, and above all, learn to trust it. Take time in your day to be still so you can hear what is being whispered. Take time in your day so you can question what needs to be questioned. Take time in your day for giving gratitude for not having to be alone and lost on this remarkable journey. You have always had your Self with you.

Connecting or reconnecting with your spiritual self is difficult for many survivors because of their deep feelings of betrayal and violation. If there is a Higher Power out there, how could this happen? If you believed in God as a child, you may feel abandoned by God because how could He let this happen to one of His children? How does abuse fit into the image of a benevolent God? For many already feeling the pain of abandonment, this is the ultimate abandonment. If this sounds like you, I'm guessing that anger has not been expressed— and it needs to be released. My dear friend Susan, whose great-grandfather was one of the founding fathers of a well-known religious group, found her deepest healing in her shouting matches with God. She yelled, she shook her fist, she held nothing back. Her heated words moved to conversations and then to deep reflection. Her talks with God brought her back to herself.

Since there is a high correlation between abusers and religiosity, many survivors have abandoned their churches as a way of rejecting their abusers. They have turned their backs on anything resembling spirituality, and in the process, they may have lost touch with their own spirits and their need for spiritual growth. Again, spirituality is about finding meaning and transcendence, not necessarily religion. Get in touch with what a transcending experience might be for you. Is it watching the sun come up? Watching your child learn to walk? Listening to classical music? What opens your heart and brings you joy?

If you consider yourself a "seeker," this may be the time to ask yourself if you are willing to explore different practices, belief systems or religious philosophies to see if any resonate with you. There is literally a buffet of ideas and principles available to you as close as your nearest bookstore or neighborhood: Eastern philosophies, New Age spirituality, personal growth gurus (who are often prolific writers), Native American rituals, non-denominational spiritual centers, revamped Christian religions, temples, and so on.

Regardless of your identification with such philosophies, what is most important is that you maintain a strong relationship with your inner spirit through meditation, prayer, or simple silence. Your spirit is alive and well and can serve as a compass and guiding light. Her wisdom can only be heard if you take the time to be still and listen.

Affirmations:

"I am whole and complete."

"My spiritual center is my true self."

"I hold my own meaning about the abuse that releases me from the legacy of the past."

"I ask my Higher Self for guidance and courage to take the risks I need to take."

Your affirmations?

Forgiveness

"Forgive others, not because they deserve
forgiveness, but because you deserve peace."
— Desmond Tutu

"Resentment is like taking poison and
expecting the other person to die."
— Unknown

"The weak can never forgive. Forgiveness
is the attribute of the strong."
— Mahatma Gandhi

"Betrayal can either make you bitter
or open your heart."
— Marian Woodman

Research shows that we need two qualities to live successfully in the present—hope and forgiveness. If you didn't have hope you wouldn't have picked up this book. If you didn't have hope, you wouldn't have considered healing from your sexual abuse wound and creating a better life for yourself. If you didn't have hope, you would have given up a long time ago. But forgiveness—that's another story. Forgiveness is a complex and complicated issue for survivors of sexual abuse. Rarely have I met anyone who is neutral on the matter; it doesn't matter whether someone was abused, had a relationship with an abused person, or only watched a story of abuse on television. Feelings are intense and confusing. We've been taught it's a Christian virtue to forgive, and yet it somehow feels too easy, too incomplete. The experts have differing opinions as well. Some say healing is not complete until you forgive; others say it's optional and individual; and still others say it's not needed for recovery.

Forgiveness refers to a change in emotion, and in my opinion it is very *late-stage* work. The Indo-European root of "forgive" means "to give up or give away anger and the associated retribution and revenge." But you can't give it up until you own it, experience it, and work through it. Forgiveness is not condoning someone's behavior. Forgiveness is not forgetting: it is not about having to be in relationship with someone who has hurt you. Nor is it about tolerating bad behavior. It is about setting limits for yourself. Forgiveness is about *you*, about freeing *yourself*—it's not about freeing the abuser from accountability or responsibility. So many survivors feel if they forgive their perpetrator, they will be letting him off the hook. This is not about condoning the selfish, abusive behavior that hurt you.

But just because someone has hurt you in unspeakable ways does not mean *you* have to suffer indefinitely. Many of us remember when Nelson Mandela was released from prison, he embraced his jailers because he said he did not want to be imprisoned twice—once by steel and concrete, and once by anger and bitterness.

Forgiveness is a *process,* not an event. It moves us from wanting vengeance and being possessed by anger to letting go, turning the perpetrator over to his own agenda, and concentrating on our own next step. Forgiveness doesn't just happen; it's an active choice. As I learned in Fred Luskin's workshops, forgiveness changes our grievance story into a story where we become the hero instead of the victim. We take our power back; we are not at the mercy of the perpetrator's attitudes, behaviors, or choices—nor is our identity formed around his despicable acts.

Forgiveness is always a choice. We forgive because:

- It's in *our* best interest—physically, emotionally, mentally, and spiritually. In a 1996 published study, researchers found that women who were abused as children experienced improvements in psychological, emotional, and physical functioning when they were able to forgive their abusers.

- We want to suffer less and stop feeling the pain.

- We want to be healthier. Studies have shown there is an impact on our cardiovascular functioning in that "blamers" have higher rates of heart disease and suffer more heart attacks. We want to improve our physical health, right?

- We want less stress and anxiety and more peace in our lives.

- We forgive so that we will not be victims of our past.

- We know that carrying hurt from the *past* affects our *current* relationships.

- And most importantly, we know that renting out so much space in our minds and hearts does not allow room for all the good stuff just waiting to come in!

When we worked on the issue of forgiveness in our workshops, I opened the workshops with: "Let's do the impossible—let's turn our pain and outrage into forgiveness." And it does seem quite impossible, doesn't it? But it is possible—though it does take time. Dr. Luskin, who is director and founder of the Stanford Forgiveness Project and author of *Forgive for Good: A Proven Prescription for Health and Happiness*, talks about what is involved in forgiving and what gets in the way of forgiveness. I think the value of his work is in his definition of forgiveness, which certainly turned my thought processes around. His definition:

> *Forgiveness is the feeling of peace that emerges as you take your hurt less personally, take responsibility for how you feel, and become a hero instead of a victim in the story that you tell. Forgiveness is the experience of peacefulness in the present moment. Forgiveness does not change the past, but it changes the present. Forgiveness means that even though you are wounded, you choose to hurt and suffer less. Forgiveness means you become a part of the solution. Forgiveness is the understanding that hurt is a normal part of life. Forgiveness is for you and no one else. You can forgive and rejoin a relationship or forgive and never speak to the person again.*

If this passage resonates with you, then I heartily recommend you read his book to see if his ideas have value for you.

"To err is human, to forgive, divine," said Alexander Pope. Is it divine to forgive? Is there a spiritual reason as well as an emotional and physical reason to forgive? Alcoholics Anonymous says, "Let go and let God." In the Bible, Matthew

6:12, we are told to "forgive us our trespasses as we forgive those who trespass against us." In the Qur'an, forgiveness is a superior moral trait. And forgiveness has been called "elevated consciousness" and "the path to true recovery" by our growth leaders.

A Baptist minister in New Jersey has offered another point of view: "It is not our job to forgive the perpetrator. We hand that over to somebody else who's a much stricter judge than we'll ever be. And then we go on." We know that detaching and letting go is a crucial aspect of every spiritual path. But does detachment and forgiveness mean we don't care? Does it mean that we are not involved, that we are turning our backs on abuse and violence? Or could it mean something else—as the Baptist minister suggests? I think this issue is an apt subject for contemplation.

EXERCISE: Contemplation

Contemplation is different from meditation. Meditation is about emptying your mind, and contemplation is about focusing your mind on a particular subject. Beyond that, instructions are basically the same: pick a time when there is no chance of being interrupted, silence your electronics, and sit in a comfortable position where your body feels supported. Take a few deep and cleansing breaths, close your eyes, and then bring up the word "forgiveness," or the word "detachment." Take 10 minutes and focus on the word you've chosen. Stay open and just let yourself be with whatever emerges in your mind. After the 10 minutes (or longer if you like), write down any thoughts or feelings you may have. This exercise is about awareness, not about decisions.

A Healing Stepper wrote after her contemplation on forgiveness:

Forgiveness means to me holding on to what is mine and letting go of what is his. I can never get him to understand my experience. There is nothing he can do to change what happened or change my Inner Child's experience of what happened. I can heal myself. I can release him so he can have the full weight of the experience in his own hands because he created it and it is his to deal with. I don't have to, nor do I want to, carry it anymore. What he did is a statement about him, his life, his choices—I just work with what is mine. Forgiveness is breaking the bond of expectation, letting go of the shame and guilt and turning disappointments from the past into hope for the future. You do your work (or not), and I'll do mine. I detach from your journey and focus on my own. I forgive you."

My favorite quote on forgiveness is one by Oprah Winfrey who, as we all know, was sexually abused at age 13 and has long been an advocate for survivors. Her message reflects a very deep understanding of our life journey:

"True forgiveness is when you can say, 'Thank you for that experience.' "

Think about that powerful statement. I do. Oprah's words speak to the question: "How does my growth in this lifetime require me to be wounded in this way in order to progress toward spiritual wholeness?"

Hank Giarretto, my first mentor and founder of one of the most comprehensive and successful programs for sexual abuse healing, once said to a group of survivors, "Have you ever considered the possibility that your present strengths—the ability to listen, to be sensitive to others, to be able to nurture others and yourself—may, in large part, stem from the fact that you were molested as a child; and that this event in your life forced you to look inward, to experience the whole *you* more fully, and therefore has made you more appreciative, more caring of yourself and the children and adults who come into your life?" Can you imagine that? Can you imagine weaving this tragic circumstance into the fabric of your being and becoming wiser, stronger, and more compassionate because of it? Can you imagine becoming more *yourself* because of your courageous healing—not less *yourself* because of what someone did to you?

The following inspirational poem, which poet Patricia Lynn Reilly released so that it could be shared with each new generation of women, is a perfect summation of the seven Healing Steps.

Imagine a Woman

Imagine a woman who believes it is right and good she is a woman,
A woman who honors her experience and tells her stories.
Who refuses to carry the sins of others
within her body and life.
Imagine a woman who trusts and respects herself.
A woman who listens to her needs and desires.
Who meets them with tenderness and grace.
Imagine a woman who acknowledges
the past's influence on the present.
A woman who has walked through her past.
Who has healed into the present.
Imagine a woman who authors her own life.
A woman who exerts, initiates, and moves on her own behalf.
Who refuses to surrender except to her
truest self and wisest voice.
Imagine a woman who names her own gods.
A woman who imagines the divine in her image and likeness.
Who designs a personal spirituality to inform her daily life.
Imagine a woman in love with her own body.
A woman who believes her body is enough, just as it is,
Who celebrates its rhythms and cycles as an exquisite resource.
Imagine a woman who honors the body of the Goddess
in her changing body.
A woman who celebrates the accumulation of her
years and her wisdom.
Who refuses to use her life-energy disguising the
changes in her body and her life.
Imagine a woman who values the women in her life,
A woman who sits in circles of women,
Who is reminded of the truth about herself when she forgets.
Imagine yourself as this woman.

The Final Step

Congratulations! You have reached the final Step. But the reality is: *there is no final Step.* We may never completely heal from our abuse wound—but we *can* change our relationship with our wound. We can change the meaning it has for us; we can modify the effect it has on our life. We were wonderful little souls before the molestation—and then the event happened. But the event was not implemented by us. It imprinted us, yes, but *it did not define us.*

Our work continues. We may need more time for healing. May, a Healing Steps survivor, expressed this reality when she wrote:

I find, after all these years of working with such determination to help my "little girl" trust the safety I am offering, that I can still wake from dreams far too chilling—a Dali reality, full of confusion and fear. I used to pace and comfort my little girl and assure her that the adult is still here. I'd pace, baseball bat ready to inflict massive pain on imaginary interlopers. Now the bat stays under the bed. Four dogs snuggle in a jigsaw against me, assuring that any bad guys either get bitten or licked before they get near me. We may do our work, but we should never expect it to be done. It takes a lifetime to evolve from the slashing scars of such disregard to the glorious beings we have become.

May is right: resolution and healing are ongoing processes. You may find it useful to go back and review some of the Healing Steps now and again. Or you may find you've been inspired to begin therapy or to join a support group. This continuum of healing has some pretty dark places along the way. Move at your own pace, and when the darkness envelops you, take a break and reach out for some light: a supportive book, a friend, a hotline, a therapist, a walk in nature, some non-socially-redeeming fun. The road to recovery has rocky places; we must learn how to struggle through them and come out the other side. We may be a bit bruised but, hey, we're survivors. We're warriors. If we survived the abuse, we can survive the recovery.

May you find grace in every Healing Step.
—Sharyn Jones

✔ *EXERCISE:* Create a Mandala

A mandala, which means "magic circle" in Sanskrit, is a microcosm of the macrocosm. Everything is present within it: it is the very definition of wholeness. The mandala has been used for contemplation and meditation since ancient times in Tibetan meditation banners, rose windows of Gothic cathedrals, Aztec calendar stones, Navajo sand paintings, and Buddhist rituals. Every mandala has a center and four directions which provide the "skeleton" or basic form. Carl Jung brought the mandala form into psychotherapy as an integrative and centering tool.

> *"Making a mandala is a discipline for pulling all those scattered aspects of your life together, for finding a center and ordering yourself to it."*
>
> — Joseph Campbell, *The Power of Myth*

The process of creating a mandala is a powerful transformational exercise—both calming and centering. While you can find mandala coloring books, I encourage you to create your own mandala. Here's how to do it:

Creating a Mandala

- Have supplies ready—paper or poster board, marking pens or pencils, scissors, glue sticks, pictures or magazines.

- First, take a few minutes to sit quietly, breathe deeply, and use your meditation techniques to connect with yourself. Take the time to be in the moment and to create a sacred space.

- Now create your mandala, using either objects or paper. Begin with a circle, as large as you want it to be. Pick an image to represent your Self, and put it in the center of your mandala. Allow your intuition to fill in your mandala with whatever images, words, or objects represent aspects of your "wholeness." Let your shadow side appear, let your hopes come forth—whatever is there, let it come out. Don't try to think your way into creating your mandala.

- You will know when the message of your subconscious is complete. When you have finished, stand back and view your creation. Admire and contemplate your truth as it is revealed to you. Reflect on the message from your inner self to your conscious self—and name it.

- You may keep your mandala, throw it away, or burn it—but I suggest if you do decide to destroy it, take a photo of it first and keep that photo in your binder or journal.

Creating a Mandala of Your Life as You Wish It to Be

- Have supplies ready—paper or poster board, marking pens or pencils, scissors, glue sticks, pictures or magazines.

- Find a symbol of your Self for the center of your mandala, or create an image that represents you. You may use a photograph or a symbolic form such as a rose, a tree, an animal—whatever speaks to you.

- Draw or create a border around your page. It can be any shape—oval, rectangular, square, or circle.

- Radiating out from your symbol in the center, create a design that portrays the most significant elements of your life as you would like them to be. Draw images or symbols, use photographs or captions from magazines, and write your own words in and around the mandala. The following are some possible themes to include in your mandala: Body, Work/Career, Creative Expression, Health, Relationships, Personal Growth, Spiritual Practice, Financial, Family.

- When your mandala is complete, look at it for a while and then write your observations.

- Place your mandala where you can see it on a regular basis. Use it as a visual affirmation that you can and will create the life you want.

Creating a Four-Part Mandala

- Divide a circle into four sections: Mental, Emotional, Physical, Spiritual. Once again, pick a symbol, photo, or picture to symbolize your Self and put it in the middle. Now put words and pictures that highlight your *goals* in each of the four quadrants. Keep working on it until you know you are finished; for some people, this remains an ongoing project.

EXERCISE: Balloon or Burning Ritual

This ritual will help you get rid of your "stumbling blocks." Think of the people or things you no longer want to carry with you, or the things that get in the way of your wholeness. Examples might be "my inability to accept help when I need it" or "worrying about people and things I cannot change." Some things may take only one word—"Bill" or "smoking."

Write each thing you want to release on a post-it note, and stick all your notes on a helium-filled balloon. (You can purchase a balloon at any party store and most drug stores.) Listen to your Inner Voice: make sure you include everything you want to rid yourself of.

When you are ready, go outdoors, take a few deep breaths, and release your balloon. Watch it float away, realizing what it is you are letting go of. Carry this image within you so that it is readily available when you run up against a block in your life. Some women have found it helpful to take a photo of the balloon floating off into the heavens and to keep that photo where they see it every day.

If you prefer, go through the same steps outlined above in collecting your "stumbling blocks," and then find a safe place to burn your notes. Ignite them and watch them go up in smoke! Again, you may want to snap a picture of your obstacles being transformed in front of you.

EXERCISE: Summing Up Your Experiences

Write your reflections on these questions in your journal or binder:

- In what ways is my life different today from the time I started the recovery process?

- How am I different?

- What new feelings am I experiencing?

- What new insights have I had?

- What changes in my behavior have people in my life noticed?

 ## Suggested Reading

Forgive for Good: A Proven Prescription for Health and Happiness, by Fred Luskin

The Power of Now, by Eckhart Tolle

Revolution from Within, by Gloria Steinem

Fire in the Soul, by Joan Borysenko, PhD

She, by Robert A. Johnson

Woman Why Do You Weep, by Sandy Flaherty

The Mindfulness Coloring Book: Anti-Stress Art Therapy for Busy People, by Emma Farrarons

The Only Road

I travel alone—a distant path
A path traveled by many before me
but a road always new to each traveler.
There are supports along the way—
Some I see—and some are lost in the
confusion of finding my way.
There are others, too—some are travelers
and some are known to me as Guides.
Sometimes there is difficulty in telling one from
the other—perhaps they are all the same.
I get so tired and need to stop and refresh
as only then can I continue.
I am, indeed, a weary traveler.
The road is one that appears to lead nowhere
and at the same time
I know it's the only road that leads somewhere.

— a survivor on the journey

Appendix
Prevention and What We Tell Our Children

We all want to protect our children from experiencing what we experienced. Discovering that your child has been sexually abused is every parent's worst nightmare. But since only 38 percent of children tell when they've been molested, what can we do? We teach our kids to take charge of their own safety in many areas—while swimming, when crossing the street, when approached by a stranger. Like any other personal safety lesson that you teach your children, sexual abuse can be explained in a non-alarming way. Even the older toddler can understand the difference between "good touch" and "bad touch" when presented in an easy-to-understand way. Private parts are easily explained by "the parts of your body covered by your bathing suit." The basic rule here is that if anyone touches you there, you come and tell mommy or daddy.

Start reading appropriate books to your kids, such as *I Said No! A Kid-to-Kid Guide to Keeping Private Parts Private,* by Kimberly King, a book that helps kids set boundaries and teaches them responses they can remember. *Your Body Belongs to You,* by Cornelia Spelman, and *It's MY Body: A Book to Teach Young Children How to Resist Uncomfortable Touch,* by Lory Freeman, can teach kids about their private parts—what's okay and what's not okay. The two classic books I used when doing counseling with children were *Your Body is Your Own* and *Sometimes It's O.K. to Tell Secrets,* both published by the Children's Justice Foundation.

Make this information part of the normal instruction you give to your children as they grow up. Talk to them about "good touch" and "bad touch," "good secrets" (birthday presents, surprises) and "bad secrets" ("don't tell your mommy because..."). And most importantly, tell them *what* to do if someone does attempt to touch them inappropriately*: "Say 'no!' and leave that place immediately."* If they can't leave: *"Say 'no!' and go tell another grownup nearby,"* or *"Say 'no! If you touch me, I'm going to tell!'"*

Children have to know what to do—so *rehearse it with them.* I used to play a game with the children I saw in therapy. I called it the "What If" game. *"What if you got separated from your mom in the grocery store—what would you do?" "What if you found a kitty in your yard and it was hurt—what would you do?"* At some point, I would ask, *"What if your friend's dad asked to see your bum?" "What if a neighbor tried to touch you in your private parts?"* Rehearse responses with them.

Start conversations early, and listen when your children talk to you. Assure them that they can tell you anything and you will still love them. Be aware that children rarely tell their secret unless you ask them directly if someone has hurt them or touched them in a way that they did not like. Kids know the difference between "an okay touch" and one that is not appropriate. Don't hesitate to ask them the hard questions. The more comfortable you are with asking, the more likely you are to evoke an honest answer.

Don't be too busy to pay attention to where your child spends his or her time—and with whom. Remember, the best protection for a child is a protective adult who teaches the child what to do. Don't hesitate to use nanny-cams (or whatever the latest technology is) to check on your child's well-being. Make unexpected visits to care providers and babysitters.

Here are some other guidelines:

- Set clear boundaries with your kids, such as *don't go into anyone else's house or get in anyone else's car without asking me first.* Eighty-four percent of all molestations take place in a residence—either yours or the offender's. Always know where your child is, and with whom.

- Tell your child never to agree to keep a secret from you when asked by another adult.

- Teach your kids how to refuse—even when someone seems friendly, interesting, or kind. We teach our kids to be obedient to adults, but we don't teach them how to say "no." It's better that they err than be overly compliant.

- Teach kids about *bait*: a new litter of kittens to look at; "come on back, I have an old bike you could have"; "come in for a glass of lemonade."

- Have your child practice yelling, saying "no," and walking away—and reinforce this lesson frequently. This is not a one-time conversation!

- Train children to act in response to unwanted touching, hitting, bullying, requests, or coercion by any person—young or old, familiar or unknown, friendly or in authority. Tell children that it's okay to be rude, make a scene, yell loudly, run away or do whatever is necessary to be safe again. Teach them to yell "no"—even if it's grandpa, their soccer coach, or your neighbor. Prevention is the key.

- Pay attention if your child becomes reluctant to go to school or sports practice—or if she or he no longer wants to stay with a relative. Gently ask why.

- Notice any regressive behavior, such as bedwetting, thumb sucking, or nightmares, fearfulness, withdrawal. Question your child.

- Note sexually explicit language or sexual behavior in your child, as these may indicate that your child is being exploited. A child will often mimic age-inappropriate sexual behavior.

- Encourage child abuse prevention programs in your schools and your community. Be an advocate. Prevention programs bring a sensitive topic into the classroom and can teach children assertiveness. Programs can help children identify inappropriate touching—what to do about it, how to tell, and how to keep telling until someone listens. Go online and check out Childhelp.org, Darkness to Light (d2l.org), and Kidpower.org for ideas on what you can do.

- My best advice to kids is: "If someone is touching you in inappropriate ways, tell and tell and tell until someone hears you and does something to help you."

If your child tells you he or she has been molested, *believe* your child. Emphasize that it is not his or her fault—it is *always* the offender's fault. Report the abuse to the police or child protective services and let them confront the alleged perpetrator. Your responsibility at this point is your child: make sure he or she is okay physically and emotionally. Don't press your child for details; just be there for him or her. I strongly recommend counseling with a well-qualified therapist for your child—and also for you. Parents need help to process their feelings and to learn the best ways to support their child. Darkness to Light offers an online sexual abuse support and information site as well as a very helpful two-hour prevention course that teaches adults how to prevent, recognize, and react responsibly to a child's sexual abuse.

The best indicator of abuse is a change in your child's behavior. Notice if she is anxious or depressed, has chronic "tummy aches," or exhibits any of the behaviors mentioned above. Running away, self-harm, drug use, isolation, animal cruelty—all may be clues that your adolescent is being abused. The most important thing you can do is ask directly: "Is someone hurting you?" Regardless of their age, kids often fear getting in trouble, or fear getting an adult in trouble, or fear that they did something to cause the abuse—so they don't tell.

The majority of the women in my Healing Steps workshop wished that someone in their lives would have looked them in the eye and asked: "Is someone molesting you?"

And, finally, keep your eyes and ears open when you are around other young people. Remember the case of Jaycee Dugard: it took just one woman seeing something odd and placing a call to authorities that led to the rescue of Jaycee and her two daughters from the horror in which they were living. This is just one case in which a stranger made a positive difference by having the courage to make a call. Let's be there for one another.

References

Step One: Breaking the Silence

Atler, M. V. 1991. "The Darkest Secret." *People,* June 10, 1991, 89–94.

Leunig, Michael. 1991. *A Common Prayer.* New York: Harper Collins.

Step Two: Where Was the Loving Protector?

Carlson, K. 1990. *In Her Image: The Unhealed Daughter's Search for Her Mother.* Boulder, Colorado: Shambhala.

Edelman, H. 1994. *Motherless Daughters.* Reading, Massachusetts: Addison-Wesley.

Flaherty, S. 1993. "A Skeptic Learns to Love Her Inner Child." *The Healing Woman* 10:1–8.

Herman, J., & Hirschman, L. 1981. *Father-Daughter Incest.* Cambridge, Massachusetts: Harvard University Press.

Hein, S. 2013. "Mother-Daughter Sexual Abuse." *Making Daughters Safe Again.* Accessed November 2016. http://mdsa-online.org/.

Mathews, R., Mathews, J.K., & Spelz, K. 1989. *Female Sexual Offenders: An Exploratory Study.* Brandon: Safer Society Press.

Tablak, P. 1994. "How to Be Your Own Good Mother." *The Healing Woman* 11:1–7.

Tracy, Natasha. 2016. "Emotional Abuse: Definitions, Signs, Symptoms, Examples," *Healthy Place*, accessed November 16, 2016, http://www.healthyplace.com/abuse/emotional-psychological-abuse/emotional-abuse-definitions-signs-symptoms-examples/.

Step Three: Facing the Perpetrator

"Men Who Molest." PBS *Frontline*, Season 3: Episode 24, April 16, 1985.

Simon, S. 1992. "Don't Play the Blame Game." *Change*, March–April.

Vanderbilt, H. 1992. "Incest: A Chilling Report." *Lear's*, February.

Vanzant, I., interview by Oprah Winfrey, *Oprah Winfrey's Super Soul Sunday*, Oprah Winfrey Network, April 24, 2016.

Zweig, C. & Wolf, S. 1997. *Romancing the Shadow: A Guide to Soul Work for a Vital Authentic Life*. New York: Ballantine.

Step 4: Then and Now

Bass, E., & Davis, L. 2008. *The Courage to Heal: A Guide for Women Survivors of Child Sexual Abuse*. New York: William Morrow.

Frawley-O'Dea, M. "The Long-Term Impact of Early Sexual Trauma." Lecture presented at the National Conference of Catholic Bishops, Dallas, Texas, June 13, 2002.

Golding, J. 1999. "Sexual Assault History and Long-Term Physical Health Problems: Evidence from Clinical and Population Epidemiology." *Current Directions in Psychological Science* 8 (December): 191–194.

Luskin, F. 2001. *Forgive for Good: A Proven Prescription for Health and Happiness*. San Francisco: Harper One.

McCauley, J., Kern D., & Kolodner, K. 1997. "Clinical Characteristics of Women with a History of Childhood Abuse: Unhealed Wounds." *Journal of the American Medical Association* 277 (May): 1362–1368.

[Unknown Author]. 1986. *Intimacy Pamphlet*. Center City: Hazelton Press.

Naparstek, B. 2005. *Invisible Heroes: Survivors of Trauma and How They Heal*. New York: Bantam.

Putnam, Frank. 2003. "Ten-Year Research Update Review: Child Sexual Abuse." *Journal of the American Academy of Child and Adolescent Psychiatry* 42 (March): 269–278.

Putnam, Frank, & Trickett, P. 1997. "The Psychobiological Effects of Sexual Abuse: A Longitudinal Study." *Annals of the New York Academy of Sciences* 821:150–159.

Step Five: Sex and Your Body

Barbach, L. 1975. *For Yourself: The Fulfillment of Female Sexuality*. New York: Signet.

Haines, S. 1986. *The Survivor's Guide to Sex: How to Have an Empowered Sex Life After Child Abuse*. San Francisco: Cleis Press.

Maltz, W. 1991. *The Sexual Healing Journey: A Guide for Survivors of Sexual Abuse*. New York: Harper Collins.

Matthews, M. 1992. "Learning to Reweave the Silken Threads That Connect Body and Mind." *The Healing Woman* 1 (August): 4.

Miller, Alice. 1998. *Thou Shalt Not Be Aware: Society's Betrayal of the Child*. New York: Farrar, Straus, and Giroux.

Step Six: Relationships

Brennan, K. 2008. *In His Sights: A True Story of Love and Obsession*. New York: Harper.

Borysenko, J. 1981. *Guilt Is the Teacher, Love Is the Lesson*. New York: Grand Central Publishing.

McGraw, P., *The Dr. Phil Show*, October 15, 2015.

Sark. 1998. *The Bodacious Book of Succulence: Daring to Live Your Succulent Wild Life*. New York: Simon & Schuster.

Vanzant, I., interview by Oprah Winfrey, *Oprah Winfrey's Super Soul Sunday*, Oprah Winfrey Network, April 24, 2016.

Step Seven: Recovery

DeCastillejo, I. 1973. *Knowing Woman: A Feminine Psychology*. New York: Harper & Row.

Reilly, P. 1999. *Imagine a Woman in Love with Herself*. Embracing Your Wisdom and Wholeness Series. Berkeley, California: Conari Press.

"Leaving behind nights of terror and fear,
I rise into a daybreak that's wondrously clear."
—Maya Angelou

Resources

National Sexual Assault Online Hotline, operated by the Rape, Abuse and Incest National Network (RAINN): 800-656-HOPE (800-656-4673)

National Sexual Violence Resource Center (NSVRC) website: https://www.snvrc.org

National Suicide Prevention Hotline: 800-273-8255

Ash Beckham: When to Take a Stand—and When to Let It Go | Ted Talk

Marilyn Van Derbur: website http://www.missamericabyday.com, and book *Miss America by Day: Lessons Learned from Ultimate Betrayal and Unconditional Love*

Darkness to Light: http://www.d2l.org

Childhelp—A Non-Profit Charity Aiding Victims of Child Abuse: https://www.childhelp.org or 800-422-4453

Dr. Phil's website: https://www.drphil.com/

The Healing Years, a Big Voices documentary available through the Big Voices website and Amazon.com

Acknowledgments

This book is the result of more than a few nudges from a community of women who encouraged me to bring *Healing Steps* to a wider group of survivors of childhood sexual abuse. I want to thank them for their stories, for their inspiration, and for all that they taught me along the way.

I also want to thank my first readers—Cheryl, Marilyn, Harriet, Vix, and Kathy—for their ongoing support; and Teresa, for her original work on the Arc of Relationship back in 1991.

I never could have realized my vision without the expertise and patience of my editor Holly Brady, and my designer Diana Russell.

And to my family, what can I say? How about: thank you, Kevin, for knowing what I could do before I did; thank you, Robyn, for your honest voice; thank you, Rebecca, for your tenacity; thank you, Pam, for always believing.

To Ron—my husband, my playmate, and my very patient partner—how can I ever thank you for the many hours I spent holed up in my office with the "do not disturb" sign on the door, the many times you quietly tiptoed into my office and put a sandwich on my desk or a bottle of water in my hand. You always listened, you were always honest, you always valued and respected what I wanted to say in *Healing Steps*. There are no words.

Sharyn Higdon Jones
is a licensed psychotherapist who has been working with sexual abuse survivors for over 35 years. She has treated victims, perpetrators, partners, and families of survivors; and she has served as an expert witness in both civil and criminal cases involving sexual abuse.

She began her training with the Sexual Abuse Treatment Program in Santa Clara, California, and with Parents United and the Institute for the Community as Extended Family, also known as the Giaretto Institute.

She is currently a consultant, a workshop leader, and a licensed psychotherapist (CA Lic.#18909) in private practice in the San Francisco Bay Area. She created the original workshop series "Healing Steps" to guide adults molested as children through the healing process.